PRAISE FOR *TRINITARIAN RESPONSES TO WORLDLINESS*

"To a post-Western Christianity, Heejun Yang has offered a compelling Trinitarian theology of inculturation—one that is admirable in its refusal to romanticize Eastern traditions in the process."

—XI LIAN, Duke Divinity School

"Heejun Yang is one of our most interesting young Christian scholars. His expansive mind, his dynamic Trinitarian faith, is just what we need to help us think about the role of the church and the Christian faith as we come up against the challenges of contemporary secular culture. Theologians, pastors, thoughtful Christians will be challenged and invigorated by this wonderful book."

—WILL WILLIMON, Duke Divinity School

"Yang gives an excellent overview of post-liberal theology, radical orthodoxy, and hermeneutic theology. . . . This well-written book offers new perspectives for a globally oriented theology in diverse secular contexts and will constructively inspire future discussion in systematic theology and intercultural theology."

—HANS-PETER GROSSHANS, University of Muenster

"A veritable theological tour de force, Heejun Yang's book offers an insightful and nuanced overview of contemporary Western theologies of the Trinity and evaluates them from the perspective of Korean theology. From this theological investigation, Dr. Yang shows that a God-centered understanding of the world will help transform Christianity into a global but non-dominating religion. I strongly recommend this book for those interested in the practical dimension of Trinitarian theology."

—PETER C. PHAN, Georgetown University, emeritus

"A bold debut from Heejun Yang. *Trinitarian Responses to Worldliness* offers a rich, thoughtful analysis of theological response to secular cultures while uniting the best of Trinitarian and decolonial theologies. Yang invites readers to embrace the Trinitarian basis of diversity and inculturation while remaining open to growth, ultimately pointing the way to genuine forms of reconciliation in our painfully fractured world."

—EDGARDO A. COLÓN-EMERIC, Dean, Duke Divinity School

"Yang's Trinitarian theology of inculturation convincingly demonstrates that worldliness is not a danger but an opportunity for theology. He creatively goes beyond the theological attempts at inculturation in North America, Great Britain, and on the European continent, because the different cultural contexts in East Asia also make different theological responses possible and necessary. Anyone wishing to continue working in this field will benefit from his work."

—INGOLF U. DALFERTH, Claremont Graduate University, emeritus

Trinitarian Responses to Worldliness

Trinitarian Responses to Worldliness

Towards a Trinitarian Theology of Inculturation

HEEJUN YANG

☙PICKWICK *Publications* • Eugene, Oregon

TRINITARIAN RESPONSES TO WORLDLINESS
Towards a Trinitarian Theology of Inculturation

Copyright © 2022 Heejun Yang. All rights reserved. Except for brief quotations in critical publications or reviews, no part of this book may be reproduced in any manner without prior written permission from the publisher. Write: Permissions, Wipf and Stock Publishers, 199 W. 8th Ave., Suite 3, Eugene, OR 97401.

Pickwick Publications
An Imprint of Wipf and Stock Publishers
199 W. 8th Ave., Suite 3
Eugene, OR 97401

www.wipfandstock.com

PAPERBACK ISBN: 978-1-6667-9109-9
HARDCOVER ISBN: 978-1-6667-9113-6
EBOOK ISBN: 978-1-6667-9114-3

Cataloguing-in-Publication data:

Names: Yang, Heejun, author.

Title: Trinitarian responses to worldliness : towards a trinitarian theology of inculturation / Heejun Yang.

Description: Eugene, OR : Pickwick Publications, 2022 | Includes bibliographical references and index.

Identifiers: ISBN 978-1-6667-9109-9 (paperback) | ISBN 978-1-6667-9113-6 (hardcover) | ISBN 978-1-6667-9114-3 (ebook)

Subjects: LCSH: Culture (Christian theology). | Christianity and culture—Africa. | Theological anthropology. | Trinity.

Classification: BR115.C8 Y36 2022 (paperback) | BR115.C8 Y36 (ebook)

07/08/22

Scripture quotations are from New Revised Standard Version Bible, copyright © 1989 National Council of the Churches of Christ in the United States of America. All rights reserved worldwide.

Trinitarian Response to Worldliness was submitted to the Faculty of Protestant Theology in the University of Münster in Partial Fulfillment of the Requirements for the PhD in philosophy of religion. Heejun Yang passed the disputation on 21 July, 2021.

*Humbly dedicated to Ingolf U. Dalferth
upon his retirement from Claremont*

Contents

Acknowledgments | xi

1. Introduction: Secular World and Trinitarian Thinking | 1
   Theological Studies in a Secular World | 1
   The Rise of Trinitarian Theologies in the Twentieth Century | 3
   The Rise of the Trinitarian Theological Movements in the Twenty-First Century | 11
   The Aim and Structure of Book | 12

2. A Postliberal Reaction (North America) | 18
   The Trends of Liberal Theology in the Twentieth Century | 19
   The Hermeneutics of Narrative Theology | 32
   The Sectarian Response to Worldliness | 46

3. A Radical Orthodoxy Reaction (Britain) | 64
   The Fallacy of Secularity | 65
   The Hermeneutics of Radical Orthodoxy | 79
   The Scandalous Cultural Hermeneutics | 90

4. A Radical Hermeneutic Reaction (European Continent) | 105
   The Development of German Hermeneutic Theology | 106
   The Radical Hermeneutic Theology: A Trinitarian Way of Orientation | 119
   The Orientation of Christian Life in a Post-secular World | 131

5. Conclusion: Towards a Trinitarian Theology of Inculturation | 143
   Towards a God-Focused-Theology | 143
   A Comparative Study of Three Theological Movements | 145
   Christian Theology in the Globalized World | 147
   The Inevitable Process of Inculturation in World Christianity | 150
   The Theology of Inculturation | 155
   The Problem of Contextual Theology | 159

Conclusion: The Trinitarian Theology of Inculturation | 163
The Application of the Trinitarian Theology of Inculturation | 172

Bibliography | 181

Index | 193

Acknowledgments

Because the Triune God created this world with relational love, we live in a relational world. This means that my book is not my own product; I am indebted to that love.

After I realized that God called me not just to be a pastor but also to be a theologian, I had to work hard without holidays and weekends to be serious about God's calling. That was why I had to suffer from a lack of sleep in most of my 20s to study in different languages and I had to be the guy who always worked from opening to closing time in the libraries. Looking back, however, I had the best youth life, because I could accompany God, while learning and communicating with many church siblings and great teachers.

It has been a long journey to get here, but now I finally stand at the ending point of my school life with so much grace. I first want to express my gratitude to Methodist Theological University for it introduced me the theology of inculturation, Wesleyan theology, and philosophy of religion. I believe that this school has one of the best curriculums for theological education in the world. I also want to express a lot of thanks to Duke Divinity School. I appreciate the generous scholarships that the School granted me in my MDiv and ThM programs. More importantly, I am so grateful that Duke offered me an opportunity to study with great teachers such as Edgardo Colon-Emeric, William Willimon, Stanley Hauerwas, Paul Griffiths, Randy Maddox, Xi Lian, Stephen Gunter, Richard Hays, Sujin Pak, Stephen Chapman, Joel Marcus, David Goatley, Mary Fulkerson, and Judith Heyhoe. I owe a lot to them. In addition, I give thanks to the heritage of the Philosophy of Religion and Theology program at Claremont Graduate University for it gave me two extraordinary teachers: Ingolf Dalferth (who now became my doctoral father) and Anselm Min (who is with Jesus now).

Just about two years ago, I could not have imagined myself studying in Germany, the home country of systematic theology and philosophy of religion. However, during the pandemic, Prof. Dr. Hans-Peter Grosshans allowed me to move to Germany and to study at his Protestant Theology Faculty in Münster where Karl Barth, Joseph Ratzinger, and Karl Rahner taught. If he did not allow me to study with Ingolf Dalferth under his supervision, I would be an academic orphan during the pandemic. So, I want to express my special thanks for his kind guidance and supervision. Also, I feel grateful for the university of Münster for having me and offering me a full-stipend scholarship during my study in Germany.

Of course, I also express my thankfulness to my doctoral father, Prof. Ingolf U. Dalferth. He has been the best teacher I have ever met in my life; his teaching was always clear and his comments on my papers were always extraordinarily precise. Without his guidance and support, I would not be able to write my first monograph. In addition, it has been an amazing honor for me to be accepted by him as his last doctoral student even after his retirement. So, I humbly dedicate my dissertation upon his retirement from Claremont.

In addition, many thanks to Angel Woodrum and Catherine Clyburn who helped with the editing of this long text. Especially, I am thankful for Catherine Clyburn because she gave me a strength and a motivation to finish my dissertation earlier. Without her help, I would not be able to write my dissertation in six months (which is going to be a new record in Korea). I also give special thanks to Pickwick Publications for publishing this work.

Most importantly, many thanks to my parents who have supported me financially, mentally, and spiritually. Without their every morning prayers, I would not be able to breathe every day. Also, I want to give thanks to my grandmother who sowed the seed of the gospel in my family for the first time. Soon, she will have the first doctorate and pastor in her family.

Finally, I give my thanks to the Lord who has never let me down. If I made any mistake in my journey, the errors come from my unsanctified temper. However, if there has been anything good, I confess that the fruits were the work of the Lord in me. "Even though I walk through the darkest valley, I fear no evil; for you are with me" (Ps 23:4).

1

Introduction: Secular World and Trinitarian Thinking

THEOLOGICAL STUDIES IN A SECULAR WORLD

How should Christian theology engage with worldliness? The Christian faith has always communicated with many different cultures and interacted with them in this world. For example, Christianity from the beginning interacted with other religious movements and earthly powers such as John the Baptist, Judaism, or the Imperial Cult of the Roman Empire. Interestingly, Christianity always has shown different reactions toward other cultures and worldly powers in its history. On the one hand, the early Christians were persecuted by the worldly powers, so that they believed that the power of worldliness would be overturned soon with the second coming of Christ. On the other hand, Christian history is replete with examples of the church exercising power over the worldly powers, the prime example being most of Europe during the Medieval period. In addition, Christianity often had a collusive relationship with political powers in the case of the first Nicaean Ecumenical Council of Christianity or the Reformation. All these examples indicate that Christianity has a complicated relationship toward worldly cultures and powers according to its different context and time, while inculturating the gospel into its different context and time.

Since modern times, however, most systems of knowledge and religious education have been measured against the secular state. In modern societies, universities produce and reflect knowledge regardless of whether they are secular or religious.[1] That was why universities have become institutions of legitimation whose task is to normalize the discourses and bodies of knowledge of society. In this light of the Enlightenment era, most academic theology could survive in a university only if it is a part of professional training of ministers, as Immanuel Kant suggests in "The Conflict of the Faculties."[2] According to Kant, the faculties in the university are traditionally divided into two kinds: three higher faculties (divinity, law, and medicine) and a lower faculty (including philosophy). Kant here regards higher faculties as higher because they are expounded to the public—the government itself. However, Kant thinks that all three higher faculties are necessarily governed by the government, otherwise there would be no fixed and universal accessible norms for their guidance. On the other hand, in Kant's philosophy, the lower facility is called lower because it may use its own judgement at least in its teaching. In this description of Kant, modern universities function within a state and therefore consistently require academic subjects to operate under the rules of secular power.[3]

Under such a circumstance, the study of theologies is not a norm of the university anymore; as Ingolf Dalferth writes, it "becomes just one option among many others."[4] In modern universities, the existence of theological studies is constantly threatened. In many major universities today, for example, PhD students in the US have to get accepted in religion departments, not in divinity schools to learn theology; in the teaching job market, there is a preference of PhDs in "religion" from secular institutions over doctoral degrees in "theology" from seminaries. In addition, many top universities in Germany today such as the Humboldt University of Berlin and the University of Münster are trying to combine their traditionally separated Protestant theology faculty, Catholic theology faculty, and Jewish/Islamic studies

---

1. Hauerwas, *The State of the University*, 5. For example, in North America, most educational institutions for educating students in theology are recognized by the United States Department of Education and the Council for Higher Education Accreditation. Likewise, in many other countries including Germany, UK, and Australia, most educational institutions are recognized by the state or its constitution.

2. Kant, "The Conflict of the Faculties," in *Religion and Rational Theology*, 233–328.

3. Frei says, "But one can note the identical duality of nineteenth-century institutions in almost all areas; the epoch of the individual's highest freedom from the state was simultaneously the epoch of statism's greatest efficiency. . . . [M]inisterial training was under the complete control of state authority, which delegated it to an educational institution whose basic intellectual and educational assumptions might well be completely at variance with those of the institution for the service of which the students were to be trained." Frei, *Types of Christian Theology*, 100–102.

4. Dalferth, *Transcendence and the Secular World*, 1.

(philosophy faculty) into one multi-religious faculty of theologies.⁵ This implies that the distinction between religions are less important than before in the perspective of secular powers; theological studies are facing a new trend due to secularism. What does it mean, then, to study a specific theological tradition in a secular university's religion department? Do Christians need to make a separate culture and system for themselves because Christianity and other cultures have totally different language and grammar? Or, does theology need to be dominant over other secular studies to claim its validity in the modern universities?⁶ On these questions, theology must re-think its stance toward worldliness in front of the push of modern secularism.

To posit a stance of Christianity toward worldliness in the current world, this book will argue that Christian theology has to *inculturate* the gospel into the current situation, while focusing on *the perspective of the Trinity*. Although many current theological movements often ignore or are hostile to the current cultures, this book will show that the concept of inculturation is the key to understand the relationship between Christianity and the external culture of the current time (worldliness), because the gospel of Christianity always communicates with other discourses in the process of understanding God's revelation. In Christian history, Christians has always developed their understanding of God under the influence of other cultures; they have evolved their teachings and understandings according to their current cultures to make their cultures be the place of God's presence (revelation), while changing other cultures as well. In this process of inculturation, Christians have communicated with others, while being open toward worldly cultures and understanding their reality as *the Trinity's creature*. To show the importance of a God-focused-perspective in this process of inculturation, my book will compare three cutting-edge post-Barthian theological movements around the world. Then, it will attempt to postulate a trinitarian theology of inculturation as an alternative Christian way of life in the current age of world Christianity.

THE RISE OF TRINITARIAN THEOLOGIES IN THE TWENTIETH CENTURY

In the face of modern secularism, much of theology has become apologetic in order to survive as a university subject. This is a trend that began in the project of the Enlightenment became more entrenched in universities. That is why theologies after the Enlightenment era often focus on human reason,

---

5. See "Theologe gegen Berliner 'Fakultät der Theologien.'"
6. See Grosse, *Theologie und Wissensahftstheorie*.

historical approach (historical criticism), and human subjectivity rather than the unique teaching of faith—the Triune God. For example, Kant attempts to treat religion within the boundaries of reason rather than focusing on God or God's perspective.[7] In Kant's philosophy, human beings need to postulate God for a practical (moral) reason;[8] Kant describes the discourse of God as a moral discipline in a sense that he postulates God for a moral reason.[9] Similarly, Friedrich Schleiermacher struggles to defend the validity of theology (and God) in the age of the Enlightenment.[10] However, unlike Kant who focuses on a moral proof of God, Schleiermacher believes that religion is not based on metaphysics or modern scientific reason, but the human nature itself which can be considered as the inner aspect of human subjectivity.[11] That is why Schleiermacher in his *Christian Faith* highlights the importance of human feeling (intuition) and self-consciousness rather than thoroughly focusing on God or theonomy (although he as a Christian theologian still argues that human-consciousness is dependent on God).[12] In those examples of Kant and Schleiermacher (who are considered as father figures of modern philosophy of religion and modern theology), we can see

---

7. Kant, "Religion within the Boundaries of Reason," in *Religion and Rational Theology*, 28–216.

8. Because human beings cannot convince themselves the certainty of God's existence with dogmatic reasoning, Kant claims that we should use practical reasoning to explain the existence of God. Kant believes that practical reason postulates God's existence as necessary. According to Kant, the concept of God "is a moral concept, the practically necessary." Kant, *Critique of Pure Reason*, 406.

9. According to Kant, within a faith in God, human beings can eventually hope to accomplish the highest good, because they can have the prototype of human predisposition under the common moral law under the divine authority. For him, a belief in God allows human beings to practically be humane and moral He says, "only faith in the practical validity of the idea that lies in our reason has moral worth." Kant, "Religion within the Boundaries of Reason," 105.

10. See Schleiermacher, *On the Glaubenslehre*.

11. According to Schleiermacher, religion starts from the inner experience of human being. He says, "There are two points of view from which everything taking place in man or proceeding from him may be regarded. Considered from the centre outwards, that is according to its inner quality, it is an expression of human nature, based in one of its necessary modes of acting or impulses . . . regarded from the outside, according to the definite attitude and form it assumes in particular cases, it is a product of time and history." Schleiermacher, *On Religion*, 13.

12. After Schleiermacher, many theologians began to utilize human experience in developing their theology. This is why Schleiermacher is often considered as the father of modern theology. He, says, "The piety which forms the basis of all ecclesiastical communications is, considered purely in itself, neither a knowing nor a doing, but a modification of Feeling of immediate self-consciousness." Schleiermacher, *The Christian Faith*, 5.

the general characteristics of nineteenth century modern liberal theology: highlighting the role of human subjectivity, the historicity of religion (historical criticism), and the ethical dimension of religion.

Although much of theology in the nineteenth and twentieth centuries was devoted to replying to the Enlightenment, theology also developed a different tendency: the renaissance of trinitarian theologies. In trinitarian theologies, theologians advocate Christian practices and Christian beliefs' self-justifying to the world; theologians begin to re-think the relationship between Christianity and culture in the modern secular world. One of the most important figures in this movement is Karl Barth. Even though the modern sciences tend to believe that Christian theology may not be justified in the light of the character of the knowledge that constitutes the modern university, Barth claims that Christian theology is an entirely self-referential enterprise. This is because its starting point is faith, not speculative reason or human experience. To be specific, Barth believes that the ground of theology is none other than the Triune God who speaks to us.[13] Here, Barth rediscovers the validity of the Reformers' motto in the modern world: "*Sola Scriptura, Sola Fide, and Sola Gratia.*"

For example, although Barth complains about Calvin's doctrine of predestination in his *Church Dogmatics*, he as a reformed theologian generally follows Calvin's idea that the knowledge of God and the knowledge of self are deeply connected; for both Calvin and Barth the knowledge of self has to be found in God's sovereignty.[14] In *Institutes*, Calvin thinks the knowledge of God lies under the ideas conveyed in the Scripture, depicting God as the unity of the divine essence in three persons. In this trinitarian understanding of God, Calvin believes that the trinitarian idea of God should be the norm of Christian life because the Knowledge of God shines forth the whole universe with God's sovereignty.[15] Likewise, Barth insists

---

13. Barth says, "The word "theology" seems to signify a special science, a very special science, whose task is to apprehend, understand, and speak of "God." . . . This is the God who reveals himself in the Gospel, who himself speaks to men and acts among and upon them. Wherever he becomes the object of human science, both its source and its norm, there is evangelical theology." Barth, *Evangelical Theology*, 4–5.

14. Calvin says, "True and substantial wisdom principally consists of two parts, the knowledge of God, and the knowledge of ourselves. But, while these two branches of knowledge are so intimately connected, which of them precedes and produces the other, is not easy to discover. For, in the first place, no man can take a survey of himself but he must immediately turn to the contemplation of God, in whom he lives and moves; since it is evident that the talents which we possess are not from ourselves, and that our very existence is nothing but a subsistence in God alone." Calvin, *Institutes of the Christian Religion*, 1.1.1.

15. Calvin says, "The doctrine of Scripture concerning the immensity and the spirituality of the essence of God, should have the effect not only of dissipating the wild

on reading the Scripture in the light of the Trinity, not of human experience. Barth thinks that theology as an academic study has its own unique grammar and base—the Triune God's talk which is the confession of the church.[16] For Barth, the Scripture is the Word of the Triune God.[17] That is why Barth believes that the Scripture and the idea of the Trinity form the reality of Christians. In this understanding of God, Christians live their lives and form a unique worldview from others. Consequently, through re-highlighting the Trinity as the real subject matter of theology, Barth opens a new era of the nineteenth century theology like "the bomb that fell on the playground of the theologians."[18]

Unlike many nineteenth century liberal theologians, Barth tries to understand human reality by the fact of Christ. Instead of depending on metaphysical philosophy, Barth's theological starting point is the Christocentric (reconciled) reality. According to Barth, *all* humanity was reconciled with God in Jesus Christ, because God has already shown divine mercy on all humanity through the crucifixion and the resurrection of Jesus Christ—the second person of God.[19] In this line, Barth claims that both Israel and the church are the pre-eminent witnesses to the grace and judgment of God's

---

dreams of the vulgar, but also of refuting the subtleties of a profane philosophy." Calvin, *Institutes of the Christian Religion*, 1.13.1.

16. Barth says, "As a theological discipline dogmatics is the scientific self-examination of the Christian church with respect to the content of its distinctive talk about God.... The church confesses God as it talks about God. It does so first by its existence in the action of each individual believer. And it does so secondly by its specific action as a fellowship, in proclamation by preaching and the administration of the sacraments, in worship, in its internal and external mission including works of love amongst the sick, the weak and those in jeopardy. Fortunately, the reality of the church does not coincide with its action. But its action coincides with the fact that alike in its existence in believers and its communal existence as such it speaks about God. Its action is 'theology' in both the broader and the narrower sense. Theology is *de divinitate ratio sive sermo*." Barth, *CD* 1/1:1.

17. Barth says, "The presupposition which makes proclamation proclamation and therewith makes the church the church is the Word of God. This attests itself in Holy Scripture in the word of the prophets and apostles to whom it was originally and once and for all spoken by God's revelation." Barth, *CD* 1/1:88. He also says, "the biblical concept of revelation is itself the root of the doctrine of the Trinity. The doctrine of the Trinity is simply a development of the knowledge that Jesus is the Christ or the Lord." Barth, *CD* 1/1:334.

18. Cross, *Dialectic in Karl Barth's Doctrine of God*, 82.

19. It is noteworthy that God who manifests in Jesus Christ has a doubleness. Here, Jesus is the electing God as well as the elected. Barth says, "The election of grace is the eternal beginning of all the ways and works of God in Jesus Christ. In Jesus Christ God in His free grace determines Himself for sinful man and sinful man for Himself. He therefore takes upon Himself the rejection of man with all its consequences, and elect man to participation in His own glory." Barth, *CD* 3/1:94.

election within the reconciled reality of Christ.[20] For Barth, because everything is based on the Christocentric reality of God, the difference between those who belong to the heirs (the Israelites or the believers) and those who do not (the pagans or the non-believers) is eliminated. Barth also asserts that the distinction between faith and unbelief is not based on particular characteristics or human experiences. In this Barth's theology, the true distinction comes instead from the perspective of transcendence—the Triune God. That is why Barth thinks that no one can attribute to oneself but to the Triune God alone because everything is based on the Triune God's action in Christian faith. Thus, in Barth's theology, Christians can overcome a particular human ideology or a partial understanding of the world because the horizontal distinctions such as the Jews and the Gentile becomes secondary, while the distinction between the Creator and creature turns out to be primary; they can reconcile with different human ideas and be a being for others in *the perspective of the Triune God*.

After Barth, many theologians rediscovered the importance of the doctrine of the Trinity and began to highlight the uniqueness of the Triune God's Word (or God's revelation) in history. That is why many twentieth century Protestant theologians such as Eberhard Jüngel, Jürgen Moltmann, Wolfhart Pannenberg (for the German-speaking world), Robert Jenson (for the English-speaking world), and Sung-bum Yun (for the Eastern Asian language-speaking world) further developed the doctrine of the Trinity with a concern toward human history.[21] Strikingly, all of these trinitarian theologians continue Barth's work of rediscovering the eschatological dimension of Christian faith within modern theology.[22] For example, Jüngel roots his theology in God's self-identification with the crucified Jesus, and focuses on the unity of the self-differentiating God. According to Jüngel, God manifests Godself as the selflessness of love through showing the trinitarian nature in God. More specifically, Jüngel highlights the communication of God toward the world; he believes that God's Word has a characteristic of "becoming" to

---

20. For Barth, God, which is the subject of theology, invites us to God's reality: "Knowledge of God in the sense of Holy Scripture and the Confession is knowledge of His existence, His action, His revelation in His work. And so, the Bible is not a philosophical book, but a history book, the book of God's mighty acts in which God becomes knowable by us. . . . This work of creation, of the covenant, and of redemption is the reality in which God exists, lives, and acts and makes Himself known. From this work we must make no abstractions if we would know God's nature and existence. Here, in this work, God is . . . thus the subject of this work. It is the work of God's free love." Barth, *Dogmatics in Outline*, 44–45.

21. Dalferth, *Crucified and Resurrected*, 187–92.

22. Dalferth, *Crucified and Resurrected*, 195.

the world.²³ In Jüngel's theology, God's Word enters into the world through its dynamic proclamation as an (word) event.²⁴ In other words, he thinks that the Trinity differentiates Godself to be a word-event toward the world, and that is why Christians can understand God in this finite world. As a result, through highlighting the Trinity's self-differentiation, Jüngel believes that God's Word becomes real in history.

Similarly, Moltmann highlights the importance of the doctrine of the Trinity with the question of the "pain of the Father at the death of the Son."²⁵ Unlike Jüngel who focuses on the unity of the Trinity, however, Moltmann emphasizes the separation of the Father and the Son at the moment of Jesus' crucifixion in order to stress the perichoretic nature of the Trinity. According to Moltmann, God the Father also feels the pain at the most despairing situation of Jesus Christ; God shows the divine love toward the world through feeling the pain of the world.²⁶ In this understanding of the Trinity, Moltmann further develops his "social doctrines" through underlining both the perichoretic unity and plurality of the Trinity. For Moltmann, God loves this world so much that God suffers with us. Here, through realizing God's endless love toward the world with the Trinity's perichoretic nature, Moltmann finds God's eschatological hope in history. Consequently, Moltmann's theology attempts to show that God works in this world through highlighting God's trinitarian (perichoretic) economy toward the social and the human history.²⁷

Likewise, Pannenberg and Jenson attempt to apply the doctrine of the Trinity to the historical dimension. Pannenberg develops the doctrine of the Trinity with a special emphasis on the difference between the Father, Son

23. Jüngel, *God as the Mystery of the World*, 317.

24. Jüngel believes that God's being corresponds to God's self-revelation in history: "In this correspondence the being of God takes place as the history of the divine life in the Spirit. And in this history which is constituted through this correspondence God makes space within himself for time. This making-space-for-time within God is a continuing event. The space of time conceived as a continuing event we call eternity." Jüngel, *God as the Mystery of the World*, 111.

25. Moltmann, *In der Geschichte des dreieinger Gottes*, 17.

26. "As well as developing a political theology, I have resolved to think more intensively than I have done up to now about the meaning of the cross of Christ for theology, for the church and for society. In a civilization that glorifies success and happiness and is blind to the sufferings of others, people's eyes can be opened to the truth if they remember that at the centre of the Christian faith stands an unsuccessful, tormented Christ, dying in forsakenness. The recollection that God raised this crucified Christ and made him the hope of the world must lead the churches to break their alliances with the powerful and to enter into the solidarity of the humiliated." Moltmann, *The Crucified God*, xii.

27. See Moltmann, *The Trinity and the Kingdom*.

and Spirit. In explaining the relation between the Father, Son, and Spirit, he explains the Spirit to be "constitutive for the fellowship of the Son with the Father."[28] Here, he believes that the reciprocity of the active relationships between the three persons of the Trinity creates the history of God. From this point of view, the world as the work of the Spirit should be understood as God's history. He claims, "the eschatological consummation is . . . the locus of the decision that the trinitarian God is always the true God from eternity to eternity."[29] In this understanding, God's history has temporality as a history, even though it moves toward eternity and God's end. As a result, through promoting the historicity of God's revelation, Pannenberg strains the temporal process of the new creation. And that is why he also attempts to interact with many natural sciences to see them as the part of God's new creation in history; his theology shows an interest in philosophy of science to affirm God's temporal process in history.[30]

In the English-speaking world, Jenson connects the doctrine of the Trinity with the historical and eschatological dimensions.[31] He says, "Israel's and the church's God is . . . identified by specific temporal actions and is known within certain temporal communities."[32] According to Jenson, because the event of Jesus Christ itself has a temporal form in history, the doctrine of the Trinity inevitably appears "to our history to what God does to and for us."[33] He additionally speaks, "the world God creates is not a thing, a 'cosmos,' but is rather a history. God does not create a world that thereupon has a history; he (God) creates a history that is a world, in that it is purposive and so makes a whole."[34] In this understanding of history, Jen-

28. Pannenberg, *Systematic Theology*, 1:268.

29. Pannenberg, *Systematic Theology*, 1:331.

30. It is also noteworthy that his student such as Philip Clayton in the US works on philosophy of science. See Pannenberg, *Theology and the Philosophy of Science*.

31. Jenson also understands theology as the hermeneutics of the church. He says, "It is the mission of the church to speak the gospel, to the world in proclamation and to God in appeal and adoration. Theology is the hermeneutic of this work." Jenson, *Systematic Theology*, 1:23. Cf. *The Knowledge of Things Hoped for*.

32. Jenson, *Systematic Theology*, 1:46.

33. Jenson, *Systematic Theology*, 1:60.

34. In developing his account of a Christian doctrine of creation, Jenson outlines eight proposals: (1) the creation narrative entails a reality other than God; (2) God creates this reality other than God through the Word; (3) God's commands and the creature's obedience show that creation has a moral significance; (4) the present tense in the creation narrative implies that God continues to sustain the life of the world; (4) God creates the world from nothing; (5) the creature has an absolute beginning; (6) God's creation has not only a beginning, but also an end, which is a particular goal; (7) the world God creates is not a thing, a cosmos, but rather a history; (8) creatures are teleological in their own being so that they are sustained by striving, by pursuit of a determinate end. Jenson, *Systematic Theology*, 2:14.

son believes that the understanding of the Trinity can be shown throughout history. For Jenson, history pursues its end in God's creation. As a result, Jenson also develops his doctrine of the Trinity in the dimension of history.

Concerning Asian theology, Sung-bum Yun, unlike Western scholars, understands eastern religious history as *a priori* of the understanding the Trinity. Yun was the first Korean theologian who received a doctoral degree from a European university. Anchored in his unique perspective bridging Western academic theology and the Eastern religious academic landscape, his work opens a theological trend called the theology of inculturation or Asian indigenous theology. After studying under Karl Barth at Basel, he finds that there are many similarities between the doctrine of the Trinity and the Korean Dangun mythology which has three personal deities: Han-in, Huan-ung, and Han-gum.[35] Looking at the similarities between Christianity and the Korean traditional religion, Yun says, "the cultural *apriori* for us is Korean culture. Although the gospel is so exceeding all, there needs a ground in order to be planted. For us, that would be our self-awareness as a Korean."[36] In this awareness of Korean history, Yun suggests the theology of *Sincerity* (誠) and the Christian ethics of *Filial Piety* (孝), based on the ethos of Korean traditional religion—Confucianism. From there, the tradition of Korean (Methodist) theology begins, and many discussions follow Yun's theological direction in Asian theology to find the *Vestigium Trinitas* in Asian cultures and histories.[37]

In sum, these Trinitarian theologians of the twentieth century develop the doctrine of the Trinity further into the historical, social and eschatological dimensions to express the mystery of the Trinity not only in the light of Jesus' crucifixion event but also in the light of the entire history, while considering their own distinctive theological contexts. In general, these theologians understand the reality of the Trinity as the reality not only of the life of Christians, but of the whole creation. Consequently, they attempt to develop the doctrine of the Trinity to the eschatological dimension of faith, in order to connect their trinitarian faith with real life and real history.

---

35. Yun says, "This legendary story is similar to the Christian doctrine of incarnation that God as Christ became human. Korean Christians see these two comparative stories in terms of the standpoint of Christian Trinitarians, that God, Jesus Christ, and the Holy Spirit are counterparts of Hwan-In, Hwan-Ung and Tan-Gun." Yun, *Theology of Sung*, 34–35. Cf. Yun, "Getting Interested."

36. Yun, *Korean Religion and Korean Christianity*, 321.

37. Yun, "The Dangun Mythology is Vestigium Trinitatis."

THE RISE OF THE TRINITARIAN THEOLOGICAL MOVEMENTS IN THE TWENTY-FIRST CENTURY

Following Barth's legacy, one of the leading motives of these twentieth century trinitarian theologians is their abandonment of the theism of the Enlightenment. In this project of trinitarian theologies, many trinitarian theologians attempt to embrace the practical use of the Christian confession.[38] As Geoffrey Wainwright pointed out in *Doxology*, these trinitarian theologians claim that Christian worship is a locus for the reception and transmission of the Christian doctrine and life, because the form of trinitarian confession (doxology) in worship predates theological reflections.[39] Here, the twentieth century trinitarian theologians commonly suggest that Christian theology is the church's internal reflection about the gospel; they tend to use their internal ecclesial confession of God to explain their reality rather than focusing on the proof of God's being or essence toward external cultures. That is why these trinitarian theologians interpret the human reality with an eschatological concern to make their faith valid to their actual lives and cultures. Through highlighting the eschatological aspect of God, "they are affirming a true and universally valid insight into God's being and the nature of his (God's) nearness to us."[40] In this perspective of trinitarian theologies, the Spirit of God opens Christians' eyes to the divine eschatological reality. In this new understanding of the reality, Christians form their unique worldview, ethics, and ontology. Because this new understanding of God involves the whole person's life and perspective, the practical consequences are unavoidable in pursuing trinitarian theologies.[41] Therefore, trinitarian theologians understand theology as a practical science that reflects on the goals, presuppositions, conditions, and means of transforming human life through God's activity and re-think how their Christian faith should react to the modern secular world based on the perspective of the Triune God.

Accordingly, the new trends of trinitarian theologies emerge in the late twentieth and twenty-first centuries, because many trinitarian theologians further develop their doctrine of the Trinity into not only the historical or eschatological aspects but also into the practical dimension. The best examples of these trends are postliberalism (George Lindbeck, Hans Frei, and Stanley Hauerwas in the US), radical orthodoxy (John Milbank, Graham

---

38. Dalferth, "The Historical Roots of Theism," in Anderson, *Traditional Theism and Its Modern Alternatives*, 15–43.

39. Wainwright, *Doxology*, 9.

40. Dalferth, *Crucified and Resurrected*, 198.

41. Dalferth, *Crucified and Resurrected*, 199.

Ward, and Catherine Pickstock in the UK), and Continental radical hermeneutic theology (Ingolf Dalferth in Germany/Swiss). Because these influential theological movements engage with the practicality of theology, they also develop their own unique stance to the modern secular world. For example, postliberal theologians claim that Christianity has its own internal logic based on their Christian narratives. To highlight the uniqueness of the grammar of Christianity, postliberal theologians tend to avoid engaging with other cultural grammars outside of Christianity. In contrast to postliberalism, radical orthodoxy theologians attempt to show a fundamentalist stance arguing that theology is the queen of the sciences. According to radical orthodoxy theologians, theology has the highest of all possible knowledge, overcoming a nihilistic circulation of secular theories. For them, Christian faith is a more radical response to the issues of postmodernity than other secular sciences. Also, the posture of Continental radical hermeneutic theology is different from the former two theological movements. Particularly, in the work of Dalferth who represents Continental hermeneutic theology, the Christian way of orientation can contribute to the post-secular society through seeing the world in the perspective of transcendence (God). For Dalferth, Christianity is always in communication with others so that Christians should engage with the secular world. Looking at these current theological trends, we find that each (trinitarian) theological trend has different attitudes toward worldliness, while sharing similar interests such as the doctrine of the Trinity, linguistic philosophy, postmodernism, and most importantly the practical response of Christianity to secularism.

THE AIM AND STRUCTURE OF BOOK

In investigating these twenty-first century trinitarian theological movements (postliberalism, radical orthodoxy, German radical hermeneutic theology), the primary goal of this book is to make a contribution to the twenty-first century trinitarian theology; this book will attempt to postulate a better relationship between trinitarian theology and the current culture beyond the age of secularism. To be specific, one of the main purposes of this book is to claim that Christian theology should inculturate its internal grammar into the current context of world Christianity within the perspective of the Triune God. This is because the gospel, due to its trinitarian nature, always communicates with new vernacular cultures and inculturates itself into worldliness. To show this, this book will investigate how twenty-first century Protestant trinitarian theologies struggle to explain the relationship between the internal grammar of Christianity and the external elements in the age of secularism. Looking at these struggles of trinitarian theologies, this book will find out that current theological movements (in the cases of postliberalism and radical orthodoxy) often fail to reconcile the two paradoxical elements within the Christian perspective; postliberalism and radical orthodoxy display ignorance or hostility toward modern secularity. However, borrowing Dalferth's theology of orientation, this book will argue that Christians can reconcile these two opposite elements when they highlight *the act of the Triune God* (the concept of transcendence) in their theology. Based on this insight of trinitarian theology, I will further suggest that *"inculturation"* can be a key concept for Christians to react to the globalization of Christianity, because the concept of inculturation (as the Triune God's action for an inevitable process of the Christian communication) allows Christians to hold their internal logic humbly, while engaging with other new cultures without ignorance or hostility.

The second purpose of this book is to investigate how trinitarian theology is accepted and inculturated in North America, Great Britain, and Germany. To engage with twenty-first century Protestant trinitarian theologies, the overall task of this book is to look at the three distinctive theological movements in the twenty-first century: postliberal theology, radical orthodoxy, and Continental radical hermeneutic theology. Although each theological movement had a tremendous impact on the entire area of theology, there has been a few works done for connecting those twenty-first century theological trends. However, in my work, I will attempt to show how these theological movements further develop trinitarian theologies in their own academic backgrounds and how they are connected to one another.

The third purpose of this book is to survey how Christians should react to other cultures in the present age of world Christianity. Interestingly, these different theological trends criticize the problem of modern secularity in the perspective of Christian theology. However, their responses to the secular world are different one another. Postliberalism tends to avoid working with interreligious dialogues or secular powers, while radical orthodoxy tries to engage with the secular sciences (without accommodation) to emphasize the superiority of Christian faith. Continental hermeneutic theology, on the other hand, claims that Christianity can bring contributions to the post-secular world; it allows Christianity to compete with other secular cultures in the post-secular society. In comparing these different responses, I will ask a fundamental question in this book: how should trinitarian theology react to the context of world Christianity? To answer this question, I will raise three questions for each chapter (each theological movement): *(1) what are the background discourses of these theological movements, (2) how do they develop their hermeneutical stance in using the doctrine of the Trinity, and*

(3) how do they react to external cultures in the modern secular age? Through comparing the three cutting-edge theological trends with these questions, I will evaluate each theological trend, and I will discern which Christian response should be applied to the context of world Christianity.

To do this, in the second chapter, I will deal with postliberalism's American response to the secular world and evaluate its contributions and limitations. The first section of this chapter will look at how postliberal theology has formed its stance toward religious studies in the age of American liberal theology through the work of George Lindbeck. In this section, I will draw attention to how postliberalism adopts Wittgensteinian theology in its context. In the second section, I will investigate how postliberalism develops its trinitarian hermeneutics through the work of Hans Frei. In North America, the Yale school has developed a theological trend called (postliberal) narrative theology. In this tradition, Frei tries to reconstruct a realistic or history-like element of the biblical narratives with the emphasis on the internal logic of Christianity (the biblical narratives). The third section of this chapter will investigate how Stanley Hauerwas connects narrative theology to the secular world with the emphasis on virtue theories. Interestingly, Hauerwas develops Christian virtue ethics under the influence of the Yale school; he further develops postliberalism to make a unique stance to the secular world. In this chapter, I will point out that postliberalism tends to avoid a vigorous interaction with secular cultures (as well as other religions) to stress the internal logic of Christianity. Thus, this chapter will argue that postliberal theology shows an insufficient sectarian response toward the secular world.

The third chapter will explore the reception of trinitarian theology in radical orthodoxy. In the first section of it, I will look at how John Milbank (the father figure of radical orthodoxy) understands the secular world. Here, I will draw attention to Milbank's critics on the modern and postmodern secular theories. Then, in the second section, I will examine radical orthodoxy's alternative ontology in the works of Milbank. According to radical orthodoxy, Christian theology has a remedy for the nihilistic circulation of the secular theories because it has a different hermeneutical understanding, assuming a transcendental reality beyond the finite secular world; radical orthodoxy suggests a theology of participation, recovering the classical Christian theology. In the final section of this chapter, I will show how radical orthodoxy takes a position toward secular cultures through investigating the work of Graham Ward. In developing Christian unique social, political, and ethical theories, radical orthodoxy argues that theology is the queen of the sciences. Consequently, this chapter will criticize radical orthodoxy for having a fundamentalist (non-accommodational) view on other secular cultures, although it engages with many different secular theories and cultures.

In the fourth chapter, I will examine how trinitarian hermeneutics is received and developed in the German-speaking world through the works of Ingolf Dalferth. In the first section, I will draw attention to how Dalferth develops his hermeneutic theology with the help of *new hermeneutics* which is succeeded by Gerhard Ebeling, Ernst Fuchs, and Eberhard Jüngel. In this section, I will investigate the background of German hermeneutic theology and how it is different from the English-speaking world theologies. For the second section, I will revisit the grammar of trinitarian theology in the light of German hermeneutic theology. For this, I will illustrate Dalferth's Christian philosophy of orientation to see how German hermeneutic theology understands and applies trinitarian theology in the modern secular world. The last section of this chapter will explain how Dalferth reacts to the post secular world with the emphasis on a God-focused-theology. Unlike other postmodern theologians, Dalferth rejects the idea of conflict between religion and secularity, while asking us to move forward toward post-secularity which allows every community to coexist and interact with one another. According to Dalferth, post-secularity allows "a differentiation of various 'public spheres.'"[42] In this sphere of post-secularity, he claims that Christianity can offer a transformative insight such as the fundamental distinction between the Creator and creation; that is, the distinction between transcendence and immanence. So, introducing Dalferth's theology, this chapter will show that Christianity can offer contributions to the post-secular world when Christians focus on the perspective of God.

For the last chapter, I will summarize the result of comparing these three different theological trends, and will argue that *the 21st trinitarian theology as the humble witness of the Triune God should work toward the trinitarian theology of inculturation. Recognizing inculturation as the act of the Triune God, this theology highlights the differences of the understanding of God according to different contexts. In doing so, rather than being indifferent or hostile to worldly cultures, this theology argues that the trinitarian nature of the gospel leads Christians to reconcile with others and inculturate the gospel into new cultures constantly in relational love.* The three compared theological trends' main idea is the centrality of God's self-revelation as a hermeneutical principle of Christian theology; I will argue that the three theological movements are correct that the understanding of the Trinity in the confession of the church should be the principle of theology in the age of secularism. However, through evaluating the different theological stances

---

42. Dalferth, *Transcendence and the Secular World*, 36.

toward worldliness, I will also point out that the trinitarian understanding of the church has to engage with the current situation of world (global) Christianity, because many Christians today live in the globalized world. To do so, in the final chapter, I will attempt to connect trinitarian theology with Korean Protestant hermeneutic theology because Korean Christian history is a good example of a global contextual response to worldliness. In this chapter, I will highlight a concept of inculturation to embrace many distinctive worldly cultures and to apply a trinitarian theology to the situation of world Christianity with a concern for the contextualization (differentiation) of Christianity. Through borrowing Dalferth's thinking, this chapter will suggest that different realities and understandings can be reconciled in trinitarian faith, because the perspective of the Triune God leads us to incorporate different cultures and understandings to one reconciled reality of the Triune God in love. So, this chapter will show that the proper role of Christian theology as the faithful witness of the Trinity is to engage with different cultures all around world and to inculturate the gospel based on a *God-focused-perspective*.

Given the structure of this research, it should be noted that this book is not intended to be a mere summary statement and detailed analysis of the trinitarian conceptions of current trinitarian theologies in the twenty-first century. The goal in and around the questions of my book is to contribute to a theological practice that opens up a new meaning to *faith-based-theology*—for the one Holy Catholic Church—by providing a clear and faithful theological analysis of our present situation for the renewal of Christian faith in the ages of secularism and globalism today. For this, this book wants to make a constructive contribution to the pressing questions of the present and not only present a theological analysis of dogmatic figures of thought; it attempts to connect the messages of the current trinitarian theologies to the context of world (global) Christianity. That is why this book will try to rediscover the importance of the centrality of God's self-revelation as a hermeneutical principle in the ages of post-secularity and globalization. In constructing a dialogue between the cutting-edge theological movements, my book will show that Christians' understanding of God can overcome the tension between theology and other cultures (or other sciences). And further, it will claim that Christian faith in fact contributes to our society through pursuing a genuine dialectics of differentiation and interdependence in the perspective of transcendence. In doing so, I will concern how trinitarian hermeneutical positions should be transferred to the new Christian contexts, and how Christian practices should be anticipated in the perspective of God that leads us to have faith, hope, and love. Consequently, I expect that my exploration of trinitarian theologies with the concept of inculturation will offer a better understanding for the inclusiveness of the Divine love which overcomes binarism, exclusivism, colonialism, racism, supersessionism, orientalism, occidentalism, essentialism, and anthropocentrism.[43]

---

43. Tillich believes that the task of theology is to bridge the gap between the eternal truth of the Christian message and the interpretation of this truth for every generation. Tillich, *Systematic Theology*, 1:5.

2

A Postliberal Reaction (North America)

The following chapter will examine the stance of postliberal theology toward worldliness. The first section will investigate the works of George Lindbeck and other religious pluralists to see how postliberalism starts its discourse from the background of liberal theology in North America. The second section will deal with Hans Frei's work to see how postliberalism develops its hermeneutic stance and how postliberalism applies the doctrine of the Trinity to the lives of Christians. The last section of this chapter will study Stanley Hauerwas' theological view on secularity to examine how postliberalism responds to worldly cultures in the age of secularism. In evaluating the view of postliberal theology, this chapter will show both the contribution and limit of postliberalism. In postliberal theology, theologians attempt to connect Karl Barth's trinitarian theology with Wittgenstein's language-game, in order to highlight the uniqueness of Christian faith and the importance of practicality in theology; postliberal theology contributes a lot to the North American theology through changing the overall atmosphere of theological studies to embrace the uniqueness and practicality of Christian theology. However, this chapter will criticize postliberal theology for avoiding an active engagement with other disciplines or secular theories outside of Christianity. Thus, this chapter will argue that postliberal theology shows a sectarian view on worldliness.

THE TRENDS OF LIBERAL THEOLOGY IN THE TWENTIETH CENTURY

The History and Types of Religious Pluralism

To examine the background of postliberal theology, what I first want to highlight is the dominance of liberal (academic) theology in the twentieth century. To be specific, one of the interesting movements of the twentieth century theology in North America is the discourse of religious pluralism within the dominance of liberal theology. In this theological trend, some theologians—including, John Hick, Paul Knitter, and Raimundo Panikkar—have gone further beyond the Christian inclusivist view with the suggestion that there is nothing unique, normative, or superior about Christianity among other world religions. The chief expounder of this view is John Hick, who first propounds it in *God and the Universe of Faiths*. In his book, Hick believes that all religions lead to the same God. According to Hick, Christianity is not the one and only way of salvation, but one among several religions. As a result, for Hick, it is the same message of God that comes distinctly to a particular religious group but in a different form from the others.[1] As Hick's suggestion became popular, some theologians began to form a stream called *religious pluralism*. The popularity of this trend is attested to by the significant meeting of theologians at the Claremont Graduate University on March 7–8, 1986. The major papers of the conference were bound in the book, *The Myth of Christian Uniqueness*.[2] In this new theological trend, many Christian theologians began to encourage active interreligious dialogues through suggesting common frames of religions.

Investigating diverse religious pluralists' methodologies, the following section will point out that there can be two general types of religious pluralism. The first type of pluralism is based on a common frame of religion. This means that scholars in this type understand there to be a common (universal) ultimate reality, and differences are coming from different cultural backgrounds to describe the same reality of God. A best example of the first type is theocentrism, which suggests a single, common God among all religions; this type is promoted by John Hick. Another example of the first type is soteriocentrism, represented by Paul Knitter. The last example I want to mention for the first type is Raimundo Panikkar's theanthropocosmic vision, arguing that each religion has the whole truth in their cosmologies without a common ground from one another. Here, Panikkar believes that every religion has their own divine-human-cosmic relational cosmology,

---

1. See Hick, *God and the Universe of Faiths*.
2. See Hick and Knitter, *The Myth of Christian Uniqueness*.

depicting their unique reality; he claims that every religion has a unique cosmology that connects human beings to the whole (cosmic) divine reality, even though each cosmology may refer to different truths one another. On the other hand, the second type of religious pluralism is based on different frames between world religions. This type does not identify a common ground between religions at all. As a result, there is no single, common ultimate reality shared by different faiths. An example of this type is George Lindbeck's cultural-linguistic approach, based on Wittgenstein's language game. Lindbeck presumes that all religions have their own cultural-linguistic grammar and thus there is no common frame. Interestingly, Lindbeck suggests that each religion has different grammars so that they are not compatible one another.

In this section, through examining different religious pluralists' views, I will show that theologians get in a trouble when they focus on the common frame of different religions to evaluate different religious doctrines, because there cannot be a perfect common religious concept to embrace many different religious teachings at once; it is worthy to highlight the uniqueness of each religion as Lindbeck suggests. To show this, this chapter will briefly summarize four important theological views on (1) the definition of religion, (2) approach to interreligious dialogue, (3) criteria for different religions, and (4) possible criticism and evaluation. Through comparing and evaluating four different theological views, this chapter will look at how Lindbeck opens postliberalism's theological stance from the background of the twentieth century liberal theology in America.

Theocentric Pluralism (John Hick)

John Hick, an English theologian who is a founding figure of religious pluralism, starts interreligious conversation with the belief that all religious traditions have one common frame. For him, the starting point is the universal religious experience of humankind.[3] He thinks both the nontheistic and theistic forms of experience may exhibit a common epistemological structure—that is, a common religious experience which changes human beings' existence.[4] For Hick, even though people have different religious experiences, there is a common frame in the fact that their religious experience has a profound effect on their existence. In this sense, he believes that all different religious experiences have a common structure, and people are experiencing the same reality. Hick expresses this as "the ultimate Reality"

---

3. Hick, *God Has Many Names*, 79.
4. Hick, *God Has Many Names*, 84.

or "the Eternal One." He says, "Let us call the ultimate object of religious worship, experience and contemplation the Eternal One—a phrase which draws upon associations both with the mystical One without a second of the Upanishads and the Holy One of the biblical and other theistic faiths."[5] In developing his theology, he aims at inclusivity through suggesting the concept of the ultimate Reality. For him, because the word "God" is strongly associated with the notion of a personal being, it fails to include religious experiences outside of Indo-European tradition.[6] By using a broader term, however, a more general understanding of religious experience may be acquired. This is why he uses the term "the ultimate Reality" to highlight that there is a common religious structure among different religious traditions.

Within this view, Hick argues that people are worshiping and experiencing the same "ultimate Reality," although they may use many different names for the same Reality. He explains that the reason why we have so many world religions is because the human religious experience may have different meanings and interpretations according to different cultural backgrounds.[7] He describes this divine Reality like this: "in itself (there is) limitless, exceeding the scope of human conceptuality and language, but which is humanly thought and experienced in various conditioned and limited ways."[8] For him, because human beings cannot understand the ultimate Reality due to their finitude, they experience the Reality within their own life experience and culture. That is why Hick believes that a way of understanding and experiencing the world depends on the complexes of conceptual, cultural, historical, linguistic conditions.[9] As a result, in Hick's theology, no one can proclaim an exclusive truth over others, because human responses toward the ultimate Reality vary according to different cultures and human conditions. In this respect, many different names for the ultimate Reality should not be judged or despised, because all of them provide a meaningful framework for the transformation of human existence in their own contexts. Thus, a certain religious experience in a specific culture cannot be regarded as an absolute exclusive truth from other religious experiences.

Because Hick is focusing on the common ground of world religions called the ultimate Reality, he establishes a criterion for the evaluation of religious beliefs based on the common frame of religions: existential transformation toward the ultimate Reality. When he compares other religions

5. See Hick, "Pluralism and the Reality of the Transcendent."
6. Hick, *God Has Many Names*, 87.
7. Hick, *The Metaphor of God Incarnate*, 134.
8. Hick, "The Philosophy of World Religions," 231.
9. Hick, *The Metaphor of God Incarnate*, 143.

with Christianity, he finds that each religion will invariably account for some phenomena better than others, while being relatively indifferent to other things.[10] As a result, any grading of a religion cannot be achieved by any intellectual test.[11] However, he believes that the important criterion for religions is their vision: "Each of the great traditions thus constitutes a valid context of salvation/liberation; but none constitutes the one and only such context, and each may be able to gain a larger understanding of the Real by attending to the reports and conceptualizing of the others."[12] In this view, each religion is an authentic response in some sense to the one divine Reality, while at the same time facing up to the immense diversity in the ways that the Reality is pictured. Consequently, the important criterion for religions is how much one can be transformed and be like the transcendent Reality encountered. In this respect, positive evaluation for Hick's religious pluralism can be given, because it is not simply based on apparent similarities of various kinds of theistic worship. It is also based on a theological reflection derived from existential awareness of and friendship with people outside the Christian faith-community.

However, the language of Hick is still adequate only in contexts where religions share or appear to share a comparably theistic understanding. For example, Daoism or Confucianism does not have a concept of the ultimate Reality based on one theistic God. Naturally, the concept of the Reality would not bear the concept of Dao (the relative contemplation), because the Dao is something that needs to be changed all the time in Eastern religions. In many world religions, the ultimate Reality has no common ground, because they may refer totally different ideas, notions, and faiths so that it is questionable whether we can put all religious experience into one theistic frame that is centered on what is called the Reality. Although each religion may have similar religious experiences, Hick overlooks that they might in fact refer to totally different realities. This suggests that Hick's theory is problematic for many who see many differences among religions rather than commonalities. Therefore, even though Hick contributes a lot to the discourse of theology through opening a new gate for the Christian pluralism, his idea is not free from distorting the views of other religious believers.

---

10. Hick, "On Grading Religions," 452.
11. Hick, "On Grading Religions," 461.
12. Hick, "On Grading Religions," 462.

Soteriocentric Pluralism (Paul Knitter)

Although many religious pluralists such as Wilfred Smith, Schubert Ogden, and John Hick, try to focus on the common frame of human existential experience or the Reality, Paul Knitter suggests an advanced approach to religious pluralism—soteriocentrism.[13] Knitter argues that we ought to cease our search for a universal theory or a common source, because those desires to establish a common essence overlook what is genuinely different: "John Hick's and my theocentric model for a Christian approach to other faiths . . . still imperialistically imposes our notions of Deity or the Ultimate on other believers."[14] Although Knitter holds a theocentric view of other religions, he recognizes that there is a tension in his theocentric view because his knowledge is originally drafted within a solely Christian framework.[15] Thus, for Knitter, the notion that world religions are a response to a single divine Reality justifying Christian faith cannot be true to other religious traditions such as Hinduism (polytheism), Confucianism, and Daoism (nontheism).

To resolve this problem, Knitter suggests a liberation theology of religion, focusing on the common goal of religions. He says, "if there is no pre-established common ground or common essence that we can invoke before dialogue, perhaps there is a common approach or a common context with which we can begin dialogue in order to create our shared shaky ground."[16] Here, Knitter focuses on the common context of religions rather than the common frame of them, because he is influenced by liberation (contextual) theology.[17] According to Knitter, although each religious concept is actually indicating different religious dimensions, each religion may share the same context: the experience of the oppressed. As a result, he avers that there are common religious concerns for the poor and oppressed, as found in Latin-American, Black liberation theology, and feminist liberation theology. Therefore, for Knitter, the common ground of religions is the situation of the present; the common goal of all religions can be the work on this unfair human reality.

According to Knitter, interreligious dialogue is necessary for building a better and more just world together.[18] Here, interreligious dialogue is not

---

13. Knitter, "Toward a Liberation Theology of Religion," in Hick and Knitter, *The Myth of Christian Uniqueness*, 187. Cf. Barker, *Paul F. Knitter's Soteriocentric Theology of Religions*.

14. Knitter, "Toward a Liberation Theology of Religion," 187.
15. Knitter, *No Other Names?*, 65.
16. Knitter, "Toward a Liberation Theology of Religion," 185.
17. Knitter, "Toward a Liberation Theology of Religion," 179.
18. Knitter, "Toward a Liberation Theology of Religion," 179.

one of winning over, but of sharing.[19] Knitter believes that what one has seen, felt, and been transformed by can also affect others, because it is about witnessing and learning, rather than converting. In this sense, all interreligious dialogues are animated by a certain mission to discover something to learn. Based on this mind set to learn from others, what is common to these cross-cultural grounds is that all of them are calling for some forms of liberation. Knitter says, "religions all over the world commonly have an awareness of the need for liberation for restoring, preserving, and fostering life."[20] For Knitter, liberation will only be able, if it breaks out of the regional confines and only if it learns to take different people's religious experience seriously.[21] As a result, Knitter believes that the primary purpose of interreligious dialogue is to speak and act together, to remove the oppression in our global world.[22] Because Knitter tries to work with other religions for the common context, while admitting different frames of divinity, his view is obviously less prone to ideological abuse than Hick's view. Thus, Knitter's view allows us to make common efforts toward liberation with other religious traditions.

Although Knitter argues for soteriocentrism to revise Hick's theocentricism, it still has a crucial weakness in that it can only embrace religions having a concern about the liberation of the oppressed. John Cobb, for example, criticizes Knitter's work, "posing such a condition on dialogue unilaterally from the Christian side is a continuation of the imperialism Knitter opposes. . . . [H]e appears to say that he seeks dialogue only with those who share his understanding of salvation."[23] According to Cobb, Knitter's view overlooks that other religions may have totally different soteriologies. For example, the plain explanation for the Confucian afterlife is to rise and gain fame in the world (立身揚名). In addition, Daoism seeks either doing nothing (無爲) or perennial youth and long life (不老長生); their concepts of salvation are not about the liberation of the oppressed. The primary concern for Eastern religions is thus totally different. This suggests that Knitter's common ground is not sufficient to embrace all other world religions because there can be different religious interests other than the common human context like the liberation of the oppressed.

19. Knitter, "Interreligious Dialogue," 22.
20. Knitter, "Interreligious Dialogue," 27.
21. Knitter, "Interreligious Dialogue," 23.
22. Knitter, "Toward a Liberation Theology of Religion," 181.
23. Knitter, "Toward a Liberation Theology of Religion," 187.

Cosmological Pluralism (Raimundo Panikkar)

Raimundo Panikkar, a third-world Roman Catholic priest, suggests a theanthropocosmic insight (which sees a unity between the divine-human-cosmic), implying that each religious tradition reflects, corrects, complements, and challenges others in its own relational cosmology.[24] He believes that religious truth is something relational, between the divine-human-cosmic. According to his theory, there cannot be a universal religious truth; he criticizes the impulse of universalization in the West, while pointing out that the concept of universalization gives a negative influence to other civilizations.[25] Rather than focusing on the universal Reality, Panikkar focuses on the absolute in the relative. Here, he believes that "truth is always relational."[26] He says, "thinking or the intelligence, covers the totality of Being only from the exterior.... Being has an untapped reservoir, a dynamism, an inner side not illumined by self-knowledge, reflection or the like."[27] According to Panikkar, no theory can be absolutely universal, while everything is relational and relative. For him, the truth cannot be abstracted from its relationship with a particular mind or a particular context. In this respect, he argues that all religious traditions can be relationally true, universal, and legitimate, even though they may have different contexts: "any alleged universal theory is one particular theory that claims universal validity, thus trespassing the limits of its own legitimacy."[28] In other words, Panikkar believes that every religion somehow deals with the relationship between the divine-human-cosmic. That is why all different religions can be true in Panikkar's theology, even while they remain incompatible in terms of language and doctrine.

From this point of view, religions are not static constructs because each concrete religious vision can be universal, even though each of them has different frames and realities.[29] To give an example, Christ cannot be an absolute truth for all. However, Christ is the mystery in the Christian sense, when Christians speak of mystery; Christians realize that their experience of the mystery is inseparable from Christ. Likewise, the Hindu who has reached realization becomes enlightened and discovers *atman-brahman*, realizing the ultimate mystery.[30] This means that each religion construes truth

---

24. Panikkar, "The Jordan, the Tiber, and the Ganges," in Hick and Knitter, *The Myth of Christian Uniqueness*, 109.
25. Panikkar, *The Invisible Harmony*, 147.
26. Panikkar, *The Invisible Harmony*, 160.
27. Panikkar, *The Invisible Harmony*, 159.
28. Panikkar, *The Invisible Harmony*, 161.
29. Panikkar, "The Jordan, the Tiber, and the Ganges," 108.
30. Panikkar, *The Unknown Christ of Hinduism*, 25.

through its own language and method. Here, Panikkar flips Karl Rahner's concept of the *anonymous Christian*. For Panikkar, a Christian can be the *unknown Hindu*, because Hinduism also has the whole truth for Hindus.[31] For Panikkar, each religious universal statement is turned toward its own center: it can be universal; it can be true. Panikkar calls this the "*pars pro toto effect*" (part for the whole).[32] In Panikkar's view, through their own traditions, people can see the whole truth, not just a partial truth. In other words, while each religious tradition has different perspectives, each has the full truth in terms of the relationship between the divine-human-cosmic. For him, "we see the whole through our window; we see and are the '*totum in partre*' (whole in the part)."[33] In addition, in Panikkar's theology, the concrete part of each religion is *pars pro toto* (part for the whole)."[34] In this methodology, Panikkar implies that each religious tradition indicates different realities and each religion has their own unique truth and true reality within themselves through their unique cosmology.

For Panikkar, the evaluative criteria for each religion is how much they can commit to the *imperative* method—"that is the effort at learning from the other and the attitude of allowing our own convictions to be fecundated by the insights of the other."[35] Panikkar rejects the comparative method in interreligious dialogue, because we do not have any neutral platform outside each religious tradition. He thinks that we can only *impariamo* (learn) from the other through opening ourselves from our standpoint to a dialogue that does not seek to win or to convince.[36] Instead of comparing, Panikkar argues that we need to search together from a different prospective, because the true concord "is neither oneness nor plurality."[37] He says, "It is the dynamism of the Many toward the One without ceasing to be different and without becoming one, and without reaching a higher synthesis. There is no harmonical accord."[38] Instead of comparing religions, Panikkar here deepens mutual understanding, although different religions cannot come up with a great universal theory.[39] In this theory, religions borrow from each other and learn from each other with a confidence that they have the whole

---

31. Panikkar, *The Unknown Christ of Hinduism*, 26.
32. Panikkar, "The Jordan, the Tiber, and the Ganges," 106.
33. Panikkar, "The Jordan, the Tiber, and the Ganges," 107.
34. Panikkar, "The Jordan, the Tiber, and the Ganges," 107.
35. Panikkar, *The Invisible Harmony*, 172.
36. Panikkar, *The Invisible Harmony*, 172.
37. Panikkar, *The Invisible Harmony*, 178.
38. Panikkar, *The Invisible Harmony*, 178.
39. Panikkar, *The Invisible Harmony*, 173.

truth; nothing is destroyed or compromised here. Thus, he believes that the fruit of interreligious dialogue is the process of *mutual learning*.[40]

While Panikkar respects other religions with considerable knowledge, his position is still limited in that not all religions have a cosmic view or cosmology. For example, in ancient Eastern religions such as Daoism or Confucianism, the cosmic (universal and eternal) concept of Li (理), Chi (氣), or Dao (道) began to develop much later, after Buddhism was introduced to East Asia. For example, Confucius explicitly says, "the subjects on which the Master did not talk, were-extraordinary things, feats of strength, disorder, and spiritual beings."[41] This implies that it is difficult to find a cosmic myth, story, or concept like the mystical or Reality, Truth, or Vision in the ancient Eastern religions, because the religiosity of the East pursues one's immanent transcendence in the mundane life rather than suggesting a universal cosmic (mysterious) story. In this ethos of Eastern religions, Eastern religious practitioners do to absolutize myths, while they tend not to develop a cosmic story to explain their reality. In this respect, even though Eastern religions also develop (cosmic) metaphysical concepts, it is hard to say that their metaphysical concepts are their primary concern in their deep heart. Therefore, we should ask again: is it really possible to have a common frame in explaining religious diversity?

Wittgensteinian Pluralism (George Lindbeck)

Looking at many liberal theologies to find a common universal frame, George Lindbeck suggests a totally different approach through borrowing Wittgenstein's idea of language game.[42] After being a delegated observer at the Second Vatican Council, Lindbeck introduces his theological methodology in his major book, *The Nature of Doctrine: Religion and Theology in a Postliberal Age*. In this book, he argues that conceptualizing one religion's doctrine allows us to trace the whole reflection of religion as Wittgenstein

---

40. Panikkar, *The Invisible Harmony*, 173.

41. Confucius, *The Analects*, ch. 7.

42. Cf. Wittgenstein here suggests that everything is a language-game that forms our life, and this idea can be applied to theology. According to Wittgenstein, human reasoning, behaviors, and even memories are mediated by language. Because everything is constituted by language, even religion can be a language-game in Wittgensteinian philosophy; he takes "theology as grammar" (§273.). He says, "So, if someone has not learned a language, is he unable to have certain memories? Of course-he cannot have linguistic memories, linguistic wishes or fears, and so on. And memories suchlike in language are not mere threadbare representations of the real experiences; for is what is linguistic not an experience?" Wittgenstein, *Philosophical Investigations*, §649.

claims: "the adoption of a particular theory ordinarily alters the meaning of the observation terms, that is, alters the fact to be accounted for."[43] According to Lindbeck, there are three theological theories of religion. One of these emphasizes the propositional aspect of religion.[44] In this view, religion stresses the ways in which church doctrines function as informative truth. This view has certain affinities to Wittgenstein's analytical philosophy with its preoccupation with the cognitive or informational meanings in religion. A second theory puts emphasis on the experiential-expressive dimension of religion.[45] This view focuses on the resemblances of religions to aesthetic enterprises and it emphasizes the human responses to different religious experiences.

In order to combine these two different emphases, Lindbeck suggests an alternative way to understand religion, the so-called "cultural-linguistic approach."[46] This approach assumes that we cannot actualize our specific human capacities for thought, action, and feeling without language and culture.[47] According to Lindbeck, religion involves languages and symbol systems. In other words, he believes that religion is the substance of culture and language.[48] For him, religion can be viewed as a kind of cultural/linguistic framework or medium that shapes our forms of life. In this methodology, a comprehensive scheme in religion is not primarily a set of propositions to be believed, but is rather the medium in which one moves, a set of skills that one employs in one's life.[49] As a result, in Lindbeck's theology, religion (the complex of language and culture) is something to use in the lives of human beings, because "the richer our expressive or linguistic system will bring the more subtle, varied, and differentiated our experience."[50] Here, Lindbeck argues that religious proclamation should be a storytelling to be used and applied into our lives. For him, when each religion's story gains power and

---

43. Lindbeck, *The Nature of Doctrine*, 11. It is noteworthy that Wittgenstein also notices that the world is pluralistic and has many different communities, as many pluralists point out; he recognizes that there are many different kinds of language-games. For example, he says in his *Philosophical Investigations*, "It is easy to imagine a language consisting only of orders and reports in battle.—Or a language consisting only of questions and expressions for answering yes and no. And innumerable others.—And to imagine a language means to imagine a form of life" (§23).

44. Lindbeck, *The Nature of Doctrine*, 16.

45. Lindbeck, *The Nature of Doctrine*, 16.

46. Lindbeck, *The Nature of Doctrine*, 18.

47. Lindbeck, *The Nature of Doctrine*, 34.

48. Lindbeck, *The Nature of Doctrine*, 34.

49. Lindbeck, *The Nature of Doctrine*, 37.

50. Lindbeck, *The Nature of Doctrine*, 37.

meaning in the scheme of someone's culture and language, it forms a strong bondage among the religious group and creates a new direction of people's life. In this view, all religions originate from culture/linguistic frames—especially narratives or stories—and the linguistic frames create certain forms of life through being used by the people in a contained cultural/linguistic community.[51]

Here, the cultural-linguistic approach emphasizes the *differences* between religions. Lindbeck is very skeptical of apologetics or conversions, because the different origins of religions relate to different cultures and languages.[52] For him, it is impossible to discuss the merits and demerits of culture and language. According to Lindbeck, even though the world of experience has a lot of similarities, we cannot unify different cultures and languages at the exact same point.[53] As a result, different religions can be incompatible and not comparable to one another because each religion has its own formulation or grammar and its own different linguistic/cultural frames and stories. According to Lindbeck, different religions just create different forms of life, causing the incompatibility between religions. As a result, the cultural-linguistic approach denies that there is a universal, experiential core to all religions, because every religion evokes fundamentally different experiences and realities. In this sense, unlike many interreligious theologians such as John Hick, Paul Knitter, and Raimundo Panikkar who focus on the common frame of religion, Lindbeck suggests an alternative (cultural-linguistic) frame, emphasizing the differences between religions.[54]

Regarding the criteria of religion, Lindbeck suggests the notion of "categorical adequacy" as his criterion of religion.[55] He claims that religious propositions are difficult to categorize as true or false statements in an ontological sense. However, Lindbeck points out that different religious propositions at least constitute idioms that make sense in their own internal grammar. In other words, although the cultural-linguistic approach

---

51. Cf. Like Lindbeck argues that we first need to be immersed into the Christian community, Wittgenstein also believes that we need to be trained in order to participate in language-games. According to Wittgenstein, when we are able to play the game, we can also say that we know the game. This is true even if we don't know any of the rules explicitly. The grammar of "understanding a game" means knowing how to go on, knowing what to do next. In other words, unless we have a technique of the game, we cannot play a game; he believes that "what we believe depends on what we learn" (§286). He says, "The game can be learned purely practically, without learning any explicit rules." Wittgenstein, *On Certainty*, §95.

52. Lindbeck *The Nature of Doctrine*, 128.
53. Lindbeck, *The Nature of Doctrine*, 129.
54. Cf. Eckerstorfer, "The One Church in the Postmodern World."
55. Lindbeck, *The Nature of Doctrine*, 48.

proposes no common framework to compare religions, Lindbeck believes that religions may have incommensurable notions of truth, experience, and categorical adequacy. As a result, in Lindbeck's theology, the reason why we need interreligious dialogue is to learn categorical adequacy in each religion's language. He says, "one of the ways in which Christians can serve their neighbors may be through helping adherents of other religions to purify and enrich their heritage, to make them better speakers of the languages they have."[56] Here, the inherited patterns of beliefs and practices of religions remain, but religious practitioners can correct anomalies in their own languages and grammars through looking at each other's different grammar. Consequently, while using Wittgenstein's language-game, Lindbeck recovers the uniqueness of each religion. For him, good religions can enable other religions to fix categorical adequacy (their own internal grammatical error) and work towards a better doctrinal system. This shows that the aim of Lindbeck's theology is to suggest a frame to keep each religious tradition's uniqueness.[57]

Although many twentieth century liberal theologians in the age of religious pluralism attempted to find some universal aspects of religion—a sense of the holy, a concern for liberation, or a cosmological vision—Lindbeck claims to move on toward the age of *postliberalism* which focuses on a narrative presentation of each religious tradition. In the postliberal culture, because everybody is aware that each religion has different realities and languages, many religious people are not interested in giving up their quest for truth. Instead, they tend to reproduce, prove, and discuss their own doctrinal confessions in their own religious community.[58] As a result, postliberal theology requires Christians to recover the importance of the truth claims in their own religious tradition.

Accordingly, one of the most important contributions of Lindbeck's work is that he emphasizes a practical dimension of religion through suggesting *a cultural-language frame*. Through borrowing insights from Ludwig Wittgenstein, Clifford Geertz, and Thomas Kuhn, Lindbeck claims that religion is a cultural-linguistic framework "that makes possible the description of realities, the formulation of beliefs, and the experiencing of inner attitudes, feelings, and sentiments."[59] Lindbeck here argues that the point of religion is to use their religious narratives to make people's life richer rather

---

56. Lindbeck, *The Nature of Doctrine*, 61.

57. For a similar view with Lindbeck's theology that each religion has different ends, see Heim, *The Depth of the Riches*; Dalferth, "Religions in a World of Many Cultures" in Sanders, *D. Z. Phillips' Contemplative Philosophy of Religion*, 158.

58. Willimon, "Answering Pilate," 83.

59. Lindbeck, *The Nature of Doctrine*, 32–33.

than suggesting a universal academic theory. So, the primary interest of Lindbeck's theology becomes using and practicing the Christian narratives in the real life of the religious community; his theology is practical.

Although the use of Wittgenstein in Lindbeck's theology makes theology practical through highlighting the uniqueness of Christian logic in a pluralistic world, Lindbeck's methodology still has a problem in that it offers a high theory of religion unlike Wittgenstein's language-game. In other words, Lindbeck's *The Nature of Doctrine* offers a modified correspondence theory of truth, while Wittgenstein rejected notions of correspondence as unhelpful and confusing.[60] This shows that Lindbeck adapts Wittgenstein's language-game for his own purpose, while modifying Wittgenstein's language-game. In Lindbeck's work, his main concern is a doctrinal disputation in the context of interreligious dialogue. Throughout his life, he was always concerned about other cultures and aimed to find an understanding of doctrine that allowed for ecumenical agreement.[61] That is why he suggests a cultural-linguistic frame in which doctrine functions as the explicit grammar of the language of Christianity. As a result, he suggests that we should understand the theory of doctrine like a computer program: "Just as genetic codes or computer programs may remain identical even while producing startling different products depending on input and situation, so also with the basic grammars of cultures, languages, and religions. They remain the same while the products change."[62] In this description, Lindbeck seeks to make another theory for the therapeutic dissolution of doctrinal problems, especially to remedy the existing formal philosophy (theory) of religion. For him, it is important to create a theory of religion to deal with doctrinal dissolutions in the pluralistic setting. However, Wittgenstein's language-game in fact wants to describe things rather than making a theory; there is a conflict between Lindbeck and Wittgenstein. In this respect, one can criticize Lindbeck for proposing a Wittgensteinian "theory" for his own purpose in an attempting to do ecumenism and interreligious dialogue,

---

60. Cf. Ashford, "Wittgenstein's Theologians?," 369.

61. Lindbeck was the son of Lutheran missionaries in China, and he was exposed to the culture of China and Korea in his early life. Also, he was an official Lutheran overseer at the Second Vatican Council. He later served as a member of the international Lutheran/Roman Catholic Dialogue sponsored by the Lutheran World Federation and the Vatican Secretariat for Christian Unity (1968–87) and was co-chairperson of the Lutheran delegation for more than ten years (1976–87). This supports that his life concern was finding ecumenical/interreligious agreements.

62. Lindbeck, *The Nature of Doctrine*, 83.

although Lindbeck is right to highlight the practicality and uniqueness of Christianity in the age of relativism.[63]

THE HERMENEUTICS OF NARRATIVE THEOLOGY

The Rise of Narrative Theology

Shortly after Lindbeck published his book, *the Nature of Doctrine*, the term "postliberalism" or "Yale school" began to be accepted as an influential theological movement. In this movement, theologians under the influence of Lindbeck begin to emphasize the cultural-linguistic frame of religion, the internal use of religious grammar, and the practicality of theology.[64] Another founder figure of this theological movement is Lindbeck's Yale colleague, Hans Frei. Both Lindbeck and Frei have a *non-foundationalists view*, holding pragmatic aspects of Christian faith. Whereas liberalism regards religions as the experiential contents of the believers, postliberalism emphasizes the uniqueness of Christian faith and the practical use of the Christian internal narratives in common. Because of the practicality of their theology, the Yale school's theology became very popular especially for the theologians who studied at Yale as its doctoral students; postliberal theology includes many Yale PhD scholars such as Brevard Childs, David Kelsey, William Placher, Stanley Hauerwas, William Willimon, Bruce Marshall, and Kathryn Tanner.[65] Through many of these followers who studied many different fields of theological studies such as biblical studies, church history, Christian ethics, and practical theologies, postliberal theology became a gigantic theological movement in North America. So, postliberal theology still has a huge impact on the American theology today.

Although Lindbeck and Frei initiate postliberal theology with a non-foundationalist view together, there are slight differences between Lindbeck and Frei. To give an example, if Lindbeck focuses on interreligious dialogue and regulative doctrine, Frei draws more attention to biblical interpretation (hermeneutics) and ecclesial practitioner to focus on the actual practice of Christians rather than suggesting another theory. This implies that many postliberal theologians do not only make a distinction from liberal theology

---

63. On this problem, other postliberal theologians such as Hans Frei and Stanley Hauerwas suggest focusing solely on the internal grammar of Christianity rather than borrowing Wittgenstein's theology for an ecumenical dialogue. I will talk more about this issue in the coming sections.

64. Hunsinger, "Postliberal theology," in Vanhoozer, *The Cambridge Companion to Postmodern Theology*, 44.

65. Hunsinger, "Postliberal theology," 42.

in an external religious study setting, because they also develop the internal usages of the Wittgensteinian cultural-linguistic frame in their internal Christian faith. Here, postliberalism develops *narrative theology* which focuses on a narrative presentation of Christian faith as regulative for the coherent (internal) grammar of theology. To show how postliberal theology further develops its cultural-linguistic frame to its internal (practical) dimension, the second section of this chapter will investigate how Frei suggests postliberal hermeneutics. To do this, the following section will investigate (1) how Hans Frei suggests narrative theology (metanarrative realism) for his hermeneutics, (2) how he uses his (internal) narrative theology in face of the modern secular reason, and (3) how he understands the doctrine of Trinity in his narrative theology.

The Eclipse of the Realistic (History-like) Reading

As I mentioned above, one of the other names of postliberal theology is *narrative theology*. This is because this theological movement emphasizes the Christian narrative's internal logic and the history-like reading in its theological method. This orientation of postliberal theology is often understood to be a Barthian influence.[66] In fact, Hans Frei's doctoral dissertation is about Barth's doctrine of revelation: "The Doctrine of Revelation in the Thought of Karl Barth, 1909–1922: The Nature of Barth's Break with Liberalism." Frei's theological journey starts from his question about God's revelation: if God speaks, how do we hear and understand? "Do the stories and whatever concepts may be drawn from them describe what we apprehend as the real world? Do they fit a more general framework of meaning than that of a single story?"[67] In his first book, *The Eclipse of Biblical Narrative*, Frei confesses that his work has been influenced by Karl Barth, Erich Auerbach, and Gilbert Ryle.[68] Frei borrows Auerbach's and Ryle's understandings of radical realism in Barth.[69] For Frei, as Ryle suggests, the text is related to the

---

66. Knight, "The Barthian Heritage of Hans Frei," 308.
67. Frei, *The Eclipse of Biblical Narrative*, 5.
68. Frei, *The Eclipse of Biblical Narrative*, vii.
69. Knight, "The Barthian Heritage of Hans Frei," 313. Frei uses both Auerbach and Ryle's books to suggest a realistic (history-like) reading. Auerbach argues that the realistic way of reading has been deeply penetrated in the Western literature history. Also, while criticizing the Cartesian dualism, Ryle claims that it is a conceptual mistake to separate the works of mind and body. Based on these two thinkers, Frei believes that Christians also should establish a realistic way of reading the Scripture. Cf. Auerbach, *Mimesis*; Ryle, *The Concept of Mind*.

person who gives (or writes) the text.[70] In this understanding of the text, Frei draws attention to the fact that the giver of the Christian narrative is none other than the Triune God because the Christian narrative is considered the Word of the Trinity. More specifically, Frei claims that the Christian narrative is a realistic telling about the person of Jesus Christ—the second person of the Trinity.

Because Frei understands the Christian narrative as the realistic form of God's Word, he claims that Christians read the Scripture as "the realistic form of the stories."[71] To support his argument, Frei highlights the observation of Barth that modern liberal theologians are largely motivated by an apologetic impulse to justify the truth claim of Christianity. Under the influence of the Enlightenment, theologians often borrow other elements outside of the Christian internal narrative in interpreting the Christian narrative. However, Barth is very suspicious of "historical relativism."[72] Instead of using the modern scientific (relative) method, Barth insists that Christians should regard their text as God's exact revelation or God's self-disclosure action, because this realistic understanding of God's revelation is in fact the subject matter of the Christian narrative. In reading the Christian narrative, Barth believes that God is analogous to "that which it creates in the recipient: faith as obedience—including rational obedience."[73] In this Barth's way of reading, Christians understand the text as the exact self-revelation God, and therefore it is important to obedient to the teaching of the text.

Following Barth's theology, Frei argues that Christians follow the guidance that the text itself suggests; they consider the Scripture as the Word of God as the text proclaims so. In addition, Frei further points out that Christians regard their process of reading (understanding) as the activity of the Holy Spirit. As a result, for Frei, there is an activity of the Holy Spirit when Christians read the Word of God;[74] there is a correlation between the Holy Spirit and the text. According to Frei, when Christians read the Scripture, the Triune God's ontology comes first because Christians read the Scripture

---

70. He says, "Ryle's work . . . is a marvelous antidote to the contorted and to my mind unsuccessful efforts of certain phenomenologists and philosophers of 'Existence' and 'Being' to tackle a similar dualism. And therefore, it serves to explain better than they do how it is that we can read written discourse with the expectation of doing it reasonably intelligently." Frei, *The Eclipse of Biblical Narrative*, vii.

71. Frei, *The Eclipse of Biblical Narrative*, viii.

72. Frei, *The Eclipse of Biblical Narrative*, 2.

73. Frei, *The Eclipse of Biblical Narrative*, 121.

74. He says, "The fundamental conviction in regard to theological theory of knowledge on the part of Biblical realists is the correlation of the Holy Spirit and Scripture in the Word of God." Frei, "The Doctrine of Revelation," 502.

in a realistic sense; in reading the Christian narrative, God is "immediately present to the believing individual."[75] In this sense, Frei believes that it is the work of the Holy Spirit who leads Christians to read their narratives in a realistic sense. In this realistic reading of the text, Frei realizes that Christians affirm positive statements about the Triune God, because they read their narratives realistically through the work of the Holy Spirit. Thus, in Frei's description, Christians interpret the text with its internal subject matter—the realistic God who manifests as the Trinity.

Within this positive statement about God, Frei's main thesis is that: "a realistic or history-like (though not necessarily historical) element is a feature, as obvious as it is important, of many of the biblical narratives that went into the making of Christian belief."[76] Here, Frei proposes a *realistic narrative hermeneutics*. Frei points out that Christians have read their narratives in a literal sense for a long time. That is why Christians assume that the Scripture is the self-revelation of God. According to Frei, in this preeminence of realistic reading, Christians develop their doctrinal traditions and ethics. He says,

> First, if it seemed clear that a biblical story was to be read literally, it followed automatically that it referred to and described actual historical occurrences. . . . The second element in precritical realistic reading was that if the real historical world described by the several biblical stories is a single world of one temporal sequence, there must in principle be one cumulative story to depict it. . . . In the third place, since the world truly rendered by combining biblical narratives into one was indeed the one and only real world, it must in principle embrace the experience of any present age and reader.[77]

In these principles of interpretation, Christians take their text as a serious realistic narrative. In this understanding, Christians believe that the subject matter of their text must be Jesus Christ who guarantees God's salvation toward human beings; they understand the world and history within their narrative because their narrative for them is a real history, suggesting the Word of God. As a result of this realistic reading, Christians can read their narrative within the text's internal logic rather than external resources to assure their text's main subject matter—Jesus Christ.

To give an example, Frei sketches the hermeneutics of the literal reading of Scripture in the works of Luther and Calvin. Frei here points out that

---

75. Frei, "The Doctrine of Revelation," 502.
76. Frei, *The Eclipse of the Biblical Narrative*, 10.
77. Frei, *The Eclipse of the Biblical Narrative*, 2–3.

the Protestant Reformers believe that "the Bible is self-interpreting, the literal sense of its words being their true meaning."[78] That is why Luther says that the Scripture is "through itself most certain, most, easily accessible, comprehensible, interpreting itself, proving, judging all the words of all men."[79] Luther thinks that the Scripture is the Word of God to be heard by all human beings to preach about Christian faith which has, at the center, Jesus Christ; he proclaims, "*sola Scriptura*" as the methodology of interpretation in order to preach about the main subject of the narrative—Jesus Christ.

Likewise, Calvin regards Jesus Christ as the main subject matter of the whole Bible. Here, Calvin goes further from Luther's idea that the text itself is the act of preaching. Calvin believes that the text "is the setting forth of the reality which simultaneously constitutes its effective rendering to the reader by the Spirit."[80] For Calvin, when Christians read the Scripture, there is a coherence between the internal testimony of the Spirit and the meaning of the text; the meaning of the Scripture is constituted by the power of the Spirit. As a result, Calvin argues that a correct doctrinal faith is to believe the literal belief sets forth in the text, because the proper knowledge of God is correlated to self-knowledge coming through the work of the Holy Spirit—as the Christian narrative suggests. In this Calvin's theology, the internal testimony of the Spirit guides Christians to see what the text means; Christians do not need external elements in interpreting their text, but the work of the Spirit. In this sense, for the Protestant Reformers, the text does not only illustrate the meaning of the narrative, but also depicts the whole reality of what it talks about.[81] In this understanding of the Reformers, the interpreters are not the independent observers of the text because they must participate into the reality of what the text describes.[82] In other words, in the Protestant way of reading, Christians must read their text as an actual realistic reference of their reality. Consequently, Frei argues that there was a unity of literal and figural (temporal) reading in the pre-critical (Reformer's) way of reading.

According to Frei, although the Reformers propose the history-like (realistic) reading to support the main subject matter of the Christian narrative, the way of Protestant interpretation changed after the Enlightenment. This is because people after the Enlightenment start to realize that the bible's description may not have literally happened in actual history; they tend to

78. Frei, *The Eclipse of the Biblical Narrative*, 18.
79. Frei, *The Eclipse of the Biblical Narrative*, 19.
80. Frei, *The Eclipse of the Biblical Narrative*, 24.
81. Frei, *The Eclipse of the Biblical Narrative*, 27.
82. Frei, *The Eclipse of the Biblical Narrative*, 36.

prove the bible with the historical/scientific reference instead of using the reference of faith. As a result, many modern theologians after the Enlightenment support figurative interpretation rather than literal reading, while using other extra-textual ideas or materials in interpreting the text. Here, the new possibilities are opened for the biblical narrative because the new idea of the Enlightenment brings many different arguments on the unity of the biblical narrative and actual history. However, Frei here argues that modernity's figurative reading conveys a total confusion to the Christians because the figurative understanding leads them to be separated from the narrative itself.

To be specific, Frei points out that many Christians suffer from the ambiguity and inconsistency of hermeneutics during the eighteenth and nineteenth centuries; many different and vague arguments coexisted all together in that era. On the one hand, some theologians held a conservative position, arguing that the Bible is literally true. For these theologians, the subject matter of the text is literally true, even though they sometimes had to ignore so many historical inconsistencies in the Bible. On the other hand, other liberal theologians believed that the bible has no ostensive sense at all. These theologians argued that the bible is not the literal Word of God, but the product of history. In addition to those two extremes, there had been constant endeavors to relate faith and actual history in interpreting the Christian narrative. That is why the myth school theologians such as David Strauss believe that the subject matter of the Christian narrative is consisted of moral and religious truths, while rejecting the supernatural elements in the narrative; For the myth school theologians, the meaning of the biblical narrative has ostensive sense in the realm of morality (which is the true subject matter they argue), not in the realm of history. Looking at these many different arguments, Frei shows that there had been a lot of struggles and inconsistencies in the hermeneutical theology during the age of biblical criticism after the Enlightenment; many Christians had struggled to understand the Christian narrative's ostensive sense.

However, Frei argues that Schleiermacher's hermeneutics brings a shift to the hermeneutical debate in regard to the issue of (internal) text and external (historical) reference. According to Frei, in Schleiermacher's theology, "the hermeneutical procedure and its logic should not be abstracted from the process of its application, and therefore, should not be stated by itself."[83] Schleiermacher believes that the understanding process is the integration of both the original text and the interpreter; he highlights two different aspects of the understanding process: the technical (psychological) aspect and

---

83. Frei, *The Eclipse of the Biblical Narrative*, 287.

the grammatical aspect.[84] On the other hand, the technical (psychological) aspect of reading highlights the autonomous role of the reader. This means that the independent role of the interpreter is important because the task of understanding can and must be performed in our consciousness. In this process of understanding, the subjectivity of the reader becomes important because the interpreter equates oneself with the text to understand the text within the individual totality.

On the other hand, Schleiermacher points out that the technical reading is not the completion of the understanding process because we also need the grammatical reading. Here, Schleiermacher draws attention to the fact that the process of understanding does not merely happen in the individual mind. This is because the individual understanding process requires certain communal agreements from others to discern whether the interpreter's reading is right or not; the individual understanding process has to have a complex dialectical harmonization between universality and individuation. In this coordination between universality and individuation, the interpreter has to understand the grammar of the text. To do this, the interpreter has to focus on a common linguistic and cultural grammar of the text. In this grammatical understanding process, the interpreter must pay attention not only to the importance of the text in their own context, but also to the linguistic and cultural background of the text. Consequently, the grammatical understanding creates a certain form of life, because the understanding process happens not in an individual's isolated mind but in a communal setting. That is, it requires the reader to participate in a certain linguistic/cultural community through the text. As a result, in Schleiermacher's works, Frei finds the eclipse of grammatical-linguistic interpretation which connects the style of an author and the expression of a reader.[85] For Frei, because the understanding process requires the reader to comprehend the grammar of the text, the right understanding of the text cannot be separated from the concrete reality (or product) of common language and culture. Thus, the understanding of the text can be more realistic in the grammatical reading.[86]

---

84. Frei, *The Eclipse of the Biblical Narrative*, 290.

85. He says, "The realistic narrative reading of biblical stories, the gospels in particular, went into eclipse throughout the period. Whether anything has change in this respect since the days of Schleiermacher and Hegel is a question for another day." Frei, *The Eclipse of the Biblical Narrative*, 324.

86. It is noteworthy that many theologians such as Barth and Frei argue that Christians should read the text in a community to highlight the importance of the grammatical reading as Schleiermacher suggests. I will deal with this issue more precisely in the following section.

The End of Academic Theology

If, as Schleiermacher suggests, we ought to be concerned with the grammar of the biblical text as well as their meaning, what would that mean for academic theologians today? According to Frei, Schleiermacher's hermeneutics is picked up again by a late nineteenth century theologian, Karl Barth; he argues that Christians should interpret the text in the church community.[87] However, Frei further develops his own hermeneutical principle in his book, *Types of Christian Theology*. In this book, Frei goes further from Schleiermacher and Barth, and argues that Christian theology is "completely internal and there is no use in comparing Christian discourse and its rules with other kinds of discourse."[88] To show his hermeneutical method, Frei suggests five types of theology, representing each with an exemplar theologian: Gordon Kaufmann, David Tracy, Friedrich Schleiermacher, Karl Barth, and D. Z. Phillips.[89]

First, Kaufman's methodology represents "theology as a philosophical discipline."[90] In Kaufmann's work, the task of theology is to investigate the use of the Word of God. Here, the concept of God is a metaphysical concept; the concept of God is the ground and limit of the world because it arises out from the richness of human experience. In such a view, there is no specific self-description of Christianity, because the concept of God just functions in the Western culture as one cultural, metaphysical concept. Kaufmann's interest here is to suggest a universal philosophy of God, showing how human beings universally develop and express the concept of God. In this Kaufmann's understanding, every religion is the part of a general intellectual-cultural inquiry as a philosophical discipline. This implies that theology is one of many philosophical disciplines in Kaufmann's theology. As a result, Kaufmann hesitates to use the self-description of Christianity. Rather, he tries to focus on the philosophical aspect of theology.

Secondly, Tracy's methodology signifies a revisionist view. Tracy thinks that our experience is our mode of being in the world, even though it is mediated externally. Here, Tracy believes that there are stable criteria

---

87. Frei, *The Eclipse of the Biblical Narrative*, 285.

88. Frei, *Types of Christian Theology*, 21.

89. Dealing with the relationship between Christianity and culture, Frei's teacher, Richard Niebuhr also suggests five types: (1) Christ against Culture, (2) Christ of Culture, (3) Christ above Culture, (4) Christ and Culture in Paradox, and (5) Christ Transforming Culture. In this sense, Frei's typology looks similar to his teacher's one although their main hermeneutical principles are opposite one another. Cf. Niebuhr, *Christ and Culture*.

90. Frei, *Types of Christian Theology*, 28. Cf. Kaufmann, *God, Revelation, and Authority*.

for meaning and truth in the condition of human experience. This implies that theology is subject to decision by certain common criteria in Tracy's theology. He says, "there is no cutting difference between external description and Christian self-description."[91] Because Tracy believes that there are common measures in human experience, he claims that the Christian self-description has to be explained in the common religious criteria. However, Tracy still thinks that there is a specific uniqueness in the Christian self-description. Even though the Christian descriptions are the part of the common expression of human experience, Tracy thinks that Christianity still has cultural and historical differences in its development from other religions. As a result, in Tracy's view, the correlation between philosophy and theology becomes an important issue.[92] That is why he attempts to explain the self-description of Christianity to the common experience of humanity. Thus, he suggests a revisionist approach, explaining Christianity's self-description to the public sphere of philosophy.

In the third type, Schleiermacher gives a correlational viewpoint on the relationship between philosophy and theology. For Schleiermacher, theology is an academic discipline which deals with the Christian self-description. In *Christian Faith*, he argues that theology is basically the self-reflection of the church community. That is why Schleiermacher argues that theology's home cannot be philosophy, but must be the church community. However, he also claims that the internal expression of Christianity can be expressed in a universal human language. That is why Schleiermacher has what he calls "the tenets from ethics." For Schleiermacher, Christians still need to use philosophical languages to deal with human cultures and humanistic studies in the Christian perspective. As a result, Schleiermacher attempts to describe the Christian self-description within the common human consciousness. And that is why he expresses the experience of the church with philosophical-technical vocabularies; in Schleiermacher's theology, the external and self-descriptive elements of Christianity are correlated. According to Frei, Schleiermacher shows an ambivalent view on the relationship between philosophy and theology because his *Christian Faith* is neither a fully dogmatic enterprise nor a philosophical enterprise.[93]

The fourth type of theology Frei chooses is Karl Barth's theology. Unlike Schleiermacher, Barth believes that the narrative of Christianity does not depend on an immediate self-consciousness. Rather, he believes that the Christian narrative exists as a self-enterprise of Christianity. For Barth,

---

91. Frei, *The Eclipse of the Biblical Narrative*, 33. Cf. Tracy, *Blessed Rage for Order*.
92. Frei, *The Eclipse of the Biblical Narrative*, 35.
93. Frei, *The Eclipse of the Biblical Narrative*, 38.

Christian theology does not fall under the universal criteria of human philosophy because it has no common ground with human philosophy. For him, theology should be a Christian self-description first. That is why he famously refuses natural theology, because God's revelation cannot be based on human experience or nature but God's self-revelation itself. Even though Barth posits theology as the Christian self-description of the church, he still believes that philosophy can help theology to describe the conceptual systems of reality.[94] In Barth's theology, the current situation of the church can be explained with anthropological and philosophical references to make the church's self-description clearer. This implies that Barth still uses philosophical (external) languages to explain the church's internal reflection, although philosophy is subordinate to theology (because Barth's primary concern is the church's self-description).[95] As a result, according to Frei, in Barth's theology, the relationship between the internal and external descriptions of Christianity "remains *ad hoc*."[96]

The last type Frei suggests is D. Z. Phillips. For D. Z. Phillips, theology is strictly the inside talk of Christianity. Phillips thinks that theology cannot adjust to conflicts with other external descriptions, because the grammar of theology is thoroughly based on the internal elements of Christianity. He says, "the criteria of what can sensibly be said of God are to be found within the religious tradition."[97] According to Phillips, we should not get confused by philosophical nor scientific methods. Although many modern philosophical and scientific methods aim at finding a universal criterion, he believes that every religion and culture has their own specific internal rules. This means that theology cannot be a plea for other sciences. For Phillips, although the meaning of religious beliefs is partly dependent on the features of human life, the qualification of Christian practices does not depend on other grounds but its own belief. As a result, Philips' theology is methodically responsible to the Christian tradition only; his theology does not have any interest in the external element, but Christianity's own internal linguistic/cultural context.[98]

Through investigating these five different types of theology, Frei goes further from Schleiermacher and Barth's hermeneutics with a favor in D. Z. Phillips' Wittgensteinian methodology. In arguing his own hermeneutical principle, Frei points out that Christian faith is formed with its internal

---

94. Frei, *The Eclipse of the Biblical Narrative*, 40.
95. Frei, *The Eclipse of the Biblical Narrative*, 43.
96. Frei, *The Eclipse of the Biblical Narrative*, 46.
97. Phillips, *Faith and Philosophical Enquiry*, 4.
98. Frei, *Types of Christian Theology*, 49.

grammar and its actual practices rather than a hypothesis based on external elements. According to Frei, because philosophy and theology are different from one another, we do not need to find a harmony between Christian self-description and external philosophy. Rather, he aims to focus on the internal practice of the church community. That is why Frei borrows Clifford Geertz's idea that "a group's ethos is rendered intellectually reasonable by being shown to represent a way of life ideally adapted to the actual state of affairs the world describe, while the world view is rendered emotionally convincing by being, presented as an image of an actual state of affairs."[99] For Frei, the Christian self-description is a matter of the use of Christian languages such as faith, hope, creation, incarnation, love, and resurrection. In the use of those Christian languages, Christians do not see their languages as a simple "hypothesis or world view, but Christian life itself."[100] According to Frei, Christians live within the internal language and practice of Christianity. In this respect, he proclaims "the end of academic theology."[101] What he means by the end of academic theology is that Christian doctrinal or scriptural statements are perfectly sufficient for themselves without other academic external elements. For him, theology is a practical matter in *the church community* which is different from other spheres of academic sciences. As a result, he envisions the collapse of the present social/academic structured theology, while suggesting a new approach for doing a practical theology which thoroughly focuses on the use of Christian language in the church community.[102]

How It Began: The Resurrection of Jesus

Because Frei proposes a realistic and history-like reading of the Bible through highlighting the internal grammar of the text itself, he claims to focus on the primary subject matter of the text when we interpret the Bible. According to Frei, because the internal logic of Christian faith presents

---

99. Frei, *Types of Christian Theology*, 27. According to Geertz, the reality, understanding and behaviors of human beings are all symbols or at least symbolic elements because they are tangible formulations of notions, abstractions from experience. Here, human symbols which constitutes human culture generates models for human beings. And there are two models: (1) Models of linguistic, graphic, mechanical, natural that express their structure in an alternative medium, and (2) Models for lead that people follow. In his book, Geertz suggests that anthropologists should focus on the models for as well. Cf. Geertz, *The Interpretation of Cultures*, 89.

100. Frei, *Types of Christian Theology*, 92.

101. Frei, *Types of Christian Theology*, 93.

102. Frei, *Types of Christian Theology*, 94.

the Bible as the Word of God, Christians should read the Bible with the understanding that it is God's self-revelation. That is, it should be read as though the Triune God wrote it about Godself, which is why Frei believes that the biblical narrative reveals the nature of the Trinity. Furthermore, because the Christian narrative requires its readers to have a faith assuming Jesus' presence in their life, the main subject of the Christian narrative should be about the story of Jesus which reveals Jesus' identity. In other words, for Frei, the right subject matter of the Christian narrative is none other than the identity of Jesus Christ, because the internal logic of the text assumes the readers to have a faith on Jesus' present in their life. In this understanding, the Christian narrative clearly describes the identity of Jesus of Nazareth as the cosmic savior; the identity of Jesus Christ stretches of time through the mysterious power of the Holy Spirit, presumed by the internal logic of the Christian narrative. As a result, the main question of the Bible becomes: "What is Jesus like?"[103] In this understanding, the main point of the Christian narrative is to preach about the identification of Jesus rather than raising historical questions.[104]

In interpreting the Christian narrative, Frei points out that the narratives in the Bible have similar patterns, showing Jesus' identity. For example, the gospel narratives describe Jesus' obedience to God; the pattern of Jesus' identification becomes both simple and complex in the story.[105] In Jesus's story, there is the coexistence of power and powerlessness: "He saved others; he cannot save himself" (Mark 15:31).[106] According to the gospel narratives, Jesus gives up his power and becomes powerless to save others. In this enact, we find that Jesus' will becomes unified with the will of God (Matt 26:39; Mark 14:36; Luke 22:42). There, we see the state of power to powerlessness in Jesus' intention and deed. Ironically, when Jesus obeyed God's will, Jesus could be resurrected from death. This implies that "Jesus' very identity involves the will and purpose of the Father who sent him."[107] Consequently, Frei suggests that we can find the common patterns of the gospel narratives: the interrelation between Jesus' intention/action and God's intention/action.

---

103. Frei, *Types of Christian Theology*, 99.

104. He says, "Reading a story, whether the Gospel story or any other is compared to understanding a work of visual art, such as a piece of sculpture. We do not try to imagine the inside of it, but let our eyes wander over its surface and its mass so that we may grasp its form, its proportions and its balances. What it says is expressed in any and all these things, and only by grasping them do we grasp its 'meaning.' So also we grasp the identity of Jesus within his story." Frei, *The Identity of Jesus Christ*, 133.

105. Frei, *The Identity of Jesus Christ*, 109.

106. Frei, *The Identity of Jesus Christ*, 111.

107. Frei, *The Identity of Jesus Christ*, 107.

Frei finds out that Jesus' intention and activity of salvation is not Jesus' own independent story, because there is an interesting unity of Jesus' intention/action with God's intention/action. Looking at those patterns in the gospel narratives, Frei further realizes that "it is essential to grasp the intimate unity of intention and action."[108] This is because he believes that the person's identity can be shown when a person's specific deeds and intentions match.[109]

In finding Jesus' identity from the unity of his intention and action, Frei says that the resurrection of Jesus is the highlight of showing Jesus' identity: "the resurrection is the vindication in act of his own intention and God's. Moreover, in the unity and transition between his need for redemption and his being in fact redeemed, Jesus' identity is focused, and the complex relation and distinction between his identity and that of God is manifested."[110] Based on the resurrection of Jesus Christ in the gospel narratives, Frei summarizes the complex patterns of interaction between God's and Jesus' action: "(1) Jesus' obedience, (2) coexistence of power and powerlessness, (3) transition from the state of power to powerlessness, and (4) interrelation of Jesus' and God's intention."[111] According to Frei, these patterns report that Jesus is God who is our savior. In other words, this Christological understanding of Jesus' identity is the primary concern of the Christian narrative. Frei says,

> It is in the interaction between God and Jesus that Jesus' identity is clarified as the one unsubstitutable Jesus of Nazareth. Indeed, at the climactic point of the divine action, the resurrection, where God alone is active, it is Jesus alone who is manifest. Jesus' enactment of his identity comes to a climax in one sense in the crucifixion and in another sense in the resurrection. . . . It comes to concrete expression in the resurrection appearance, where Jesus identifies himself most fully as Jesus who is the Son of Man, the promised one of Israel, the Christ. . . . He reestablishes that connection and its titles, by 'demythologizing' the savior myth."[112]

---

108. Frei, *The Identity of Jesus Christ*, 100. Cf. Frei borrows Gilbert Ryle's idea that intention and action logically involve each other in verbal usage: "To perform intelligently is to do one thing and not two things." Ryle, *The Concept of Mind*, 40.

109. For Frei, identity description "locates the identity of an individual at the point at which his inward life, coming to outward expression, is linked with or meshes into the train of public circumstances." Frei, *The Identity of Jesus Christ*, 154.

110. Frei, *The Identity of Jesus Christ*, 124.

111. Frei, *The Identity of Jesus Christ*, 164.

112. Frei, *The Identity of Jesus Christ*, 175.

A POSTLIBERAL REACTION (NORTH AMERICA) 45

From this understanding of the Christian narrative, Frei realizes that the Bible demonstrates the identity of Jesus Christ who is present with us. For Frei, the concrete expression of Jesus' resurrection shows Jesus's identity as Christ by demethylating the savior myth. In this Christological reading of the Bible, Frei claims that Christians should read the Christian narrative in a realistic sense. This is because the internal grammar and pattern of the Bible leads the reader to understand Jesus (the primary content) in a Christological or trinitarian sense. In this trinitarian understanding of Jesus, Jesus must be presenting with us; the Christian narrative becomes so real that it leads Christians to live within the story.

In sum, through developing Schleiermacher and Barth's theologies further, Hans Frei argues that the understanding of the Christian narrative should be based on the internal grammar of the text. In this way of interpretation, Frei reads the Bible in a literal (history-like) sense. For him, the Christian narrative presents both Jesus' vivid presence and Jesus' identity; the main subject matter of the Christian narrative is the identity of Jesus, revealing Jesus' presence with us. Frei believes that the internal pattern of the Christian narrative requires the reader to read the text in Jesus' presence. As a result, he thinks that Christian theologians should never lose the realistic sense of reading the Bible. In other words, their starting point must be Christian faith—believing that God's revelation is present to them. According to Frei, in this realistic reading of the Bible, "nothing is more naturally congruent and coherent than saying, 'do justice, love kindness, and walk humbly with your God' (Mic 6:8)."[113] This is because the realistic reading of the narrative necessitates the reader to live within the realistic story. In this respect, Frei's understanding of Christianity becomes very practical, because it asks Christians to pursue concrete Christian ethics within the logic of the Christian narrative. That is why, in the works of Frei, the primary concern of Christian theology is how to practice the internal rules of Christianity rather than creating a new universal theory. Therefore, through highlighting the internal grammar of Christianity, Frei shows a radical view that the primary concern of Christian theology is to obedient to God in people's real lives.

---

113. Frei, "On the Thirty-Nine Articles," in "Unpublished Pieces," 112.

THE SECTARIAN RESPONSE TO WORLDLINESS

The Development of Postliberal Christian Ethics

After Hans Frei's work, the understanding of postliberalism toward worldliness reaches its peak in the works of another Barthian/Wittgensteinian theologian, Stanley Hauerwas. In his works, Hauerwas includes a wide range of subjects such as philosophical theology, church fathers, political theology, law, education, bioethics, and mostly criticism on liberal democracy, capitalism, and militarism. Perceiving various theological perspectives such as Methodism (his home church), Anabaptism (John Howard Yoder), Anglicanism (his current church), and Catholicism (Thomas Aquinas/virtue theory), Hauerwas connects classical theologies with virtue ethics within the postliberal influence; his theology shows a huge practicality. Especially, Hauerwas as a Christian ethicist further develops a postliberal theological response toward the American secularism. Because he shows how to apply postliberal views to the concrete Christian life, postliberal theology's interest and stance become clearer in the works of Hauerwas. So, he is considered as one of the best successors of postliberal theology.[114]

Accepting the reality of secularism in America, Hauerwas draws attention to the fact that many Christians believe that the secular state has an authority and power over people's educational visions, public/political issues, and even ethical principles. He is generally critical of this situation because the American secularism follows Constantinianism. For Hauerwas, American secularism elevates the importance of the secular state over that of God. That is why, borrowing Barth and Yoder's theology, Hauerwas develops a sectarian response toward worldliness in order to criticize the American secularism. In his works, Hauerwas as a postliberal theologian tries to focus on the Christian narrative as the grammar of Christian ethics. Based on this postliberal understanding, he argues that Christians should live as a faithful witness of God in a small colony called "the church." Here, Hauerwas is very direct in his assessment of the secular world, and his influential theology has typified the postliberal theology's stance towards the secular world. To understand Hauerwas' postliberal response toward worldliness, this section will investigate Hauerwas' theological reflection. In this section, I will deal with (1) how Hauerwas develops his Christian ethics under the influence of postliberal theology, (2) how he develops a sectarian response to the secular world, (3) how we can evaluate the contribution of postliberalism, and (4) the limits of the postliberal response toward worldliness.

---

114. Dorrien, "Truth Claims," 22–29; Reno, "Stanley Hauerwas," 302.

The Witness of God in the Secular World

Following Lindbeck and Frei's postliberal approach, Hauerwas "tries to do theology to be practical."[115] In his recent book, *The Work of Theology*, he shows among many other things how he writes theological sentences. As a Wittgensteinian theologian, Hauerwas argues that language explains more about our thinking than we might realize at first: "we often say more or less than we think we say."[116] For Hauerwas, "we find our life fated in the language of our ancestors, in the language we inherit from them . . . to understand what words mean we must understand what whose who use them mean."[117] As a result, he attempts to examine his own use of theological language to see how he understands theology and the world, that is, "the difference Christian convictions can make for how the world is understood, as well as how we live in the world."[118] In Hauerwas' theology, the work of theology should focus on "how" to write a theological sentence, rather than on constructing a universal theory. In this respect, he as a typical postliberal theologian looks at "how theology is conceived as an exercise in practical reason."[119]

Hauerwas points out that every practice forms its concepts within a particular language. This suggests that we need a particular training in order to acquire practical reason (or to act) in a certain community: "the person of practical reason must have a capacity for perception of particulars that comes from being well trained."[120] Since training is required, Hauerwas emphasizes the importance of practical reason to see how we become virtuous in each community. He says:

> It is the virtue that makes the experience of some people not simply an accumulation of actions from the past but a dynamic orientation to bring this systematization into play and allow it to be tested by present circumstances, to draw from it what is relevant and to see where it does not fit.[121]

---

115. Hauerwas, "How I Think I Learned to Think Theologically," in *The Work of Theology*, 13.

116. Hauerwas, "How I Think I Learned to Think Theologically," 2.

117. Hauerwas, "How I Think I Learned to Think Theologically," 2.

118. Hauerwas, "How I Think I Learned to Think Theologically," 4.

119. Hauerwas, "How I Think I Learned to Think Theologically," 7.

120. Hauerwas, "How I Think I Learned to Think Theologically," 15. Although Hauerwas, McIntyre, and Lindbeck put more emphasis on the differences between communities, Donald Davidson emphasizes the similarities between human languages. So, it is good to know that there are other interpretations of Wittgenstein. Cf. Davidson *Inquiries into Truth and Interpretation*, 83–198.

121. Hauerwas, "How I Think I Learned to Think Theologically," 16.

For Hauerwas, our past experiences are resources that enable the present. He thinks that rational agency cannot stand alone but must be supplemented by virtue because virtue gives us integrity and constancy. He says, "the virtues he commends, integrity and constancy, are no doubt crucial for sustaining the habits necessary for the flourishing of people of practical reason."[122] Practical reason, Hauerwas argues, entails a politics and social intelligence, because we are prompted to ask "why did I so act?"[123] In other words, practical reason demands the acknowledgment of authority, and this authority should depend on the ethos that makes argument possible. As a result, for Hauerwas, it is important to know "how language makes possible a common life"[124] because language is "a disposable vehicle of the subject it serves."[125] In other words, Hauerwas thinks that the language of a particular community produces a narrative that constitutes a discourse because the particular community's language leads us to act and form virtues in us. In this respect, he attempts to see how we use language in a particular community to see how we act with virtues in our society. Therefore, what Hauerwas cares about is not a theory, but what makes us virtuous and what makes us genuine Christians.[126]

Because he focuses on how to be a faithful Christian, Hauerwas draws upon virtue ethics and the Christian narrative to support the positions of Christian theology and Christian practice.[127] In particular, he as a Christian ethicist tries to see how the church forms habits of language and how it shapes Christians' understanding in the world. He says, "you can only act in the world you can see and you can only see what you have learned to say."[128] Hauerwas claims that we should look at what the church says to us to understand and practice the Christian language; he argues that Christian

---

122. Hauerwas, "How to Be an Agent," in *The Work of Theology*, 81.

123. Hauerwas, "How to Be an Agent," 88.

124. Hauerwas, "How I Think I Learned to Think Theologically," 18.

125. Hauerwas, "How to Write a Theological Sentence," in *The Work of Theology*, 130. Cf. Wittgenstein says, "Christianity is not based on a historical truth; rather it offers us a narrative.... Here you have a narrative, don't take the same attitude to it as you take to other historical narratives.... Now believe! ... Then you will see that you are holding fast to this belief ... then everything will be different and it will be no wonder if you can do things that you cannot do now." Wittgenstein, *Culture and Value*, 32–33.

126. Hawerwas says, "That theology became for me an exercise in practical reason meant the church became central for how the world was to be understood." Hauerwas, "How I Think I Learned to Think Theologically," 29.

127. He says, "Rational agency cannot stand alone, however, but must be supplemented by the virtues." Hauerwas, "How to Be an Agent," 79.

128. Hauerwas, "How I Think I Learned to Think Theologically," 27.

theology first needs to focus on the church's own language.[129] According to Hauerwas, Christians can worship the risen Christ who created and reconciled all of us, when they speak and live within the Christian language. This implies that theology should be based on practicing our actual ethics because there is no way for Christians to understand the Christian language without actual training and practicing. If we do not actually speak the (Christian) language, the language will be no use at all. In this sense, Hauerwas believes that theology is inseparable from ethics. Thus, the work of theology for Hauerwas is *practical reason* to train Christians how to speak and practice the Christian language.

Because theology is something to be performed rather than theorized, Hauerwas believes that Christians do not need to make coercive arguments toward the secular world. He thinks that Christians just need to focus on God' revelation as the internal grammar of Christian theology suggests.[130] In other words, if Christians believe in God, they will not need to be apologetic to the world. This is because they are already called as the witness of God in the reality (grammar) of Christ.[131] In Hauerwas' theology, what is important for Christians is about how to live as a faithful Christian, not about how to explain their doctrines to others.[132] Hauerwas points out that

129. It is noteworthy that Hauerwas' theology is heavily influenced by MacIntyre: "Narrative history of a certain kind turns out to be the basic and essential genre for the characterization of human actions." MacIntyre, *After Virtue*, 209.

130. As I mentioned above, Stanley Hauerwas and Hans Frei are skeptical about Lindbeck's use of Wittgenstein's language game in the setting of interreligious dialogue. For Hauerwas, language game is more about depicting the world with language rather than making another Wittgensteinian theory.

131. He says, "My refusal to 'do' epistemology I learned from philosophers such as Wittgenstein, Anscombe, and MacIntyre. That I have tried to do theology in a manner that reflects what I learned from them makes the charge that I 'reject' what can be learned from 'secular sources' seem quite odd to me." Hauerwas, *The State of the University*, 167.

132. In the Gifford lectures, Hauerwas talks about natural theology from the perspective of trinitarian theology. Here is the summary he suggests in the book: "James, in a curious combination of Darwinism and pragmatism, utterly fulfills Lord Gifford's stated wishes. He turns natural theology—the discovery of God in God's creation—into religious psychology—the discovery of humanity's worth in human subjectivity. A young Niebuhr adopts James pragmatism and his 'empirical approach' to religion, little realizing that his Christology would have to empty itself fully in order to be compatible with a methodologically atheist approach to theism. The god he discovers is the ultimate fulfillment of human needs, who, conversely, sets a standard so perfect that attempts to adhere to it are but "a new form of egoism, namely, pharisaic pride." Barth, in contrast, begins not with human reason or human religious experience or human scientific discoveries, but by talking about God, insisting that God is the subject of theology—natural or otherwise. The theology that God reveals (and not vice versa) makes claims on persons' lives—it has something to say about humans, though it begins with God, and it tells humans who they are and how they should be." Hauerwas, *The State of the University*, 132.

being a witness of God is already the work of the Spirit because it is the Holy Spirit who makes Christians be faithful in the message of the Scripture. He quotes Aquinas, "Sacred Scripture, since it has no science above itself, can dispute with one who denies its principles only if the opponent admits some at least of the truths obtained through divine revelation; thus we can argue with heretics from texts in Holy Writ, and against those who deny one article of faith we can argue from another."[133] Here, Hauerwas agrees with Aquinas that Christians do not seek to defend their faith out of fear or other elements, when they live according to the teaching of the Bible. This is because Christians believe that their faith (and their Bible) is given by God; the understanding of God (and God's Word) is already God's work.[134]

Accordingly, instead of suggesting cognitive claims, Hauerwas argues that what the Christian narrative makes is ethical claims, asking us to *be the (faithful) witness of God*. To be specific, Hauerwas believes that Christian practices are the best way to witness God who is the Father, Son, and Holy Spirit.[135] Here, he borrows a theology of testimony from Barth and Rosenzweig: "a theology that is based on the notion that knowledge of God is possible only in the context of the ethical labor of the elect individual who seeks through her moral endeavor to testify to the loving act of the transcendent God."[136] According to Hauerwas, Rashkover's account of a theology of testimony (from Barth and Rosenzweig) has a similarity to his emphasis on being a witness of God. This is because witness is the necessary condition for the truthful Christian convictions. For Hauerwas, what Christians believe has a particular shape through believing God's relation to the world. In this shape, Christians act and live according to their exact convictions which require them to be a witness. For example, as Bruce Marshal

---

133. Hauerwas, *The State of the University*, 135. Cf. Aquinas, *Summa Theologica*, 1.1.8.

134. As I mentioned above, the view of Hauerwas (believing that the understanding of the text is the work of the Spirit) resonates with the views of the Reformers, Karl Barth, and Hans Frei.

135. Hauerwas, *With the Grain of the Universe*, 134. Cf. Marshal says, "The triune God grants us true beliefs in order to give us a share in his own life. Countless beliefs about creatures are tied up with beliefs about the triune God and his purposes in the world, and there is probably no clear or effective way to draw a line between those which are and those which are not. The Spirit cannot, it therefore seems, lead us into the life of God without seeing to it that we hold most true beliefs, not only about God, but also about everything else. Since we hold beliefs at all only insofar as they fit with the rest of what we supposed to be true, this is to say that the Spirit guarantees that our beliefs are generally—though of course not always—true when we take them to be." Marshall, *Trinity and Truth*, 281.

136. Hauerwas, *The State of the University*, 3. Cf. Rashkover, *Revelation and Theopolitics*, 3.

notes, the martyr "dies because he believes the gospel and loves the gospel's God, not in order to believe it. . . . The more excellently or successfully a person participates in the church's practices, the less need he has to treat those practices as evidence for the church's beliefs."[137] In this sense, once the Holy Spirit leads Christians to be the witness of the Triune God, academic arguments become irrelevant in Christian faith. Rather, Christians simply confess and live to be the part of the work of the Spirit and to be the part of the Christian narrative, as the martyrs do.

Because Christian arguments rest on the witness which is the work of the Spirit, Hauerwas claims that the Christian conviction requires "the pragmatic display of the fact that the God who has created and redeemed the world has done so from the love that constitutes the life of the Trinity."[138] Unlike scientific knowledge, which can be shown by the success of experiment, Hauerwas points out that the truth of Christian convictions exists only through the life of faithful witness. According to Hauerwas, Christians understand themselves to be the part of the Christian narratives so that they continue to primarily enact the ongoing work of the Holy Spirit; they are not interested in a way of attracting other convictions of the world. Rather, they pursue living carefully as the witness of God to be the part of the Christian story. In this sense, theology has to be done through being faithful to the gospel (or the Christian language). This implies that Christians cannot have a priority on the accommodational view toward the secular world because they first have to chase being a witness of the truth that they practice in the church community. As a result, as Marshal notices, the practices of Christians inevitably encounter "an epistemic affliction."[139] This is because they reject the worldly views and practices, while living based on their own beliefs, practices, and lives in the church community. In other words, according to Hauerwas, Christians are not interested in answering to the threat of relativism or secularism because it is enough for them to live according to the inner belief of the church community as the faithful witness of God. Thus, for Hauerwas, the view of Christians must conflict with the views of other secular cultures.

---

137. Marshall, *Trinity and Truth*, 190.

138. Hauerwas, *With the Grain of the Universe*, 132.

139. Hauerwas, *With the Grain of the Universe*, 134. Cf. Marshall also says, "Christians will inevitably encounter a kind of epistemic affliction, because they not only hold true, but insist on treating as epistemically primary across the board, beliefs which will be rationally contestable until the end of time." Marshall, *Trinity and Truth*, 216.

The Sectarian Understanding: Christians as Resident Aliens

If there comes an epistemic affliction for Christians in the face of relativism, how should Christians react politically to solve this epistemic affliction, coming from the conflict between the life of the church community and the life of other communities? On this question, Hauerwas argues that Christians should pursue to be the member of the non-Constantinian church. Hauerwas agrees with Charles Taylor that there has been "a certain kind of social imaginary in modern society—that is, the market economy, the public sphere, and self-governing people are simple assumed to be unquestionable givens."[140] Accordingly, modern political society has been understood as the instrument to serve individuals for mutual benefits and prosperity; the public sphere should be secular rather than founding on some divine foundation. Here, as Taylor notes, secularism requires the necessity of legitimating discourse for a "peace" that serves the state. In this trend of modernity, Hauerwas points out that Christians have difficulty making their lives meaningful in the dominance of secular ideas and secular legitimations.[141] In such a situation, many Christians in the age of modernity attempt to translate Christianity into existentialism to be apologetic. However, in this setting, American Christians become confused because they often fail to find a clear distinction between Christian ethics and American secular ethics (or social activism).[142] Here, Hauerwas complains that many modern Christians in America tend to focus more on the welfare of America, instead of being a truthful Christian.

In front of this confusion of American Christians, Hauerwas clearly argues that the Bible's concern is to be faithful to the gospel, and thus the job of theologians is "not to make the gospel credible to the modern world, but to make the world credible to the gospel."[143] According to Hauerwas, the challenge of Jesus to the matter of politics is about "how to be faithful to a strange community, which is shaped by a story of how God is with us."[144] For him, both conservative and liberal churches assume that their task is to inspire their people to get involved in politics and to change the world. However, he criticizes those public churches for overlooking the spiritual dimension of the church, while holding the accommodationist (Constantinian) social ethics. In modern societies, people believe that society is formed

---

140. Hauerwas, *The State of the University*, 37. Cf. Taylor, *Modern Social Imaginaries*, 1.
141. Hauerwas, *The State of the University*, 38.
142. Willimon and Hauerwas, *Resident Aliens*, 17.
143. Willimon and Hauerwas, *Resident Aliens*, 24.
144. Willimon and Hauerwas, *Resident Aliens*, 30.

to supply our needs so that society it necessary and good. In Hauerwas' theology, however, giving too much power or credibility to secular society is idolatry. Instead of believing in the power of secular societies, he claims that the primary task of the church is to be the community of the cross. He says, "the political task of Christians is to be the church rather than to transform the world."[145] For Hauerwas, the church is not an alternative social strategy. Rather, the church's first job should be being "the witness of God." As Hauerwas notes, Jesus is not interested in Caesar or the power game of the world (Matt 22:21), because the church clearly proclaims that God rules the entire world, not just a few nations.[146] In this respect, Hauerwas describes the modern Christians as "resident aliens" who live a colony life of the church within the dominance of the society of unbelief.[147]

To show how he further develops his theological view on secularism, Hauerwas derives Yoder's theology of politics. In Hauerwas' theology, John Howard Yoder represents "the recovery of the politics necessary for us (Christians) to understand why witness is not simply something Christians "do" but is at the heart of understanding how that to which Christians witness is true."[148] According to Hauerwas, Yoder learned from Barth that theology should be confident to follow its one master who desires to us to be faithful to the church.[149] As it is well known, Yoder is a strong supporter of Christian nonviolence and his view on nonviolence is deeply connected to the doctrine of God, because Yoder's conviction cannot be separated from the Christian conviction that God is the Creator and Redeemer. Yoder notes:

> Christ is agape; self-giving, nonresistant love. At the cross this nonresistance, including the refusal to use political means of self-defense, found its ultimate revelation in the uncomplaining and forgiving death of the innocent at the hands of the guilty. This death reveals how God deals with evil; here is the only valid starting point for Christian pacifism or nonresistance. The cross is the extreme demonstration that agape seeks neither

---

145. Willimon and Hauerwas, *Resident Aliens*, 38.

146. Hauerwas says, "The church has its own reason for being, hid within its own mandate and not found in the world. We are not chartered by the Emperor." Willimon and Hauerwas, *Resident Aliens*, 39.

147. Willimon and Hauerwas, *Resident Aliens*, 49.

148. Hauerwas, *With the Grain of the Universe*, 136. Hauerwas mentions that his Gifford lecture and its title, "With the Grain of the Universe," has its background from Howard Yoder's understanding of politics.

149. Hauerwas, *With the Grain of the Universe*, 138. Cf. Nation, "The Ecumenical Patience and Vocation of John Howard Yoder."

effectiveness nor justice, and is willing to suffer any loss or seeming defeat for the sake of obedience.[150]

For Yoder, the Christian conviction of nonviolence has its origin from the character of God who has revealed by Jesus Christ. Here, the conviction of Christians does not teach Christians to withdraw from the world, but to confront to the world with the power of the Spirit. In other words, the lordship of Christ and the obedience to God are the central positions that guide them to their central convictions and behaviors in Yoder's theology.

Based on the lordship of Christ, Yoder and Hauerwas criticize the Constantinian assumption: "what God is doing through the framework of society as a whole and not through the Christian community is the presumption that lies behind the Constantinian accommodation of the church to the world."[151] For Yoder and Hauerwas, it is a mistake to translate the Christian language into the dominant language of worldly cultures. For them, God's revelation does not rely on the capacity of our democratic or intelligent societies. Rather, God's revelation relies on itself. Yoder notes,

> What we need to find is the interworld transformational grammar to help us to discern what will need to happen if the collision of the message of Jesus with our pluralist/relativist world is to lead to a reconception of the shape of the world, instead of rendering Jesus optional or innocuous. To ask, "Shall we talk in pluralist/relativist terms?" would be as silly as to ask in Greece, "Shall we talk Greek?" The question is what we shall say. We shall say, "Jesus is Messiah and Lord." . . . Let us use the more biblical phrases "witness" and "proclamation" as naming forms of communication which do not coerce the hearer.[152]

For Yoder and Hauerwas, the conviction of Christianity can be conveyed through the life of witness, not apologetics. Here, the more historically dominant position, which Yoder and Hauerwas both describe as "Constantinian," demands the church to be unified with their society to keep the worldly Empire together. However, Yoder and Hauerwas point out that the early Anabaptists did not withdraw from the world and confronted to be

150. Hauerwas, *With the Grain of the Universe*, 139. Cf. Yoder, *The Original Revolution*, 59.

151. Hauerwas, *With the Grain of the Universe*, 142. Cf. Yoder, "Christ, the Hope of the World," in *The Royal Priesthood*; Carter, *The Politics of the Cross*, 96–111. Cartwright notes that Yoder's definition of Constantinianism does not start with Constantine's legalization of Christianity because Yoder believes that what he calls Constantinianism has a longer history. For him, the forms of Christians, involving accommodation and violence to the world, are also Constantinianism.

152. Yoder, "But, We Do See Jesus," in *The Priestly Kingdom*, 56.

the church to be the witness of God; they were killed by Calvinist, Lutheran, and Catholics.[153] Following the faith of Anabaptists, Yoder continues to say, "We still have no proof that right is right. We still have not found a bridge or a way to leap from historical uncertainty to some other more solid base. . . . But we do see Jesus, revealing the grace of God by tasting death for everyone (Heb. 2:8–9)."[154] According to Yoder and Hauerwas, it is enough for Christians to witness about the revelation of God in Jesus Christ, because their conviction is coming from the witness of Christ—the true revelation of God. In this respect, Hauerwas argues that it is the life of witness which reveals "the grain of the universe."[155]

Because Yoder and Hauerwas' version of Christianity is based on the Christological understanding of the world, Hauerwas thinks that Christians cannot escape from being in mission to be the witness of Jesus Christ; they should be *the heralds of Jesus Christ*. For Yoder, Christians must preach about their truth—Jesus Christ, because the primary concern of Christianity is Jesus Christ. However, Yoder believes that the tone of Christians should be non-coercive heralds. He says,

> If it were not true the herald would not be raising his or her voice. Yet, no one is forced to believe. What the herald reports is not permanent, timeless logical insights but contingent, particular events. If those events are true, and if others join the herald to carry the word along, they will with time develop a doctrinal system, to help distinguish between more or less adequate ways of proclaiming; but that system, those formulae, will not become what they proclaim.[156]

According to Yoder, the witness of Christians must remain non-coercive because they believe their witness as true. For Yoder, Christians believe in Jesus Christ not because the message of Christ concerns a contingent event

---

153. Yoder, "But, We Do See Jesus," 42.

154. Yoder, "But, We Do See Jesus," 61. This attitude (focusing thoroughly of the proclamation of the church to the secular world) has a similarity with Barth's *Barmen Declaration*: "Jesus Christ as he is attested for us in Holy Scripture, is the one Word of God which we have to hear and which we have to trust and obey in life and in death. We reject the false doctrine, as though the Church could and would have to acknowledge as a source of its proclamation, apart from and besides this one Word of God, still other events and powers, figures and truths, as God's revelation." Cochrane, *The Church's Confession under Hitler*, 239.

155. Hauerwas, *With the Grain of the Universe*, 146. In introduction, Hauerwas addresses that the title of his Gifford lecture is to remind people of Yoder's theology of politics.

156. Yoder, "The Disavowal of Constantine," in *The Royal Priesthood*, 256.

or a relative reporting. They believe it because it is true so that it is enough for them to be a herald of what they believe. However, in this understanding, the herald must be vulnerable in the world of relativism. Yoder says, "what makes the herald renounce coercion is not doubt or being unsettled by the tug of older views. The herald believes in accepting weakness, because the message is about a Suffering Servant whose meekness it is that brings justice to the nations."[157] Here, Yoder's view on politics reminds us of sectarian position toward worldliness because his view does not accommodate or fight against the worldly views. Instead, Yoder and Hauerwas want Christians to do what they should do, no matter how others respond.

In this respect, Hauerwas' theology shows a non-Constantinian approach to worldliness.[158] Because he puts emphasis on the internal logic of Christianity, he focuses on the practical use of the biblical narrative. As a result, even in the threats of modern pluralism and relativism, he is not interested in making an interdisciplinary theory or an accommodational position toward other secular cultures. Instead, he believes that the primary concern of the church is to preach about the gospel. For him, Christians need to show their truth through their lives to be a faithful witness of God. That is why Hauerwas believes that it is more important for Christians to focus on what the church teaches rather than changing the world with social programs or secular politics.[159] He says, "Which, I hope, is one way to sat that the church does not have a politics, but rather the church is God's politics for the world. If Christians are well formed by that politics, they hopefully will serve the world well by developing 'an ecclesial squint.'"[160] Consequently, Hauerwas' postliberal view shows indifference to the secular culture or politics, while first concentrating on how Christians can be the genuine witness of God. In this respect, as the Anabaptists do, Hauerwas holds a sectarian response toward the secular world through holding a strong conviction to the truth of Christianity.[161]

157. Yoder, "The Disavowal of Constantine," 256.

158. Hauerwas, "How to (Not) Be a Political Theologian," in *The Work of Theology*, 173. Cf. Yoder believes that Niebuhr's idea that Christ is above culture is wrong, because Christ is also a cultural reality (fully human). This means that Yoder and Hauerwas in fact know that Christians cannot fully withdraw from the world. Yoder, "How H. Richard Niebuhr Reasoned," 68.

159. Hauerwas, "How to (Not) Be a Political Theologian," 185. Hauerwas says, "From Yoder's perspective, the church best serves the social orders that claim to be democratic by taking seriously the internal calling of the church rather than "becoming tributary to whatever secular consensus seems strong at the time. . . . It is a strategy that makes any identification as a "political theologian" doubtful."

160. Hauerwas, "How to (Not) Be a Political Theologian," 190.

161. It is noteworthy that Hauerwas recognizes that he holds a sectarian view by

The Contribution of Postliberalism

Looking at the responses of postliberalism, we can notice that postliberal theology has made many contributions to theological studies in North America.[162] In my perspective, one of the most important points is that postliberal theologians highlight the internal grammar of Christianity. In the history of Christianity, one of the major jobs of theologians has been promoting healthy Christian practices such as worshipping to God, prayer, and martyrdom. This implies that theology is different from other academic disciplines because its ground is not modern scientific reason but God's revelation which leads Christians to have faith in God and Christian practices. That is why one of the primary jobs of Christian theologians must be talking about God to promote the unique practice of Christianity. Here, it is important to note that postliberal theologians rediscover the uniqueness of Christian theology in the American secular setting through focusing on God's trinitarian revelation. As postliberal theologians indicate, the primary concern of Christianity is to be the faithful witness of God rather than cooperating with other secular perspectives.

Another influence of postliberal theology I want to highlight is that postliberal theologians focus on the actual practices of Christianity. As postliberal theologians indicate, many Christians in the Church are not interested in making a theory, but in practicing what they believe to be a faithful witness of God. This indicates that the primary job of theology should be promoting and helping the practices of the Church, because Christian theology is based on the Christian practice rather than hypothetical theories. In the face of modernity, many Christian thinkers concentrate on making philosophical explanations of their faith to the world. However, postliberal theologians recover the importance of the practice of Christian theology; they give a huge impact on the development of practical theologies in America. Here, it is noteworthy that postliberal-influenced divinity schools such as Yale, Princeton, and Duke have a strong emphasis on practicality in their education compared to other seminaries. This shows that postliberal theology in fact encourages the practicality for their education

---

himself: "What I learned from Yoder meant I was to be labeled a sectarian, fideistic tribalist because I was allegedly tempting Christians to withdraw from political engagement. Nothing could have been further from the truth." Hauerwas, "How to (Not) Be a Political Theologian," 181.

162. For further evaluations, see Placher, "Revisionist and Postliberal Theologies and the Public Character of Theology"; Jones and Stewart, "The Unintended Consequences"; Michener, *Postliberal Theology*; Hunsicker, *The Making of Stanley Hauerwas*.

and congregation, while many other theologians still overlook the importance of the actual training and practice of Christianity.

In addition, I believe that postliberal theologians rediscover the importance of truth claims in the age of relativism. Borrowing Wittgenstein's idea of language games, postliberal theologians are more interested in examining their own truth claims epistemologically. That is why postliberal theologians argue that they cannot dismiss their Christian truth claims in front of other truth claims. For them, their truth claims are not formed by an individual alone, but by their faith community. As a result, their truth claims can be considered as God's revelation within their culture and practice. That is why postliberals think that, if the Christian belief is coming from God's revelation, it is enough for them to focus on their own truth claims which are not subject to other external elements or criticisms. As a result, postliberal theologians attempt to restate their truth claims confidently in front of other worldly cultures.

Conclusion: Epistemic Uneasiness

Although postliberal theology with many contributions has a huge impact on theological studies in North America, it has a critical flaw in that it tends to ignore the question of historicity.[163] For example, because Frei intends to focus on the Christian narrative, he denies to use any historical references in interpreting the narratives as Carl Henry suggests.[164] In Frei's realistic interpretation, the historical dimension of the text becomes less important because conveying accurate historical data is not a primary concern. For Frei, the meaning of the narrative is within the narrative itself. However, Nicholas Wolterstorff complains that Frei simply ignores the author's intention (or the historicity of the text), even if the meaning of the text itself is important.[165] William Placher also points out that the narrative needs to refer to God's actual action in history, instead of merely focusing on the narrative itself.[166] In this respect, the method of Frei overlooks that the narrative is also the product of God's action in history. That is why many theologians criticize postliberalism for being insular toward worldliness,

---

163. For further criticisms on postliberalism, see Placher, "Scripture as Realistic Narrative: Some Preliminary Questions"; Knight, *Liberalism versus Postliberalism*; Moyaert, "Postliberlism, Religious Diversity, and Interreligious Dialogue."

164. Henry, "Narrative Theology." You can also find Hans Frei's response: Frei, "Response to 'Narrative Theology.'"

165. Wolterstorff, "Evidence, Entitled Belief, and the Gospels."

166. Placher, "Paul Ricoer and Postliberal Theology." Cf. Knight, *Liberalism versus Postliberalism*, 260–62.

because postliberalism tends not to deal with the historicity of the text or Christian theology.

Likewise, I believe that Hauerwas' response toward worldliness is problematic, mainly because he ignores all other questions coming from others in the age of relativism. We can see this problem more clearly in the work of Hauerwas' colleague at Notre Dame and Duke, Paul Griffiths. As Hunsinger implies, "Griffiths owes an obvious debt to Lindbeck's influential "cultural–linguistic" theory of religion."[167] Even though Griffiths is retired as a Catholic theologian, he was devoted to interreligious studies for his early career because he studied Sanskrit Buddhism for his doctoral work. In pursuing interreligious dialogue, Griffiths under the postliberal influence defines religion as a form of life: "a religion, then, I shall take to be a form of life that seems to those who inhabit it to be comprehensible, incapable of abandonment, and of central importance."[168]

From this outset, Griffiths focuses on the possible epistemological responses to the awareness of religious diversity. He argues that making a religious claim involves acceptance so that each one's religious beliefs ought to be taken seriously as truth claims. He gives himself as an example. For him, religious claims are simply given to him because he has decided to be a faithful Catholic: "Jesus rose from the dead, God is triune, and I have a duty to attend Mass at least weekly."[169] In his religious beliefs, "acceptance requires choosing to treat a claim as true."[170] Since Griffiths accepts Jesus as God, Jesus is the Lord and the truth for him. That is why he prays and worship to God regularly. Likewise, if someone accepts that the Buddha is the unsurpassed refuge for suffering humanity, the acceptance will involve other actions like chanting for refuges regularly.[171] Consequently, the action of acceptance produces the response of assent; it will affect the respondent's cognitive life. In other words, religions typically require acceptance of its claims central to its believers. As a result, when each religious believer meets other religious claims, they should ask about a question raised by religious diversity, because each religion's claim is regarded as a truth claim for each believer.[172]

In the encounter with other religious cultures, Griffiths points out that people realize of contradictoriness among their religious truth claims because their religious claims are totally incompatible with other religious

---

167. Hunsinger, "Postliberal Theology," 54.
168. Griffiths, *Problems of Religious Diversity*, 7.
169. Griffiths, *Problems of Religious Diversity*, 26.
170. Griffiths, *Problems of Religious Diversity*, 28.
171. Griffiths, *Problems of Religious Diversity*, 28.
172. Griffiths, *Problems of Religious Diversity*, 30.

claims. He writes, "there are conflicts or incompatibilities among the doctrines of different religions."[173] For example, Griffiths as a Christian believes a claim that there is one God. Although this claim is thoroughly true for him, Buddhists may claim that there are many gods in this world. Here, two religious claims are contradictory if each makes a claim to be truth because both cannot be true while one must be true.[174] Even more, religious claims prescribe right actions according to their positions; each truth claims even suggests contradictory actions each other. For example, Christians believes that the Bible is the most important book in the world and the book allows them to eat whatever they want, while Muslims argues that Quran is the most important so that they do not eat pork according to their scripture. Consequently, people can easily find that there exist incompatible truth claims among different religions.

If each religious claim brings "epistemic uneasiness" through their own private logics, how can people know which one is true religion in the face of contradictions among religions? According to Griffiths, in Wittgenstein's thought, "some forms of life use the predicate is true in connection only with hypotheses; and in those forms of life religious claims cannot be true."[175] For example, the claim, *Jesus is Christ*, is taken as absolute, non-negotiable, and insulated truth for Christians. In this form of life, only religious claims can be the bearer of the predicate "*is true.*" However, in this argument, other artifacts of science cannot be true. In other words, although every religious claim must be true for its believers, no religious claim can be true, because a different understanding of what it is to use the predicate "*is true*" is in

---

173. Griffiths, *Problems of Religious Diversity*, 32.

174. Here, Griffiths overlooks that the truth claim of the church is confession. Although truth claims are contradictory one another, it is noteworthy that confessing has different tones from claiming something to be true. For example, if I claim something, I expect others to agree. If they do not agree, I would start questioning my claim. However, if I confess something, I invite others to do so as well. Even if others do not agree, I do not change my confession because my confession is different from scientific truth. Because Griffiths misunderstands the church's confession as a mere scientific truth claim, he shows exclusive response toward other religious claims. Griffiths, *Problems of Religious Diversity*, 32. Cf. Grosshans would argue that Christian theology should be based on realism, not just non-foundationalism: "Thus, religion must also mirror the reality of our relationship with God, and this, I have argued is a relationship whose hallmark is freedom. Therefore, true religion is alive to the element of surprise in human life, the times when we grapple with the extraordinary. God marks, therefore, the open point in the horizons and lobal understandings that we have conceived from power-theoretical, moral or aesthetic perspectives (limited though these invariably are *de facto*)." Grosshans, "And The Truth will Set You Free," 203.

175. Griffiths, *Problems of Religious Diversity*, 46.

play in each statement.[176] Therefore, Griffiths concludes in front of religious diversity: "I do not know."[177]

Even though Griffiths argues that Christians must have tolerance for other religious traditions, he is not sure about the result of confronting other external cultures within the perspective of Christianity. As a result, postliberal theology creates epistemic uneasiness rather than solving those problems when it deals with other external cultures. That is why postliberal theologians appeal to the privatization of religious belief or the sectarian response to worldliness in order to account for the reason why they should keep one's own religious tradition. For example, Griffiths argues that religious diversity does not reduce each one's religious beliefs, because religion has been privatized in our society. He points out that the court of the United States of America firmly locates religious belief in the private sphere as William James indicates.[178] As a result, there is a room for sufficient independent reason in each one's religious doxastic practice. According to Griffiths, although religious diversity leads people to realize contradictions among religious truth claims, it does not reduce epistemic confidence because each religious claims will be well-established and provide significant self-supports by themselves in their own logics. In privatization, religious claims do not lose their epistemic confidence, because they operate their reason within a their own distinct cultural/linguistic grammar. Looking at postliberals' sectarian response toward worldliness, even those who are not postliberals may agree that Jesus is not interested in answering to the questions of relativism according to the internal logic of the Christian narrative. However, as I will elaborate in later chapters, this view is problematic because it ignores the complexity of Christian history and faith. Thus, there remain questions unsolved in postliberal theology.

Here, it is noteworthy that radical orthodoxy and German radical hermeneutic theology also criticize postliberal theology. Regarding the response of postliberal theology toward worldliness, John Milbank, the father figure of radical orthodoxy, argues that postliberal theology should go further to Christian realism. He says, "if it is true that virtuous ends are

---

176. Griffiths, *Problems of Religious Diversity*, 47.

177. When I asked the outcome of interreligious dialogue, Paul Griffiths answered in his class, "I do not know. We are just doing it because diversity is just there." Here, Griffiths is not sure about what we can exactly learn from studying other religious traditions, while he is doing it with considerable tolerance.

178. James says, "Religion . . . shall mean for us the feelings, acts, and experiences of individual men in their solitude, so far as they apprehend themselves to stand in relation to whatever they may consider the divine." James, *The Varieties of Religious Experience*, 36.

internal to activities, then it follows that no ethical objective, which is not to some degree intrinsically realizable by some known process of activity, is genuinely 'moral' at all."[179] Postliberal theologians honor their place called church so that their communities are internally constituted with people who want to live in an alienating city (called church) for the sake of holding the truth. However, Milbank notes that every community is always "a being with" other communities because communities always encounter otherness or friend as their gift.[180] As a result, each community has to have a series of exchanged and binding gifts from one another in a shared *polis*. This implies that the church community is also the result of a constant binding and re-binding of others. In this sense, Milbank criticizes the postliberal response toward worldliness for overlooking the fact that there can be many different narrative plots in our society other than the Christian narrative. According to Milbank, although the response of postliberalism toward pacifism is a good account to realize God's order without an imperative force, postliberal response is just a partial representative rather than the whole Christian explanation.[181] And this is mainly because postliberal theology shows a sectarian view on worldliness, ignoring the fact that Christian theology always has to mingle with other cultural products in the realm of history. Consequently, Milbank criticizes postliberal theology for being an "alienated acting."[182]

Likewise, Dalferth, a leading German hermeneutic theologian, claims that postliberal theology should go further to explain their internal logic. On the one hand, he sees that the realistic reading of postliberal theology is right because there is "no understanding of the resurrection confession unless it is interpreted both Christologically (in relation to the person of Jesus) and soteriologically (in relation to us)."[183] As postliberal theologians argue, the understanding of Christianity should be done in a trinitarian

179. Milbank, *The Politics of Virtue*, 77.

180. Milbank, *The Politics of Virtue*, 78.

181. Milbank says, "Hauerwas's insistence that the way of peace, the way of exemplary persuasion and forgiveness, is always the more final way, not on account of a sublime imperative, but because it belongs to a more desirable way of life that we should strive to realize-a way of life no more and no less 'imaginary' than existing social practices which always write violence into their scripts. . . . A Historicist theology knows that the whole thing-God, heavens, and the economy of their relation to our finitude (the counter factual of angelology by imagining 'another finitude' reminds us that we have not transcendental knowledge of finitude 'as such')—is the product of our representation, and it is this whole picture which must be—if anything is to be considered such—and imperfect registration of final reality." Milbank, *The Word Made Strange*, 31–32.

182. Milbank, *The Word Made Strange*, 32.

183. Dalferth, *Crucified and Resurrected*, 54.

way according to the internal grammar of the Christian narrative; the understanding of the Christian narrative should be realistic and connected to the practical actions. On the other hand, Dalferth claims that postliberal theology fails to consider a third decisive factor: "the action of God."[184] According to Dalferth, when we consider the confession of Christianity as an act of God, the other worldly elements also should be discussed in Christian theology because worldliness is also the part of God's creation. Consequently, the critic of radical orthodoxy and German hermeneutic theology on postliberal theology implies that we need a further discussion to talk about Christians' response to worldliness with the question unsolved in postliberal theology.

---

184. Dalferth, *Crucified and Resurrected*, 55.

3

A Radical Orthodoxy Reaction (Britain)

The following chapter will investigate the theology of radical orthodoxy through the works of John Milbank and Graham Ward—two father figures of this theological trend. In doing so, this chapter will try to understand the contribution and limit of radical orthodoxy's stance toward worldliness, while inviting radical orthodoxy to a dialogue with other post-Barthian (trinitarian) theological movements. In this chapter, on the one hand, I will argue that radical orthodoxy shows a strength in that it actively engages with secular theories and postmodernity; radical orthodoxy contributes a lot to the discourse of Christian theology. On the other hand, pointing out the limit of radical orthodoxy, this chapter will criticize radical orthodoxy for holding a problematic view on worldliness. That is, radical orthodoxy shows a hostility toward worldliness, while holding a fundamentalist view that Christian theology is an absolute answer to solve the problem of modern secularism in history. In engaging with many secular philosophies and theories, radical orthodoxy often condemns secular theories for overlooking the transcendental dimension of this world in God. In criticizing secular theories, however, radical orthodoxy absolutizes the view of Christian theology, even though the view of Christianity is also a (imperfect) cultural product in the dimension of history like other secular theories; this chapter will claim that radical orthodoxy has a contradictory argument. To show this, the first section of this chapter will look at John Milbank's criticism on secular theories as the backdrop of radical orthodoxy's stance toward worldliness. The second section will study how Milbank suggests an alternative answer to secular theories through utilizing Augustine's trinitarian theology. And the last section will deal with Graham Ward's cultural hermeneutics to examine how radical orthodoxy engages with worldly cultures outside of Christianity and to see how radical orthodoxy understands the relationship between Christianity and culture.

THE FALLACY OF SECULARITY

The Rise of Radical Orthodoxy

Radical orthodoxy begun to be recognized as an important theological movement after radical orthodoxy theologians published a book called *Radical Orthodoxy: A New Theology* in 1999. If postliberal theology has been developed by Yale PhDs in America under the influence of George Lindbeck and Hans Frei, radical orthodoxy has been raised by Cambridge scholars in the UK, because all the contributors of the book studied theology at Cambridge.[1] The founder figures of this movement are Anglican theologians, John Milbank and Graham Ward. Although chief founders of this movement are Anglican theologians working in England, the movement includes theologians from other ecclesial traditions and different countries such as Catherine Pickstock, William Cavanaugh, or James K. A. Smith.

Here, radical orthodoxy's characteristics can be found in its name. In explaining its name, what *orthodox* means is that the theological movement re-affirms "a richer and more coherent Christianity which was gradually lost sight of after the late Middle Ages."[2] In emphasizing the importance of orthodox Christianity, the movement also upholds the influence of the Barthian *neoorthodoxy* "refusing all mediations through other spheres of knowledge and culture."[3] In addition, what *radical* means in its name is that the movement radically tries to "return to patristic and medieval roots and especially to the Augustinian vision of all knowledge as divine illumination."[4] This shows that the movement seeks to recover Christian vision to be "more mediating, but less accommodating" toward the current postmodern era.[5] As its name indicates, the aim of radical orthodoxy is to recover the orthodox Christian tradition (especially the classical Medieval theology) in the current secular era. While criticizing modern secularism for producing a humanistic/nihilistic viewpoint in the light of orthodox theology, radical orthodoxy claims to restore a trinitarian viewpoint which

---

1. Milbank et al., *Radical Orthodoxy*, xi.
2. Milbank et al., *Radical Orthodoxy*, 2.
3. Milbank et al., *Radical Orthodoxy*, 2.
4. Milbank et al., *Radical Orthodoxy*, 2.
5. Milbank et al., *Radical Orthodoxy*, 2.

leads people to participate into the real *causa sui*—the Triune God. Through recovering trinitarian view toward the world, radical orthodoxy suggests "a new theology" to re-envision traditional (orthodox) Christian theology toward various contemporary issues.

Comparing with postliberal theology, radical orthodoxy shares many similar interests with postliberal theology, such as classical theology (especially Cappadocian church fathers, Anselm, Augustine, and, Aquinas), analytic language philosophy, Karl Barth's theology, virtue ethics, Christian liturgies, theological hermeneutics, and most importantly criticism on modern secularism. In fact, Milbank expresses his indebtedness to Hauerwas in his books several times;[6] radical orthodoxy shows a similar theological lineage with postliberalsim in criticizing modern secularism. However, the scope of radical orthodoxy's criticism on modernity and its engagement with secularity are much broader than those of postliberal theology. This is because radical orthodoxy admits that Christian theology is also the product of history in this world; radical orthodoxy, unlike postliberal theology, promotes actively engagements with many social theories to show the validity of Christian faith against many questions from secular cultures. Thus, regarding the relationship between Christianity and worldliness, radical orthodoxy shows a different stance from postliberal theology, because radical orthodoxy attempts to answer many questions from modern secular theories, including political, economic, and sociological perspectives in history.

To show where radical orthodoxy starts its theological journey, the first section of this chapter will look at how radical orthodoxy criticizes modern secular reason. Interestingly, Milbank believes that the essence of modern philosophy is nihilistic because modernity only involves a finite reality. According to Milbank, modern secular philosophies do not go beyond the finite human understanding, even though they often try to find the ontological depth behind finite phenomena. In criticizing modern secularity, Milbank's criticism on modern secularity is so broad because it includes, not only philosophers like Duns Scotus, Baruch Spinoza, and Thomas Hobbes, but also social and economic theorists such as Adam Smith, Emil Durkheim, and Max Weber. Because Milbank defines secular philosophy so broadly that he includes many modern social theories and philosophies, this section will highlight few important themes of Milbank's criticism on secular theories to look at the philosophical background of radical orthodoxy's stance on worldliness. Investigating how radical orthodoxy criticizes false positivism in modern secularity, this section will include: (1) what the origin of secular reason is in Milbank's theology, (2) how Milbank understands

---

6. Milbank et al., *Radical Orthodoxy*, 2; Milbank, *The Word Made Strange*, xi.

the genealogy of modern secularity, and (3) how he allies with and separates from postmodern theories to criticize postmodern secular philosophies.

The Separation of Philosophy and Theology

Milbank argues that, before modernity, "there was no secular."[7] This indicates that the community of Christendom in the Western world once did not understand their time and space with secular reason, but with the theological/eschatological worldview which led people to justice and humbleness in front of God. According to Milbank, secular theories started to be instituted and imagined in the modern era to advocate false positivism on human reason. In the pathos of modernity, many modern theorists recognized human autonomy and freedom as the core elements of understanding the world; many modern theorists developed a reduction of religion to social theory, because they investigated religion within secular bias, based on the positive affirmation of one's freedom and reason. As a result of the positive affirmation of the human self, the secular began to appear as a domain, governing social rules in the politics, economics, and even ethics. Later in the postmodern era, however, the left-Nietzscheanism has been developed, because people began to realize the problematic implication of modern positivism. For Friedrich Nietzsche, Western society, which was grounded in the legacy of platonism and Christianity, showed nihilism. This was because the philosophy of the Western modernity was trapped in the realm of finite. In Nietzsche's critique, as Milbank notes, "nihilism is the conclusion of 'pure reason' . . . fully honest Western reason realizes that reason itself is but a pathetic human projection."[8] From this Nietzsche's critic, Milbank finds the problem of modern secularism that cuts off the dimensions of faith and transcendence. To find an alternative way to overcome the finite circulation of modern secular reason, Milbank in his first book, *Theology and Social Theory* examines the problem of modern secular reason through borrowing Nietzsche's method of genealogy.

Milbank discovers the root of modern secular reason from the arguments of Duns Scotus.[9] As Catherine Pickstock indicates, radical orthodoxy believes that typical modern philosophies such as the Cartesian and the

---

7. Milbank, *Theology and Social Theory*, 9. Although Scotus' influence has been huge for modern thinking, it is noteworthy that Scotus is also considered as a root of post-modern philosophers by Gilles Deleuze, Alain Badiou, and Jaques Derrida. See Cross, *The Physics of Duns Scotus*; Cross, *Duns Scotus*.

8. Milbank, *Theology and Social Theory*, xvii.

9. Milbank, *Theology and Social Theory*, xxv.

Kantian understandings are developed within Latin scholasticism;[10] radical orthodoxy theologians draw attention to that modern philosophy also has its indebtedness from Scotus' scholasticism. According to Scotus, when the human mind tries to understand abstract properties such as being, good or truth, they do not simply mirror the finitude concepts to the abstract properties, because they understand the abstract notions with a certain elevation of their reality.[11] In other words, Scotus realizes that human beings cannot describe abstract notions in an exact way without conceptual elevation. For Scotus, that is why there are so many different interpretations of human life, because everybody has a different conceptual elevation process.

In Scotus' theology, because there is no full convertibility in describing being or truth due to many different conceptual elevations, human beings only have a subtle picture to describe their reality with diverse interpretations.[12] He says, "When one of those that come together is incompatible with certainty, then certainty cannot be achieved. For just as from one premise that is necessary and one that is contingent nothing follows but a contingent conclusion, so from something certain and something uncertain, coming together in some cognition, no cognition that is certain follows."[13] According to Scotus, the fact that there are many different interpretations implies that the proofs of abstract concepts proceed from a finite contingent world rather than a universal truth transcending all differences. Because Scotus advocates human understandings in a contingent world, he suggests voluntarism which emphasizes God's will and human freedom rather than holding illuminationism, believing human thought needs to be illuminated by God's transcendent grace. For Scotus, God already gave us voluntary freedom, allowing us to have rational thinking in this contingent world.

Examining Scotus' theology, Milbank asserts that Scotus' theology brings the metaphysical liberal era, which affirms *positive* universal laws, human wills, and even different interpretations within "a contingent world."[14] This is because the theology of Scotus "opens up the possibility of

---

10. Pickstock, "Duns Scotus," 545. Cf. Ford, "Radical Orthodoxy and the Future of British Theology."

11. Pickstock, "Duns Scotus," 546. Cf. Duns Scotus, *Ordinatio*, I.8.3.n50.

12. Pickstock, "Duns Scotus," 546. Cf. Duns Scotus, *Ordinatio*, I.3.1.nn31–151.

13. Duns Scotus, *Ordinatio*, I.3.1.n221.

14. Milbank, *Theology and Social Theory*, 15. He also says, "In the thought of the nominalists, following Duns Scotus, the Trinity loses its significance as a prime location for discussing will and understanding in God and the relationship of God to the world." Scotus also mentioned that Scotus "for the first time established a radical separation of philosophy from theology by declaring that it was possible to consider being in abstraction from the question of whether one is considering created or creating being." Milbank, *Theology and Social Theory*, 23.

considering being without God."[15] In this respect, Milbank's concern with Scotus' theology is that it separates philosophy from theology. And furthermore, after Scotus' theology, there has been a process of developing secular reason which advocates human freedom and human intelligence within this contingent world without referring to God who can give us transcendental freedom beyond the finite human mind.[16]

The Genealogy of Modern Secular Reason

To examine the genealogy (development) of modern secular reason after Scotus' theology, Milbank investigates many different secular theories in the Western society. According to Milbank, secular reason (which separates philosophy and theology) is further developed through the implication of modern *political theories*. In the works of modern political theorists such as Hugo Grotius, Thomas Hobbes, and Baruch Spinoza, political theory begins to have a certain autonomy from theology through embracing the notion of humanism as the destiny of autonomous human freedom.[17] The modern political theorists claim that the natural laws are already given to us; the

---

15. Pickstock, "Duns Scotus," 548. Milbank summarizes Scotus' acknowledgement and its later development in *Theology and Social Theory*, xxvi. Although Milbank thinks that Scotus opens a new era through advocating nominalism, Milbank interprets Scotus in Aquinas' influence: "1. Scotus implicitly and cogently asks how, if created being simply shares in Being, it can really, integrally be. 2. Scotus and Ockham rightly question whether analogy of attribution does not violate the principle of non-contradiction, since there is no third term between the univocal and the equivocal. 3. Ockham likewise tends to suggest that certain realist conceptions of universals and real relations tend to violate the principle of identity. (How can a particular form as this form—which might, for example, in the case of the form of a man, be white or black—also be, or be able to become, the same form as universal—which, as denoting nominally a genus like 'humanity', might be determined as either white or black? How, likewise, can a thing be by necessary relation also what it is not?) 4. According to Ockham, every supposed grasp of a universal has clearly been arrived at through a process of linguistic naming. 5. Since Being is now univocal, it becomes less clear than it was for Aquinas that *ens commune* can only be the effect of an infinite cause. Already Ockham suggests, following the implications of univocity of Being (and well before the 'Renaissance') that while creatures cannot cause totally, they can still bring about finite being as such, in collaboration with God, on the same ontological level. And although we have no experience of this, even a human productive action presupposing no pregiven substrate, cannot be logically ruled out." See Milbank, *Theology and the Political*, 393–427, esp. 416–17.

16. Cf. For a similar discussion, Habermas deals with the separation between faith and knowledge. As its background, the book's chapter six also engages with Duns Scotus's theology. Habermas, *Auch eine Geschichte der Philosophie*.

17. Milbank, *Theology and Social Theory*, 10.

universal natural laws are "known *etsi Deus non daretur*."[18] For example, Hobbes says in his *Leviathan*, "The right of Nature, whereby God reigneth over men, and punisheth those that break his Lawes, is to be derived, not from his creating them, as if he required obedience as of gratitude for his benefits; but from his *Irresistible Power*."[19] For the modern theorists like Hobbes, there is a sheer human freedom in response to God's grace, because human beings have an *irresistible power* to control over other objects in this contingent world. For Hobbes, because human beings have freedom and power to control over other objects in this contingent world, the knowledge of power comes from an analysis of *factum*. In other words, in the thinking of modern political theorists, the analysis of *factum* becomes "an area of human autonomy by making dominium into a matter of absolute sovereignty and absolute ownership."[20] This means that modern theorists understand the world based on scientific/material knowledge (*factum*). Because of this *factum* understanding of the world, they argue that political knowledge has a material foundation—*conatus*, which is the production of humanity. That is why they believe that their political society in fact constitutes of human contracts. As a result, for modern political theorists, the conception of society becomes a human production rather than a pure creation of God.[21]

Under the circumstances of "the new science of politics," Milbank points out that secular *political economy* is also developed with the discovery of a regularity in human affairs—the operation of the market. According to Milbank, modern economic theories accelerate the process of secularization. For Milbank, the modern political economy is raised by the Scottish scholars such as David Hume and Adam Smith. Here, while Hobbes and Spinoza focus on the natural law tradition which construes norms from self-preserving *conatus*, Hume situates the human morality into the pre-moral or the sub-rational within the realm of human experience. In other words, Hume believes that human ethics are based on emotions rather than abstract (universal) moral principles. In this understanding of Hume, ethics can be found in every individual, because the interest of individuals shows a certain mechanism, allowing the individuals to be moral.[22] As a result, Hume believes that human sentiments lead human beings to have a casual determinism which promotes a practical reason, pursuing (utilitarian) benevolence.

18. Milbank, *Theology and Social Theory*, 10.
19. Hobbes, *Leviathan*, II.31.
20. Milbank, *Theology and Social Theory*, 16.
21. Milbank, *Theology and Social Theory*, 11.
22. Hume, *A Treatise of Human Nature*, III.2.1.

Likewise, Adam Smith, an Edinburgh Christian ethicist, sees that human morality is "principally recommended to his own care."[23] For Smith, conscience arises from dynamic and interactive social relationships, seeking mutual sympathy of sentiments. For him, that is why human beings can develop negotiations of trade and contracts of peace by their deliberate utilitarian calculation in their sentiments. His famous "invisible hand" controls the market with a providential and Newtonian-like rule in the world of human sentiment. For the Scottish theorists such as Hobbes and Smith, the invisible mechanisms of emotion lend themselves to social goods by leading human beings to pursue benevolence.[24] According to Milbank, because the conclusion of these modern political economists affirm providence (regular mechanism) in human affairs, their economic theories "help to construct an amoral mechanism which allows not merely the institution but also the preservation and the regulation of the secular."[25]

Along with political and economic theories, Milbank believes that modern sociology is also part of defining the logic of secular reason, in that it adds the scope of (social) positivism. According to Milbank, modern sociology focuses on the idea that individuals are always situated within society. For the French sociologists such as Auguste Comte and Emile Durkheim, for example, society is a whole prior to any individual because a social system precedes any politics or individuals. For them, the social is an ahistorical category.[26] Unlike Adam Smith, these modern sociologists think that the differentiation of labor process is not linked with individualism or the marketplace, but the given organic complexity of society. Based on this wholistic understanding of society, the French sociologists attempt to explain religion within their sociological frame. That is why Comte, for example, claims that "all religious beliefs were more or less imperfect approximations to 'sociology', or to the truth of the ultimate determining power of the social whole."[27] In this sociological view, religion should be demystified, because it is the part of social reality. For Comte, sociology has to find a prior and external influence of individual existence with the aspect of *datum*.

Later, Durkheim embraces Comte's metaphysics of the *fait sociale* and further develops sociology with neo-Kantian liberalism. Durkheim says, "obedience to the general will does not contradict our autonomy because

---

23. Smith, *The Theory of Moral Sentiments*, II.2, 119.
24. Milbank, *Theology and Social Theory*, 40.
25. Milbank, *Theology and Social Theory*, 47.
26. Milbank, *Theology and Social Theory*, 53.
27. Milbank, *Theology and Social Theory*, 61 Cf. Comte, *The Crisis of Industrial Civilization*, 24–27, 187–88.

we are thereby willing a freedom greater than the freedom of the state of nature."[28] According to Durkheim then, human freedom does not conflict with social structure which is a *priori* element of every human behavior. Because Durkheim presupposes that social structure is found in every human behavior, he argues that even religion should be considered as a part of the social structure. That is why he investigates religion not starting from the ideas of practitioners, but from its function: "definition (of religion) is to be sought from reality itself."[29] Here, Milbank criticizes the French sociologists for reducing all religious phenomena to the sociological/factual dimension. He says, "an adequate 'transcendental' reflection on the conditions of possibility for social action discovers the inevitability of historiography, but finds no room whatsoever for 'social science.'"[30]

On the other hand, Milbank believes that modern secular reason also draws on the works of German father figures of sociology such as Max Weber and Ernst Troeltsch. Like the French sociologists, these German sociologists presuppose *a priori* promises of relationship between individuals and existing social elements.[31] However, unlike the French sociologists, the German sociologists think that religion does not only rely on social structures, because religion has its own unique factor to have an impact to other social spheres in economics and politics.[32] For example, Troeltsch says that the medieval town has an unique economic system from other regional community because it has a Christian ethos in its deep heart.[33] Likewise, Weber argues that religion impacts people's ethics and, further, their economic system.[34] This implies that every religion has its own moral affinity because every religious belief is associated with a certain social form of life. However, in these German sociologies, each religion still holds a general patterning in this world. This indicates that the German sociologists, like the French sociologists, attempt to grasp an understanding of religion within the secular world of modernity, not beyond the world of *datum*.

---

28. Milbank, *Theology and Social Theory*, 63.
29. Durkheim, *The Elementary Forms of Religious Life*, 22.
30. Milbank, *Theology and Social Theory*, 74.
31. Milbank, *Theology and Social Theory*, 75.
32. Milbank, *Theology and Social Theory*, 90.
33. Troeltsch, *Social Teaching of the Christian Churches*, 254.

34. Weber claims that each religious belief forms a certain collective ethics. So, Weber attempts to explain that religious beliefs impact ethical behavior in human society and even promote the development of capitalism (which is an economic behavior). Weber, "The Sociology of Religion," 519–89.

As a result, Milbank points out that the German sociologists have a few problems in understanding religion.[35] According to Milbank, one of the main critiques for the German sociologists is that their understanding of society is solely based on the Western bases, especially on Christianity.[36] Weber and Troeltsch both find a formal rationality in monotheism, while condemning other polytheistic forms of religion as private values. That is why Weber claims that the understanding of capitalism can be fully developed only in the Protestant ethics, not in others.[37] For Milbank, another problem of the German sociologists is that their understandings of religion "deny the convertibility of the transcendentals with objective being, and yet try to establish the objectivity of knowledge, aesthetic judgment and ethical will in terms of the necessary a priori modes of operation of these three faculties."[38] Milbank here believes that modern social theories (including both the French and German sociologies) fail to incorporate religion as the whole because they tend to understand religion as an ideology or a mere social element within the world of *factum*. According to Milbank, modern secular reason tends to understand everything within a limited contingent understanding of the world, while denying the transcendental aspects of humanity; everything remains in the spheres of politics, economics, and socials without imagining transcendence beyond human finitude.

Looking at the genealogy (and the reinforcement) of modern secular reason in the modern era, Milbank realizes the fallacy of modernity. Although modern secular theorists open up the institutionalization of the secular, which is governed by a positive human power with the emphasis of the world of *factum*, Milbank raises a question about the connection of *factum* and the secular.[39] According to Milbank, to identify the aspect of

35. For further criticism on modern sociologists, see Jonas, *Die Maxcht des Heiligen*.

36. Milbank, *Theology and Social Theory*, 94.

37. Weber, *The Protestant Ethics and the Spirit of Capitalism*. Cf. Milbank once said, "It is precisely the Protestant (and also Jansenist) reduction of the this-worldly to a merely instrumental significance for the pursuit of material ends, or else to a ledger-book register of spiritual privilege, which has helped to create the space within which a pure capitalism can so successfully flourish. Thus, the fact that the most capitalist country in the world, the United States, is the most imbued with this Weberian version of the Calvinist legacy is not at all accidental." Milbank et al., *Paul's New Moment*, 32.

38. Milbank, *Theology and Social Theory*, 129.

39. Milbank summarizes four pillars of modern ontology: "(1) the univocity rather than analogy of being; (2) knowledge by representation rather than identity; (3) the priority of the possible over the actual; and (4) causality as 'concurrence' rather than 'influence'. These assumptions are all profoundly linked to the equally important invention of a novel space of 'pure nature', independent of the human natural orientation to the supernatural as taught by the Church Fathers and the high Middle Ages, but then largely abandoned by late medieval and early modern theology." Milbank, *Beyond Secular Order*, 3.

factum with the secular, modern secular theorists begin to regard Adam's (the first human being's) *dominium* over power, property, and morality as a granted gift of God.[40] Milbank points out that dominium over oneself and external objects in modern secular reason justifies a sheer power of human being to control over all things within the arbitrary human mind.[41] For many modern theorists like Hobbes, Smith, and Weber, the human will is already given; human beings can arbitrarily control over other objects in this contingent world. That is why many modern secular theorists attempt to understand their reality from a priori conditions of human knowledge and power. In this atmosphere, many modern theorists overlook the importance of *praxis*, while investigating the concepts of society and religion only within the world of *factum*.

Because secular reason advocates positive human powers over understanding and controlling other objects, Milbank finds that the essence of secular reason is the "'metaphysical' liberal era of universal laws," promoting both the powers of others and of oneself.[42] According to Milbank, the notion that one has a positive free will to control over the reality is false, because the human free will merely exists within one's own anthropocentric mind without considering other objects or God seriously.[43] That is why Milbank defines the root of modern liberalism as the individualist model of *dominium* which allows unrestricted private property, voluntary sovereignty, and active rights to other objects.[44] For Milbank, modern secular theories allow unrestricted sovereign authority to capricious human power; it allows human beings to arbitrarily control over everything, including the realm of transcendence.[45] Consequently, Milbank believes that modern secular theo-

---

40. Milbank, *Theology and Social Theory*, 13.

41. He says, "self-identity, the *suum*, is no longer essentially related to divine rational illumination, or ethics, but is a sheer 'self-occupation' or 'self-possession.'" Milbank, *Theology and Social Theory*, 14.

42. Milbank, *Theology and Social Theory*, xiv.

43. Milbank summarizes the problems of modern political theories in its three denials: "firstly, of 'Baroque poesis', or the idea that human making is not a merely instrumental and arbitrary matter, but itself a route which opens towards the transcendent; secondly, of the Christian doctrine of creation, in favour of a reversion to an antique mythology of rational action as the 'inhibitor of chaos'; thirdly, of Aristotelian ethics/politics, with its central notions of praxis, virtue and prudence." Milbank, *Theology and Social Theory*, 148.

44. It is noteworthy that Milbank sees the Reformation as one of the contributions of modern nominalist voluntarism. Milbank, *Theology and Social Theory*, 18.

45. Milbank further says, "Clearly, then, in theological terms *Theology and Social Theory* radically broke with most twentieth-century theology in two principal ways: First, it refused to say that theology must conform to secular knowledge, which is regarded as established independently of theology, and it refused a Barthian-style fideism,

ries commit inevitable "violence toward a given ontological reality," that is, against the perspective of Christianity which supports the dimension of transcendence and the importance of actual *praxis* in the world.

The Genealogy of Postmodernism

If modern theories brought the development of secular reason which reduces the human orientation toward transcendence in a realm of pure modern scientific reason, how can we overcome the fallacy of modern secularism? Milbank points out that there have been many attempts to solve the problem in secular reason. He groups them into two schools: the Hegelian dialectics (including Karl Marx, Karl Rahner, and Gustavo Gutiérrez, Leonardo Boff),[46] and the Nietzschean philosophy of differentiation (including Martin Heidegger, Michael Foucault, Jacques Derrida, and Gilles Deleuze).[47] According to Milbank, especially, many thinkers in the Nietzschean postmodern philosophies attempt to refute modern metaphysics through highlighting the importance of *differences*. In the current postmodern era, absolute universality is no longer valid; modernity is viewed as fundamentally flawed. In the perspective of postmodernity, modernity reduces everything into the product of subjective humanity, while suggesting a universal theory of everything and disregards the diversity of the given world. And that is why many postmodern thinkers emphasize the necessity of the ontology of difference to overcome the problem of modernity.

However, according to Milbank, the challenge of postmodernity is not enough to rebut the problem of modernity, because these postmodern thinkers do not fully overcome dualism, relativism, and malign egotism based on one's will-to-power.[48] In Milbank's theology, although it is right to claim the ontology of difference in the age of pluralism, postmodern philosophies still have a nihilistic description on the human reality, because they are still founded on the humanistic understanding of reality, ignoring the realm of transcendence. Thus, Milbank also criticizes postmodern philosophies for missing the aspect of transcendence.

---

which says that theology simply expounds the givens of faith and ignores rational deliberations. Second, it broke with the approach of most twentieth-century theology that thinks there is a sphere of secular theologically 'neutral knowledge.'" Milbank et al., *Paul's New Moment*, 11–12.

46. Although Milbank precisely deals with the problem of Hegelian dialectics including the Catholic thought and liberation theology, I will skip this part due to the limit of space in my work. Milbank, *Theology and Social Theory*, 145–256.

47. Milbank, *Theology and Social Theory*, 278.

48. Milbank, *Theology and Social Theory*, 281.

To criticize postmodern philosophies, Milbank locates the origin of the secular postmodern philosophies as Friedrich Nietzsche, because many postmodern thinkers such as Martin Heidegger, Gilles Deleuze, Jean-Francois Lyotard, Michael Foucault, and Jacques Derrida follow Nietzsche's "historicist genealogy," "ontology of difference," or "nihilistic moralism."[49] According to Milbank, one of the most important characteristics of the postmodern philosophies is an absolute historicism which tries to overcome Kantian philosophy, based on the finite human subject. Unlike Kantian philosophy, the Nietzschean genealogy denies a single story based on human freedom or finite human subject. Instead, Nietzsche sees many different moral values and stories in his *Genealogy of Morals*.[50] In Nietzsche's philosophy, there is no eternal moral value, because existing different cultures require human beings to have different moral interpretations. In the face of different cultures and moral stories, Nietzsche claims that we need to celebrate those differences and competitive struggles, and that we should recover primitive myths about power struggles between charismatic heroes.[51] For Nietzsche, that is why the chaotic Dionysian philosophical concept should be praised instead of the formal Apollonian philosophical concept.[52] Because Nietzsche celebrates chaotic struggles, he supports "will-to-power" and "nihilism" for human morality.[53] That is why Nietzsche criticizes Christianity for oppressing the Dionysian struggles, while bringing the Apollonian concepts to the Western society.

Although Milbank finds a beauty in the Nietzschean philosophy because it promotes the philosophy of difference, he criticizes the Nietzschean philosophy of difference. The first critique of Milbank is on Nietzsche's will-to-power.[54] Nietzsche believes that Christianity leads human beings to have ascetic repressions toward human nature, sexuality, and differences;

---

49. Milbank, *Theology and Social Theory*, 278.
50. See Nietzsche, *On the Genealogy of Morals*.
51. Milbank, *Theology and Social Theory*, IX.
52. See Nietzsche, *The Birth of Tragedy*.
53. He says, "2. The end of Christianity—at the hands of its own morality (which cannot be replaced), which turns against the Christian God (the sense of truthfulness, developed highly by Christianity, is nauseated by the falseness and mendaciousness of all Christian interpretations of the world and of history; rebound from 'God is truth' to the fanatical faith 'All is false'; Buddhism of action). 3. Skepticism regarding morality is what is decisive. The end of the moral interpretation of the world, which no longer has any sanction after it has tried to escape into some beyond, leads to nihilism. 'Everything lacks meaning' (the untenability of one interpretation of the world, upon which a tremendous amount of energy has been lavished, awakens the suspicion that all interpretations of the world are false)." Nietzsche, *The Will to Power*, 9.
54. Milbank, *Theology and Social Theory*, 284.

Christianity appears to be the enemy of dynamic human struggles. However, Milbank argues that Christianity carries "the total inversion of any heroic identity of virtue with strength, achievement or conquest. It celebrates dependency and claims to refuse violence."[55] This indicates that Christianity is an opposite of nihilism, because it refuses violence against Nietzsche's philosophy. Milbank also points out that the Nietzschean celebration of differences falls into "a limitless ambition to obliterate all others."[56] According to Milbank, through advocating will-to-power, Nietzsche does not see the true (transcendental) nature of human being, but a mere care of the self. For Milbank, the Nietzschean philosophy produces a modern military society rather than solving the problem of modern egoistic subjectivism.

In addition, Milbank believes that Nietzschean postmodern ontology has a huge problem in advocating an anti-realist position. Nietzsche regards Western metaphysics as the child of Christian theology which assumes a transcendent reality or a transcendent concept such as moral good.[57] In the Nietzschean philosophy, the postmodern critique of metaphysics seeks to de-Christianize Western philosophy; Nietzschean postmodernism rejects the traditional Western metaphysics through suggesting a nihilist anti-realism.[58] For example, Heidegger, a leading postmodern thinker, believes that an authentic human existence is in the life of *Dasein* which is a mode of a being thrown into this contingent world.[59] Against his teacher, Edmund Husserl, Heidegger claims that human beings as "being-in-the-world" are thrown into a particular time and place without choice. For Heidegger, human beings get lost in "the forgetfulness of Being," when they are forgetful of their thrownness in this world. This implies that human beings can know only what has come to them in a certain time and space as an event.[60] Based on this distinction between Being (*das Sein*) and beings (*das Seiende*), Heidegger in his early works shows a hermeneutic endeavor to constitute human beings in time. That is why he suggests "the ontological difference" which allows different interpretations among others. For Heidegger, everybody has different understandings, because human beings cannot avoid a distortion in thinking other beings (in time). According to Heidegger, everybody merely stands in their own subjective position when they think of others.[61]

55. Milbank, *Theology and Social Theory*, 286.
56. Milbank, *Theology and Social Theory*, 291.
57. Nietzsche, *The Will to Power*, 7.
58. Milbank, *Theology and Social Theory*, 298.
59. Cf. Müller-Lauter, *Heidegger und Nietzsche*, 303.
60. See Heidegger, *Being and Time*.
61. Heidegger believes that we live on the age of nihilism. What it means by that,

Looking at the non-transcendental (finite) description of Nietzsche/Heideggerian postmodernism, Milbank criticizes postmodern philosophies for supporting a nihilistic version of historicism.[62] Although Nietzsche and Heidegger's philosophy is further developed than other Western metaphysics through affirming the importance of differences, they still suggest that human beings are trapped in the finite hermeneutic circulation by philosophy alone without theological imagination. For Milbank, this perspective of infinite differences from the structure of thrownness exemplifies the emptiness at its root, because unless this system commits some epistemic violence to transcendence, there is only arbitrary and groundless insistence on some values. As a result, for Milbank, the postmodern philosophy of difference (possibly including Deleuze and Derrida's philosophies of difference)[63] is "a fundamental rift sundering ourselves from ourselves and ourselves from others."[64] Because Nietzschean philosophers do not have a realistic ontology suggesting something beyond this chaotic finite world, their ontology of difference in fact does not propose any particular moral evaluations; their arguments are essentially nihilistic. For Milbank, these postmodern philosophies of difference rather cause arbitrary power struggles to fulfill each one's will-to-power, because they fall into a moral nihilism in the end without suggesting any concrete ethical virtue or truth.[65] Therefore, he believes that nihilistic postmodern philosophies are fallacious because they merely offer the *dominium* of an arbitrary, humanistic, and voluntarist god.

In short, investigating the genealogy of secular reason, Milbank criticizes both modern secular theories and postmodern philosophies, because they are missing the aspect of transcendence and gets trapped in the nihilistic circulation of this contingent world. For Milbank, secular reason is based on the positive affirmation of human freedom in this world, as Scotus first suggests. Because secular reason is stuck in the finite circulation of human

---

when we think, we do not see things from the perspective of other beings. Instead, in the Western philosophy, we try to find a beauty or the truth from our observation or our thinking; we focus on a "beauty" which is "subjective" rather than on the beauty that presences right before our very eyes in that being. Heidegger, *What Is Called Thinking?*

62. Milbank says, "If beings are entirely constituted by their relationship to Being, then this is not a relationship we can survey, and Being remains forever absent, forever concealed behind its presentation in the temporal series of beings." Milbank, *Theology and Social Theory*, 302.

63. Milbank here criticizes Deleuze and Derrida for missing a realistic ontology; they share the same lineage with the Nietzschean philosophy. Milbank, *Theology and Social Theory*, 309–14.

64. Milbank, *Theology and Social Theory*, 304.

65. According to Milbank, the Nietzschean philosophy here includes Deleuze, Lyotard, Derrida, and Foucault. Milbank, *Theology and Social Theory*, 318.

will, Milbank believes that secular reason cannot offer genuine (transcending) reconciliation in front of others. For Milbank, in the finite realm of secular reason, there merely exist one's own will-to-power and *"bellum omnium contra omnes"* in its deep heart.[66]

THE HERMENEUTICS OF RADICAL ORTHODOXY

The Other City

If both modern and postmodern secular theories aggravate a nihilistic *dominium* over oneself and others, where can we find an alternative explanation to elucidate our reality in a meaningful way? On this question, Milbank believes that Christian theology articulates an alternative social science against the nihilistic circulation of secular reason. This is because Christian theology aims to establish a new and unique community based on the Church which is something more than a social subsystem in our society.[67] According to Milbank, Christian theology proposes a distinguishable Christian mode of action and practice, because it is first and foremost based on ecclesiology. Here, Milbank draws attention to the fact that Christian theology has developed different *Sittlichkeit* from the secular world through the constant re-narration of its social practices in history; Christian theology has shown "counter-history," "counter-ethics," and further "counter-ontology," offering salvation from the nihilistic secular theories. Thus, Milbank believes that the Church has an alternative answer to remedy the nihilistic circulation of secular reason.

In suggesting a counter-ontology against the nihilistic characteristics of secular philosophies, Milbank draws attention to Augustine's *City of God*. Milbank thinks that Augustine proposes a unique Christian explanation over worldliness throughout his works. This is because Augustine's theology depicts different history, ethics, and ontology from earthly philosophies. Here, Milbank develops radical orthodoxy's hermeneutics based on Augustinian theology. In this section, to show how Christian theology articulates a different ontology from secular theories, I will deal with how Milbank borrows Augustine's *City of God*. For this, I will investigate the three aspects

---

66. Cf. Hobbes, *Leviathan*. Nietzsche says, "Insofar as the individual wants to preserve himself against other individuals, in a natural state of affairs he employs the intellect mostly for simulation alone. But because man, out of need and boredom, wants to exist socially, herd-fashion, he requires a peace pact and he endeavors to banish at least the very crudest *bellum omnium contra omnes* from his world." Nietzsche, "On Truth and Lies in a Nonmoral Sense," in *The Portable Nietzsche*, 35.

67. Milbank, *Theology and Social Theory*, 383.

of Augustinian theology in Milbank's work, and will study how Milbank applies Augustinian theology into postmodernity. So, the coming section will contain: (1) how Augustinian theology develops a counter-history, (2) how Augustinian theology has a counter-ethics against ancient philosophies, (3) how Augustinian ecclesiology affirms a counter-ontology, and (4) how Milbank applies Augustine's trinitarian theology into postmodernity.

The Counter-History

According to Milbank, one of the most important characteristics of Augustine's theology is that it has a *counter-history* against worldliness. Milbank points out that postliberal theology is correct to see that the modes of Christian experience are coming from a particular culture and practice. To be specific, as D. Z. Phillips suggests, "the whole of Christian practice refers to the absolute."[68] This is because the Christian practice is internally derived from a response to the Absolute which the Christian narrative suggests. That is why D. Z. Phillips agrees with Hans Frei that only Christian narratives identify God, because the narratives invent the idea of God to Christians. In this postliberal understanding of metanarrative realism, Christians eventually articulate their entire form of life from the Christian narrative, because they develop the idea of God-become-incarnate through the Christian narrative. For Christians, the idea of God is so real, because they believe that the world is situated within their stories; they keep finding "the absolute" in their lives. In this mode of being, Christians develop different ethical forms of life in history from others, because they interpret the world with the idea of the absolute within the Christian narrative. Here, Milbank agrees with postliberal theology that the Christian narrative forms a different ethical life through formulating metanarrative realism.

However, Milbank criticizes postliberal metanarrative realism because postliberal theologians insulate "the Christian narrative from its historical genesis."[69] Against postliberal theologians, Milbank asserts that the entire practice of Christians cannot be in isolation. This is because the real implication of Christian practices is the creation of a "real history" which includes all kinds of different interpretations and diverse world views. As a result, Milbank believes that a true Christian metanarrative realism should embrace other worldly histories and different interpretations, because he pleads that one must behave theologically in the same way as secular thinking with inverted (theological) signs. In other words, Milbank points out

68. Milbank, *Theology and Social Theory*, 384., Cf. Phillips, "Lindbeck's Audience."
69. Milbank, *Theology and Social Theory* 388.

that the Christian narratives are not free from the context of the materialistic world. At this point of metanarrative realism, Milbank returns to Augustine's *Civitas Dei* to embrace different stories within a real history. He says, "a true Christian metanarrative realism must attempt to retrieve and elaborate the account of history given by Augustine in the *Civitas Dei*."[70] Milbank believes that Augustine's theology offers a true Christian metanarrative realism, because it embraces worldliness in finite time (history) based on the transcendental perspective of Christianity.

According to Milbank, Augustine envisions peaceful reconciliation to human history through suggesting an *altera civitas*, which has no connection with the city of violence.[71] Rather than explaining the world with conflicts or dialectical relationships, Augustine's city of God is "grounded in a particular, historical and 'mythical' narrative and in an ontology which explicates the beliefs implicit in this (Christian) narrative."[72] For Augustine, the *Civitas terrena* is none other than the world of denying God—the world of sin. Augustine believes that we cannot find justice in this earthly city because of its essential structure of *dominium*. In Augustine's theology, human beings fall into the situation of sin when they worship idols instead of God. On the other hand, Augustine states that there is a possibility of alteration in the *Civitas Dei* because it offers the vision of peace based on its self-exposed offering of reconciliation to enemies.[73] Instead of supporting constant battles or dominances over others, Augustine finds new possibilities from the heavenly city embracing all the abandoned losers and rivalries through worshiping the one unified God of love.[74] For Augustine, in this city of God, all violence is disdained through the work of Jesus Christ, because the Bible's narrative of Jesus shows the self-sacrificial love based on forgiveness, refusing mimetic violent rivalries. In other words, Augustine believes that the idiom of Jesus articulates the emergence of the Church which aims to bring the peaceful kingdom of God into the sinful world until the last days come.[75] In this different story of God, Milbank believes that we can develop a different history against the nihilistic history of finite *dominium*.

70. Milbank, *Theology and Social Theory*, 391. For an additional description of radical orthodoxy's interpretation on Augustine's *City of God*, look at Ward, *Cities of God*.
71. Milbank, *Theology and Social Theory*, 392.
72. Milbank, *Theology and Social Theory*, 392.
73. Augustine, *City of God*, X.5.6.
74. Unlike the worldly city, the city of God here is a nomad city because it does not have a site or walls. It is rather based on pilgrimage through this world. Augustine, *City of God*, 2.
75. Augustine says, "man cannot be rescued from it (the source of error) without toil.... The divine governance does not altogether abandon man in his condemnation,

The Counter-Ethics

For Milbank, the second important characteristic of Augustine's theology is that Augustine offers different ethics from other Western antique philosophies. Augustine recognizes the state (*res publica*) as an association united by a "common sense of right and a community of interest."[76] In this understanding of the state, because a political sphere only concerns with positive goals of finite wellbeing, the states necessarily leads the division between what is secular and what is spiritual; the view of the state is problematic. Instead of proposing a finite welfare, what Augustine offers is "the association of a multitude of rational beings united by a common agreement on the common objects of their love."[77] In antique thought, the direction of desire is the key element for determining what true justice is. This is because the ancient philosophers believe that only a true *eros* can discern the Good. Here, Augustine criticizes the Roman commonwealth for following a wrong desire—the pursuit of individual *dominium*.[78] According to Augustine, the false conception of the state leads people to desire wrong and coercive justice in the name of social welfare. For Augustine, this coercive political

---

and God does not in his anger restrain his compassion and so his prohibitions and instructions keep watch in the feelings of mankind against those dark influences which were in us at birth and resist their assaults; an yet those commandments bring us plenty of trouble and sorrow." Augustine, *City of God*, XIV.22. In this description, God gives us sorrow and pain in order to save us from ignorance and condemnation. For Augustine, in other words, pain is profitable for human beings, yet also in itself a punishment. According to Augustine, like the way parent might beat their beloved child for a pedagogical reason, the point of God's punishment is to let humans to overcome ignorance and to bridle corrupt desire. Consequently, in Augustine's theology, the reason why Christians face an existential struggle in the world is because of their eschatological destiny. Because the image of God can only be fulfilled in the vision of God (eschaton), Augustine's anthropology is the teleological process of becoming "like" God or "participating" in God till the days of eschaton. For further understanding of Augustine's concept of the Church, it is helpful to look at Schleiermacher's understanding of the Church. For Schleiermacher, the decisive contrast is not between church and world, but this contrast must be overcome from the kingdom of God. The decisive point here is that one must not identify the Church with the kingdom of God. Consequently, we must understand the church as an eschatological entity rather than the kingdom of God itself. In doing so, we can understand the contemporary debates about the abuse of minors in the Church.

76. Milbank, *Theology and Social Theory*, 404; Cf. Augustine, *City of God*, XIX.21.

77. Milbank, *Theology and Social Theory*, 404; Cf. Augustine, *City of God*, XIX.24.

78. Augustine criticizes antique ethics and politics for pursuing a commonwealth which is based on one's own enjoyment: "No-one should be brought to trial except for an offence, or threat of offence, against another's property, house or person; but anyone should be free to do as he likes about his own, or with others, if they consent." Augustine, *City of God*, II.20.

structure belongs to the part of the *civitas terrena*, which has a pagan mode of practice "with different faith, ad different hope, a different love."[79] In Augustine's theology, the *civitas terrena* merely refers limited and finite goods without indicating the infinite Good—the Triune God. For Augustine, the city of pagans only offers false worship to oneself or to the dominant powers (which he considers idols)—the essence of sin.[80] Consequently, Augustine claims that the worldly city brings bad ends, because it allows the use of a coercive, arbitrary, and excessive force of worldliness rather than directing a true desire towards God.[81]

Instead of a life of sin which is based on individualistic self-love, Augustine believes that the Church offers a true society which has agreement in desire among its members. For Augustine, because the Church has a concern for all members of its community regardless class, gender, or tribe, the Church is a political reality which is based on divine love, rejecting any heroic excellence.[82] In contrast to the ancient Stoics pursuing inner peace within the world of materialism, Augustine thinks that a true state of inward self-government leads people to have further relationships both with God and neighbors. For Augustine, the internal souls of human beings are the part of an external sequences. Here, Augustine's communal understanding of the self requires us to have a fellowship with others. This implies that freedom of will is not separated with the community. In this Augustinian understanding of human will, the goal of the Church is not pursuing a collective glory or an individual heroic life, but a relational life based on forgiveness and love.

According to this Augustinian ecclesiology, everybody is the body of Christ even though each member is different. In the Church, Christians do not separate their identity from their peaceful kingdom; they chase justice,

---

79. We should notice that Augustine does not the earthly city as a state in the modern sense of government. Augustine, *City of God*, XVIII.54.

80. Augustine, *City of God*, XV.6.

81. Augustine basically sees the result of original sin and habituated custom as the tragic inability of the will continues in this finite world. For Augustine, humanity, in its fallen state, is subject to punishment so that "there is not a human being who does not sin (Job 14:4; 1 King 8:46; Eccl 7:21; Ps 14:1)" as he indicates in *Nature and Grace*, VIII.8. Because the descendants of Adam are still trapped by the first wrong choice no one can easily obey to God and avoid God's punishment for their transgression. Augustine points out in his *City of God*, XIV.25: "But even the righteous himself does not live as he wishes, until he has arrived where he cannot die, be deceived, or injured, and until he is assured that this shall be his eternal condition. For this nature demands; and nature is not fully and perfectly blessed till it attains what it seeks . . . therefore it shall then only be blessed when it is eternal."

82. Augustine, *City of God*, XXII.30.

humility, and will to pardon within the relational sequence. As a result, the genuine Christians pursue reconciliation, forgiveness, and harmony with all other goods.[83] In advocating forgiveness, it is noteworthy that the reason why Augustine condemns the Donatists is because they pursue an inward purity of intention rather than a divine love of forgiveness. For Augustine, it is not right to cut off others from the body of Christ.[84] In Augustine's theology, God is capable of creating unity without erasing differences, because God is relational (triune) by Godself—one in substance, but three persons. Within this trinitarian understanding, the distinctiveness of Christianity lies in its reconciliation of virtue with differences. Looking at Augustine's trinitarian understanding of God, Milbank realizes that Augustine's *City of God* offers an alternative ethics to the postmodern age, because it seeks harmonious consensus based on fraternity, allowing "something like the 'peaceful transmission of difference,' or 'differences in a continuous harmony.'"[85] In this Christian theology, virtue is in a new positive relation to difference unlike many other ancient philosophies. Therefore, Christians can develop their unique virtue with others in harmonious unity because they know about their failures and why they need constant repentance, forgiveness, and conversion before God.

The Counter-Ontology

Milbank reflects that the reason why Christian theology can offer different history and ethics is because it provides a different ontology from secularity. For Milbank, Christian belief belongs to the Christian practice, affirming God who creates, redeems, and preserves by enacting a metanarrative understanding. In this Christian belief, Christian theology confirms three major mechanisms in its ethics: "the practice of charity and forgiveness," "the reconciliation of difference with virtues," and "the treatment of peace as a primary reality."[86] According to Christian theology, as Dionysius the Areopagite realizes, God is the Creator who creates all differences in the world.[87] For Christians, God is the Triune God who differentiates everything from nothing. In the doctrine of the Trinity, God the Father first differentiates the Son and then the Spirit in the relation of charity; God's differentiation comes from God's own harmonic unity through the gift of

---

83. Augustine, *City of God*, V.24.
84. Augustine, *On Baptism*, I.15.23–26.
85. Milbank, *Theology and Social Theory*, 422.
86. Milbank, *Theology and Social Theory*, 429.
87. Dionysius, *The Divine Names*, 588B, 542D–593A.

relations. In this doctrine of the Trinity, Christians also discover that God can only speak to us through the Word who incarnates.[88] This incarnation theology implies that the infinite God has an external relationality to the world. Thus, for Christians, "the created world of time participates in the God who differentiates."[89]

To be specific, as Augustine notices, the Triune God is not a material being that can be quantified, so the true being of the Trinity does not have any modification (or *accidentia*). Because the Trinity is the substance that needs no qualification to be without qualities, quantities, times, positions or any other modifications (accidents),[90] Augustine understands God as a relational reality. He says,

> Nor are they [the names of Trinity] said modification-wise, because what is signified by calling them Father and Son belongs to them eternally and unchangeably. Therefore, although being Father is different from being Son, there is no difference of substance, because they are not called these things substance-wise but *relationship-wise*; and yet this relationship is not a modification (or accident), because it is not changeable.[91]

In Augustinian theology, God has three persons in one substance. In this Trinitarian understanding, the three persons of God do not bother one another, and have a harmonious unity, and thus God has intimate relationships within Godself. As a result, the Triune God can be also intimate and relational to other God's creatures, because the world was created from the trinitarian nature of God. In this understanding of creation, because the Triune God as a relational being contains the all world and gathers all of us together, every creature is related to one another within the Trinity. Therefore, Christian theology suggests an alternative understanding of beings from other philosophies: everything is in the trinitarian relation of God, allowing differences within harmonic unity.

Based on this Augustine's trinitarian ontology, Milbank tries to understand creation as a gift of God. For him, God's grace and incarnation are the supreme gift of God, while the Fall and evil are the refusal of gift, and while

---

88. Milbank, *The Word Made Strange*, 171–94.
89. Milbank, *Theology and Social Theory*, 431.
90. Augustine says, "We should understand God . . . to be good without quality, great without quantity, creative without need or necessity, presiding without position, holding all things together without possession . . . everlasting without time, without any change. . . . God is substance, or perhaps a better word would be being (*ousia*). But God cannot be modified in any way." Augustine, *On Trinity*, V.2.3.
91. Augustine, *On Trinity*, V.5.6. Emphasis added.

atonement is the renewed gift allowing diverse gifts through the work of the Spirit in the church community.[92] Milbank points out that the *donum* in Augustine's theology "is not a free one-way gift, but the realization of a perpetual exchange between the Father and the Son."[93] In this understanding of gift, Milbank develops the theology of participation and further extends the theology of participation to language, history, and culture. For Milbank, the human realities such as language, history, and culture are constituted by exchange. In other words, because this world is created by the gift-exchange of God who is relational (trinitarian) in nature, Milbank believes that the human realities are also based on the gift-exchange of the relational God.

In Milbank's theology, however, the circumstance of fallenness requires human beings to restore the exchange of gift through participating into God again. In Augustinian theology, there cannot be nihilistic illusions because everything is created by the Trinity who differentiates all of us in unity. This is why Augustine explains false or evil beings as deficiencies of God's fullness.[94] In Augustine's theology, although everything is created by the Triune God's grace, all creatures sin. This is because the creatures of God cannot have the fullness of God. In other words, for Augustine, the created world may lack God's goodness because it is originally created from nothingness or darkness. Facing the fallen nature of worldliness, Augustine sees the necessity of God's grace which can be condensed in Jesus Christ: "it is not those who are in good health who need a physician, but those who are sick. I came not to call the righteous, but sinners . . . it is a reliable message worthy of complete acceptance that Christ Jesus came into the world to save sinners (1 Tim 1:11)."[95] For Augustine, without the help of God, Jesus Christ, and the Spirit, there is no way for human beings to be healed and be healthy again because every reality comes from the triune God in Christian theology. Consequently, Augustine's theology necessitates us to participate into the Triune God's grace—the relational exchange of gifts. In recognizing the necessity of the exchange of gifts, Milbank believes that participating into God's grace leads us to accomplish "the peace of the *altera civitas*."[96] In this *altera civitas*, Christians with the grace of the Trinity can embrace differences and promote all persons' participation in the Divine love without

---

92. Milbank, *Being Reconciled*, ix.

93. Milbank, *Being Reconciled*, x.

94. Augustine says, "Evil has no positive nature; but the loss of good has received the name evil." Augustine, *City of God*, XI.9.

95. Augustine, *Nature and Grace*, 21.23.

96. Milbank, *Theology and Social Theory*, 440.

exclusion through recovering the relational nature of the Trinity and the exchange of the Triune God's gift.[97]

Postmodernity and God's City

If Christian theology offers an alternative vision unlike other secular theories as Augustine and Milbank suggest, how can we apply Christian theology to the contemporary world? Milbank summarizes the characteristics of the current postmodern world in four ways: (1) the blurred distinction between nature and culture, (2) the merging of public and private, (3) the rise of the information economy, and (4) the emerging of economic/political globalization.[98] First, Milbank points out that people in postmodernity no longer find the connection between nature and culture in human affairs, because there are so many different ways of producing new cultures today. Although people before postmodernity tend to predict what human nature is and what human nature produces, the ethos of postmodernity denies that humans are governed by natural laws or their inborne nature. Rather, they see human affairs in terms of the processing of the complex communications to value diversity. Secondly, Milbank contends that there is no boundary between public and private in postmodernity because people can no longer have their own private idea or territory due to the complex web of the current society. In postmodernity, one can choose anything anywhere, but these choices are always really the choices of others. In postmodernity, people cannot depend on inalienable private possession because, between the internet abolishing privacy, and the hyper-specialization of all goods and knowledge, neither privacy nor property truly exist. Thirdly, Milbank draws attention to the fact that we live in the age of information. In postmodernity, productions immediately get into the exchange of the product, because all the traditional economic categories are merged together; the human culture and production multiply faster and larger in postmodernity. Lastly, Milbank argues that we live in the globalized world. For example, to be a big professional singer, one should not compete with only other local singers but also with all other global famous figures. This means we are forced to live under the intensity of global capitalism to compete one another. Under these characteristics of postmodernity, Milbank realizes that the organization of exchange is reduced to the economic one in our postmodern society.[99] Thus, postmodernity leads us to live in the age of global capitalism.

---

97. For further discussion see Ward, *Cities of God*.
98. Milbank, *Being Reconciled*, 187–94.
99. Milbank, *Being Reconciled*, 165.

Looking at those four characteristics of postmodernity, Milbank believes that *socialism* is the answer to fight against the giant tyranny of postmodern capitalism.[100] However, he thinks that the secular postmodern philosophies do not offer a healthy socialism. Secular socialism, according to Milbank, has three major problems: (1) it explains reality without reference to transcendence, (2) it sees finite reality as self-explanatory and self-governing, and (3) it regards this finite reality as *saeculum* (a fixed amount of time without Christianity's eschatological dimension).[101] To be specific, many leading postmodern thinkers such as Gilles Deleuze, Antonio Negri, and Michael Hardt, often absorb the post-Marxist pathos. According to Milbank, these secular thinkers ignore the aspects of transcendence in human affairs or religions, while solely focusing on the economic/capitalistic exchanges; they often value community as the absolute thing. As a result, these post-Marxist philosophers absolutize finite human community to be a perfect answer to remedy the problem of capitalism. In addition, because the Marxist version of postmodern philosophies understands religion within the plane of immanence, Milbank points out that the secular postmodern philosophies bring a new age of religions, locating salvation "in a higher self, above the social, temporal, remembered self."[102] In this view of religion, new (postmodern) religions show an extreme individualism because they affirm the holiness of an empty mystical self in the name of a true life. In the deep heart of these postmodern religions, there is only a care for oneself because they do not admit the aspect of transcendence or overcoming self-interest. Consequently, Milbank thinks that the secular postmodern philosophies do not in fact suggest an answer to fully get over the threat of postmodern capitalism.

In the face of the false responses of the secular postmodern philosophies, Milbank points out that Christianity can be an alternative postmodern answer to overcome capitalism, because Christianity is "the religion of the obliteration of boundaries."[103] In Christianity, one's life does not stay in the tradition of the Law by God's grace; there is neither Jew nor Gentile, neither slave nor free, nor male and female in Christ Jesus (Gal 3:28). Looking at the similar point between postmodernity and Christianity (which blurs the boundaries), Milbank proposes that the Church is uniquely capable of responding to the problems of postmodern capitalism because the Church has different history, ethics, and ontology from the secular world.

100. Milbank, *Being Reconciled*, 162.
101. Milbank, *Being Reconciled*, 195.
102. Milbank, *Being Reconciled*, 195.
103. Milbank, *Being Reconciled*, 196.

Here, he gives five specific reasons why the Church can be an alternative answer to the age of postmodernism.[104] First, on the question of the merging of nature and culture, Milbank thinks that the Church suggests an open-ended transformation of the natural world, because it understands the world as God's creation. In Christian theology, the created world has to be restored with the grace of God; Christians expect the bonds of love in the Christian community to overcome the division between Creator and creation. To heal the world, Christians highlight the importance of affinity or belonging together in their community rather than pursuing individual efforts. In this theology of affinity, Christians can work together to fight against the high-handedness of modern capitalism; there is a right form of socialism in Christianity. Second, in regard to the aspect of the blending of private and public, Milbank avers that the Church offers reconciliation, not locking doors to others. In the Church, because Christians recognize one another within the relational God, Christians offer a practice of reconciliation to others through embracing differences. So, for Milbank, there is a right form of virtue in the Church. Thirdly, in the age of information, Milbank draws attention to the fact that the Church has a concertedness as the body of Christ. For Milbank, the Church does not offer an abstract concept. This is because the Church's theology is based on the concrete body of Christ which includes the concrete practices and ethics of Christians. Fourthly, regarding globalization, Milbank sees that the Church proposes the city of God which can be a counter-empire against the globalized capitalism. For Milbank, the city of God does not offer the same mistake as the worldly city. Instead, it offers a totally new counter-ontology against the worldly city so that it has a power to fully overcome the problems of the worldly city. Lastly, in addition to affinity, reconciliation, embodiment, and counter-empire, Milbank claims that the Church adds the aspect of transcendence beyond the world of immanence; it brings hope to the believers that the transcendence of God can overcome the arbitrary and oppressive control by a sovereign empire. Therefore, Milbank believes that the Christian Church unlike many other secular postmodern philosophies has an alternative answer to overcome postmodern capitalism in these five different responses toward postmodernity.

To summarize, in the face of fallacious secular theories, Milbank believes that Augustinian theology can offer an alternative answer to remedy the problems of secular theories and postmodern philosophies. In investigating Augustine's ecclesiology, Milbank finds that the Church offers different history, ethics, and ontology from secular theories. This is because the Church

104. Milbank, *Being Reconciled*, 198–211.

offers affinity, reconciliation, embodiment, and counter-empire through highlighting the relational (trinitarian) nature of the Triune God and God's creature. In this account, Milbank points out that the Church is also the part of the exchange of the Triune God's gift; the Church must engage with many secular theories. In this respect, Milbank asserts that Christians should engage with many secular theories to invite other worldviews to the city of God, where God offers genuine reconciliation with relational love.

THE SCANDALOUS CULTURAL HERMENEUTICS

Radical Orthodoxy's Response to Secular Cultures

While John Milbank articulates an ideal posture for the Church to take towards the problems of the secular world, another thinker in the school of radical orthodoxy, Graham Ward, takes a different approach and pronounces an ideal posture for the Church to take towards culture (or other secular discourses), in and of itself. According to radical orthodoxy, theology has to engage with social, political, and cultural theories, because it rejects the dichotomy between theory and practice and the dualism between philosophy and theology. For radical orthodoxy, the Christian mission does not only preach the gospel, but also brings cultural and historical transformations with its vision. This implies that Christians should examine their place and time to carry forward their tradition in the age of postmodernity and to change the world. Because radical orthodoxy pursues active engagement with worldliness, it seeks a new relationship between culture and Christianity to promote cultural transformations toward postmodernity in the perspective of orthodox Christianity.

To show radical orthodoxy's view on the relationship between culture and Christianity in postmodernity, Graham Ward develops *cultural hermeneutics* in his book, *Cultural Transformation and Religious Practice*. In this book, Ward attempts to show how radical orthodoxy thinks about other cultures through investigating how cultural transforms are achieved in the postmodern society. Here, Ward draws attention to the fact that Christianity as a social practice brings cultural transformations like other social activities. Then, how is Christianity different from other cultural activities which also carry cultural transformations? And what is the exact relationship between Christianity and other cultures? To answer these questions, this section will explore Ward's cultural hermeneutics. To do this, the coming section will include: (1) where Ward speaks from to posit radical orthodoxy's stance toward other cultures, (2) how he develops cultural hermeneutics to explain the process of cultural transformation in postmodernity, (3) how he understands the relationship between Christianity and cultural transformation, (4) how radical orthodoxy contributes to theological studies, and (5) the possible criticisms on radical orthodoxy as a conclusion.

The Stance of Radical Orthodoxy

In order to demonstrate how radical orthodoxy places Christian practices with other cultural practices, Graham Ward draws attention to Karl Barth's unique theological stance, rejecting apologetics. According to Ward, Christian belief has two aspects: "the personal and the social."[105] This indicates that the discourse of Christianity has "a radical exteriority," even though it starts from one's own faith, coming from the revelation or grace of God. This is why Ward points out that Christians always talk with other discourses outside of Christianity in history to preach about the gospel and to explain what they believe to others. As a result, Ward believes that Christian theology (understanding God's revelation) is an ongoing activity because it always speaks out to the world. For Ward, Christian theology is always inter-relational with other cultures. According to Ward, theology's primary concern is to address about the infinite God who revealed in Jesus Christ. However, he thinks that the revelation of God must be spoken in human language and culture because human beings can understand the infinite God only when God reveals or incarnates Godself to the finite world—the realms of human language and culture.[106] This infers that Christian theology also gets constructed out of the cultural material like other cultural products. In this respect, Ward argues that Barth's non-apologetic response is also "a cultural activity."[107]

Interestingly, Barth explicitly tries to separate the discourse of Christian theology from other secular discourses. Barth believes that the Church's distinctive talk about God "has no role to play vis-à-vis the 'secular or pagan.'"[108] On this topic, Ward thinks that Barth's theological polemic against secular cultures is the product of agency who experiences diverse theological, cultural, and social exchanges.[109] Even though Barth believes

---

105. Ward, *Cultural Transformation and Religious Practice*, 13.
106. Ward, *Cultural Transformation and Religious Practice*, 6–7.
107. Ward, *Cultural Transformation and Religious Practice*, 48.
108. Barth, *CD* 1/1:5.
109. Through investigating Barth's life, Ward points out that Barth's life has a complex mixture of diverse backgrounds such as German theological liberalism, pastoral experience, communism, personal marriage life, etc. Ward here believes that Barth's

that Christian theology renders a "self-enclosed circle" of concern in the Church community, Ward asks: "Who defines and maintains the autonomy of discourses?"[110] According to Ward, although Barth believes that the Church's theological discourse is distinctive from philosophical, scientific, or historical discourses, Barth's reflection cannot be a self-enclosed discourse because his theological reflection is a production from a particular place, time, and practice, as Michel de Certeau suggests.[111] In other words, Barth's rejection of apologetics is the part of Barth's reaction to other discursive practices throughout his life. As a result, Ward unlike other (postliberal) Barthian theologians realizes that Barth's radical separatism to the secular world in fact holds a mode of dialectical thinking, containing other external discourses in it.[112]

According to Ward, Hegel lies behind Barth's theology more than Schleiermacher in regard to the relationship between Christianity and worldliness.[113] This is because Barth reengages Hegel' dialectical thinking from his earlier edition of *Epistles to Romans* to his later works, when he deals with his categorical assertion between theology and philosophy. In Barth's theology, the negations (of other external cultures) are the key to recognize how theology needs to proceed. As Barth indicates in his *Epistle to the Romans*, Christian theology deals with "the infinite qualitative difference (God)" which human beings cannot understand in their finite language and time.[114] In Barth's theology, to explain the discourse about God, human beings have to think through a dialectic connection between God and culture. That is why Barth concludes that "'the Task of Dogmatics' . . . is only possible 'on the basis of divine correspondence to this human attitude:

---

work cannot be separated from his life journey because theological reflection presupposes its cultural/temporal backgrounds. Ward, *Cultural Transformation and Religious Practice*, 19–33.

110. Ward's view is different from the postliberal stance that the Church as an unique community has its own language and grammar within the autonomy of language-games. According to Ward, Barth's text includes the question of authority with what jurisdiction and to whom it addresses. For Ward, Christian utterance is not constructed out of the cultural materials because it also shows up to us as a social science as Barth suggests. Ward, *Cultural Transformation and Religious Practice*, 47. Cf. Tanner, *Theories of Culture*, 96.

111. Ward, *Cultural Transformation and Religious Practice*, 38. Cf. Certeau, *The Writing of History*.

112. Ward, *Cultural Transformation and Religious Practice*, 41.

113. Ward, *Cultural Transformation and Religious Practice*, 48.

114. Barth says, "If I have a system, it is limited to a recognition of what Kierkegaard called the "infinite qualitative distinction: between time and eternity, and to my regarding this as possessing negative as well as positive significance: 'God is in his heave, and thou art on earth.'" Barth, *The Epistle to the Romans*, 10.

'Lord, I believe; help thou my unbelief.'"[115] This implies that Barth's *dogmatics* deals with the dialectical encounter of human beings toward the Word of God.[116]

Although Barth in his *Protestant Theology in the Nineteenth Century* condemns Hegel's univocity of *Geist* and reason, he says, "Doubtless, theology could and can learn something from Hegel as well. It looks as if theology had neglected something here, and certainly it has no occasion to assume an attitude of alarm and hostility to any renaissance of Hegel that might come about."[117] According to Barth, Hegel's dialectical thinking leads us to see theology as a material practice participating into the history of God's self-revealing. Under the Hegelian influence, Barth recognizes theology as a discursive practice, holding the historical (material) dimension.[118] Barth notes:

> History, the theological practice of participating in that history and the need to consider more carefully that biblical witnesses speak as men, and not as angels or gods. . . . Thus we have to reckon on their part with all kinds of human factors, with their individual and general capacities of perception and expression, with their personal views and style, as determined by age and environment, and of course with the limitations and deficiencies of these conditioning factors—in this case the limitations of their imagination.[119]

For Barth, the understanding of God or Biblical witnesses has to be discerned in the historical dimension because Christian theology talks about God's story in the place where the hearer is situated. As a result, Christian theology must be implicated in cultural negotiations, when it fulfills the apologetic task of theology or when it talks about God with other cultures. In Barth's theology, Christian theology is a reflexive practice to other historical (materialistic) human cultures based on the Christian position—Jesus Christ. For Barth, Christian theology seeks to understand a divine event— the incarnation of God into this material world. Succeeding Barth's stance to worldliness, Ward concludes, "Theology's task with respect to culture is

---

115. Ward, *Cultural Transformation and Religious Practice*, 44. Cf. Barth, *CD* 1/1:24.

116. We need to acknowledge that Jesus Christ in Barth's theology is both the absolute subject and the absolute object because he "who is the subject and object of the basic act of God, the subject and object of the consummating act of God that reveals that basis." Barth, *CD* 4/1:361.

117. Barth, *Protestant Theology in the Nineteenth Century*, 403.

118. Barth here thinks that theology is conceived as "the covenant grace as the theme of history." Barth, *CD* 3/1:60.

119. Ward, *Cultural Transformation and Religious Practice*, 93.

to allow for that searching by Christ, in Christ, of the cultural imaginary."[120] In this respect, for Barth and Ward, Christian theology starts from a prayer which leads the human culture to understand its own limitations, while hoping social transformation based on the Christian imagination coming from Jesus Christ.[121]

Cultural Hermeneutics

If Christian theology includes a dialectical movement to other external cultures as Ward indicates, Christian theology must then modify and transform itself and other cultures in its dialectical process. This is because the dialectical interpretation process as a political engagement will affect the myriad symbolic exchanges. That is why Ward believes that Christian theology requires *cultural hermeneutics*, reading the signs of the time to extend a hermeneutical project into the cultural product. Here, Ward points out that cultural production involves "the formation of both knowledges and subjectivities."[122] In Ward's cultural hermeneutics, different forms of interpretative reasoning engage each other, and they transform one another within the dimension of the cultural products. This implies that cultural hermeneutics is about engaging with other cultural products between horizons as Hans Gadamer and Alain Bourdieu suggest.[123] In the process of understanding, human beings perceive the world through events, eventualities, and experiences in a specific time and space; knowledges are produced from the local reflection or the situated ones. Although each hermeneutic event comes from a concrete situatedness, Ward realizes that there are consistencies in the hermeneutic events.[124] This implies that specific vocabularies and sets of ideas invoke universals or a transcendental vocabulary within their own philosophical tradition. Looking at the consistencies (repetitions) of similar hermeneutical interpretations, the situatedness of knowledge cannot deny that there are general observations in hermeneutics. In other words, because the same way of interpretation happens over and over again within a tradition, each hermeneutical tradition develops their own creeds,

---

120. Ward, *Cultural Transformation and Religious Practice*, 59.

121. Ward, *Cultural Transformation and Religious Practice*, 59. Cf. It is noteworthy that Karl Barth was always interested in socialist politics, although he was not interested in apologetics. And that is why he is often described as a "red pastor of Safenwil." Hunsinger, *Karl Barth and Radical Politics*.

122. Ward, *Cultural Transformation and Religious Practice*, 63.

123. Ward, *Cultural Transformation and Religious Practice*, 67.

124. Ward, *Cultural Transformation and Religious Practice*, 87.

confessions, and normative laws, while believing their beliefs as true and real. Consequently, cultural products produce certain beliefs, practices, and ethics based on their unique situated interpretations.

In this understanding of hermeneutics, Ward argues that "a hermeneutical ontology does not necessarily mean interpretative relativism."[125] According to Ward, the standard of interpretation should be measured by how the interpreter is faithful to the one's own philosophical traditions, texts, or practices as George Lindbeck, Clifford Geertz and Gilbert Ryle suggest. For Ward, interpretations are based on one's own practice's grammar which may conflict with other cultural practices. This indicates that there cannot be democracy of interpretation, because every interpreter is based on one's own cultural grammar and language.[126] In this respect, Ward argues that the situatedness of knowledge is not a concern for Christian theology because Christians firmly believe in the universal truth that the reality of God is constant.[127] For Christians, creation is constantly given to them and there is "real gratuitousness," as Henri de Lubac suggests.[128]

Because Ward supports the non-foundational understanding of hermeneutics, he attempts to examine where we are and how we reinforce one's own hermeneutical belief within cultural exchanges. According to Ward, every cultural practice's criteria for evaluation is an internal enquiry.[129] At the same time, however, each cultural practice is discursive, because every act of interpretation is "always implicated in hierarchies and therefore political struggles in which knowledge and power are profoundly interrelated."[130] In this endless dialectical process of understandings, the hermeneutic process keeps producing cultural transformations both in one's own cultural tradition and other cultural traditions.[131] In sum, the transformation of cultures implies two points in Ward's theology. First, our understanding process comes from a situated standpoint. Second, the understanding process is embodied in each person's life as a real thing and it produces *habitus* through engaging with other cultural products.

---

125. Ward, *Cultural Transformation and Religious Practice*, 70.
126. Ward, *Cultural Transformation and Religious Practice*, 71.
127. Ward, *Cultural Transformation and Religious Practice*, 69.
128. Cf. Lubac, *The Mystery of the Supernatural*, 68–96.
129. Ward, *Cultural Transformation and Religious Practice*, 77.
130. Ward, *Cultural Transformation and Religious Practice*, 69.
131. Ward Here draws attention to Schleiermacher's hermeneutics emphasizing the non-foundationalism. According to Ward, Schleiermacher's hermeneutics brought the development of radical forms of contemporary hermeneutics. Ward, *Cultural Transformation and Religious Practice*, 69. Cf. Frank, *Das individuelle*; Schleiermacher, *Hermeneutics and Criticism and Other Writings*.

Because each hermeneutical tradition produces a certain cultural product or a cultural practice based on their own situated standpoint, Ward claims the standpoint of hermeneutics should be how much each hermeneutical tradition achieves cultural transformation in the ongoing cultural exchanges. According to Ward, we cannot judge which hermeneutical tradition describes the world more accurately. This is because every cultural tradition comes from their own standpoint. Instead, what becomes important for Ward is how we can promote a better cultural transformation based on one's own situated hermeneutical point, because he supports the non-foundational view of hermeneutics. As a result, rather than rendering investigation into interpreters or acts of interpretation, Ward's cultural hermeneutics attempts to focus on how each situational practice "operates" its own grammar within cultural exchanges.[132]

Cultural Transformation and Christian Imagination

To examine how each cultural practice operates in cultural exchanges, Ward pays attention to feminist theorists (Patricia Hill Collins, Donna Haraway, Lynn Nelson, and Alison Jaggar) and colonialism theories (Edward Said and Gayatri Chakravarty Spivak).[133] According to Ward, feminist and post-colonial theories attempt to avoid fixing one's identity and social imagination to one cultural product, while promoting cultural exchanges to encourage social transformations through highlighting the marginalized views. In these theories, the theorists aim to offer a better account of the world in negotiating with other cultural standpoints.[134] Here, because each unique standpoint is filled gradually through dialogues with others, there is no pure subject standpoint. Rather, every standpoint addresses "itself to other standpoints and maybe combine."[135] This implies that the subject-position is reflective and relational to others. That is why every cultural practice rejects, modifies, and syncretizes each other in the process of sharing their different standpoint. In this respect, for Ward, the task of interpreting is always "*in medias res.*"[136] In other words, although the process of interpreting begins with an "I" or "we," its horizon keeps moving through encountering other cultural products. Thus, there comes cultural transformations, when each cultural standpoint gets into political struggles with other cultural standpoints.

132. Ward, *Cultural Transformation and Religious Practice*, 172.
133. Ward, *Cultural Transformation and Religious Practice*, 85.
134. Ward, *Cultural Transformation and Religious Practice*, 83–85.
135. Ward, *Cultural Transformation and Religious Practice*, 77.
136. Ward, *Cultural Transformation and Religious Practice*, 85.

Because social transformation comes from the operation of recognizing others, Ward believes that "the economy of recognition bears the project towards its future."[137] This means that our imagination is an important tool for a better cultural transformation. In a competitive set of spheres, the power to make one's own rhetoric credible is very important. That is why Ward thinks that social imaginaries (which make the rhetoric more credible) are influential in postmodernity as Charles Taylor and Paul Ricoeur indicate. In a shared cultural space, according to Taylor, a social imaginary is both a cultural product and a produce, because it is "expressed in theoretical terms . . . that common understanding which makes possible common practices."[138] Taylor argues that social imaginaries are not just ideology, because they are inducted into new practices while producing the new culture; they are forms of *poiesis*. In addition, Ricoeur "explicitly relates the imagination to *poiesis*."[139] According to Ricouer, because the social imaginary functions between people, "our images are spoken before they are seen."[140] In Ricouer's theory of metaphor, the language of reference has three levels of the mimetic process: the prefigured (the perceived as), the configured (the written), and the refigured (the read).[141] This suggests that all our language expressions are metaphorical. Based on this understanding of metaphor, Ricouer claims that imagining as a metaphor "is above all restructuring semantic fields."[142] In Ricouer's philosophy, imagination is *poiesis* of our society, because it exists before our realization; imagination as a *poiesis* enables us to see better possibilities through producing better metaphors toward the future world. Following Taylor and Ricouer's philosophies, Ward also argues that social imagination is at the heart of transformative possibilities for a culture, because social imagination as a *poiesis* leads us to forge new connections, new relations, and new standpoint-projects.[143]

In conclusion, according to Ward's cultural hermeneutics, each cultural product can bring social transformations through communicating with other cultural products, even though each cultural product has its own unique cultural grammar and ethos. Ward thinks that every cultural transformation involves a dialectical movement, leading us to exchange

---

137. It is noteworthy that the importance of the idea and activity of recognition here is another Hegelian legacy. Ward, *Cultural Transformation and Religious Practice*, 90.

138. Taylor, *Modern Social Imaginaries*, 16.

139. Ward, *Cultural Transformation and Religious Practice*, 130.

140. Ricouer, "Imagination in Discourse and Action," in *From Text to Action*, 171.

141. Ward, *Cultural Transformation and Religious Practice*, 132.

142. Ricouer, "Imagination in Discourse and Action," 173.

143. Ward, *Cultural Transformation and Religious Practice*, 150.

with different cultural products to have a better social imagination. In this process of cultural transformation, Ward claims that Christian theology as a cultural product also offers cultural transformation through bringing a social imagination of Jesus Christ which shows us the possibility of God's transcendent reconciliation. Here, because Christian imagination has a power to work toward the realm of transcendence, Ward believes that Christian theology offers a new standpoint to overcome the nihilistic circulation of secular theories.

The Contribution of Radical Orthodoxy

I believe that radical orthodoxy's response to worldliness makes three good points.[144] The first is, it is right for radical orthodoxy as a theological movement to vigorously engage with other cultural products in this materialistic world, while rejecting a sectarian view through highlighting the dialectical mode of Christian theology. Radical orthodoxy points out that Christian theology does not come from a vacuum. Rather, for radical orthodoxy, Christianity always mediates with the material world throughout its dialectical movement in history. Indeed, when we look at many different theological traditions in history, every theological argument has its own social context. In this sense, as radical orthodoxy suggests, it is better for Christians to read the time and engage with other cultures, because theology itself is not free from the sociopolitical context.[145] Another strength of radical orthodoxy which comes from its active engagement to worldliness is that it does not overlook the importance of embodiment. Christian theology does not merely talk about the invisible and transcendental God, but also produces bodily activities, practical ethics, and certain cultures. This implies that Christian theology should not disregard human desire, physical body, and actual practice; as radical orthodoxy suggests, it is important to stress the importance of the Church's liturgy, people's erotic desire, and the sociopolitical aspect of the Church. The other asset from radical orthodoxy's active engagement is that it rediscovers the communal aspect of salvation; it promotes active political struggles rather than depoliticizing Christians. According to radical orthodoxy, the dialectical movement of Christian

---

144. For further responses to radical orthodoxy, see Crockett, *A Theology of the Sublime*; Hyman, *The Predicament of Postmodern Theology*; Smith, *Introducing Radical Orthodoxy*; Slater, *Radical Orthodoxy in a Pluralistic World*.

145. Ward says, "theology, in order to understand itself as a discipline and its culture relevance, must reflect upon this socio-historical context." Ward, "Theology and Postmodernism," 440.

theology leads Christians to have political struggles with other cultures. In this process, Christian theology can reinforce its stance and bring actual cultural formations in this world. In this sense, radical orthodoxy holds "practicality," because the view of radical orthodoxy promotes actual cultural transformations in the public sphere unlike many other metaphysical or sectarian theologies.

The second legacy of radical orthodoxy is that it talks with postmodernity, which is one of the dominant cultural movements today. It is noteworthy that radical orthodoxy theologians actively talk with other postmodern figures and even publish books together.[146] Radical orthodoxy theologians do not miss that many important postmodern left-wing thinkers such as Alain Badiou, Slavoj Zizek, and Giorgio Agamben bring religious discourse for their political radicalism.[147] Instead of ignoring these secular philosophies, radical orthodoxy theologians talk with the cutting-edge postmodern philosophers to discuss about transcendence, religion, and the sublime in human life together. In doing so, they open a public sphere to talk about Christianity without foundationalism. In addition, Ward points out that postmodern thinking creates a new space for theological reflection, because it promotes different places and practices as Maurice Blanchot, Jean-Francois Lyotard and Jean Baudrillard suggest.[148] For radical orthodoxy theologians, the new visibility of religion in postmodernity gives new opportunities for the religious practitioners to explain their distinctive practice and religiosity. In this respect, we can give a good evaluation to radical orthodoxy for opening a new public space to express the uniqueness of Christian tradition in the postmodern society.

The final point of radical orthodoxy's inheritance is that radical orthodoxy offers an alternative answer against modern secular nihilism through giving a counter-ontology which highlights the aspect of transcendence. Radical orthodoxy brings contemporary philosophical resources (Nietzsche, Heidegger, Levinas, Derrida, Foucault, Irigaray, Rorty, and others) "into dialogue with Augustine, Irenaeus, Aquinas, and other resources."[149] In this effort, radical orthodoxy stresses that classical Christian theology has a counter-history, counter-ethic, and counter-ontology which can overcome the problem of nihilistic circulation in contemporary secular philosophies. Through highlighting the importance of transcendence in the classical tradition, radical orthodoxy claims that our ontology should be based on

---

146. Cf. Davis et al., *Theology and the Political*; Milbank et al., *Paul's New Moment*.
147. Ward, *Politics of Discipleship*, 143.
148. Ward, "Theology and Postmodernism," 435.
149. Ward, *Politics of Discipleship*, 10.

realism, which overcomes the dualistic understanding of philosophy and theology. For radical orthodoxy, Christianity throughout its theology and practice gives us a hope to have a reconciling power to transcend our limitations in the world of immanence. Here, radical orthodoxy rediscovers the value of the classical theology, offering a wholistic view to remedy many problems of the contemporary world. In this respect, radical orthodoxy deserves to get a good credit for successfully renewing the classical tradition of Christianity to the postmodern world.

Conclusion: The Scandalous Cultural Hermeneutics

Although radical orthodoxy makes many contributions to the contemporary theological studies as I indicated above, it is very controversial within academic theology.[150] For example, D. M. F. Strauss points out that radical orthodoxy's position of considering theology as the queen of the sciences is problematic.[151] According to radical orthodoxy, theology is the queen of the sciences because theology deals with the ground of *all beings* and reveals that every creature is related to God. Here, because everything is grounded by God, Milbank does not draw a sharp distinction between nature and grace as Aquinas suggests.[152] In another context, however, Milbank divides our reality into two different realms: the natural world and the God-related-world;[153] there exist a clear distinction between the earthly city and the heavenly city within the theology of radical orthodoxy. In this line, radical orthodoxy criticizes modern secular theories and postmodern philosophies for they are merely grounding on an immanent foundation—the earthly city. As a result, radical orthodoxy has a conflicting argument. Further, radical orthodoxy simply presumes that modern secular theories and postmodern philosophies are pagan and thus evil, because they are not grounded by God. However, Strauss would argue that it is God's role to save the world, rather than Christian theology's role. This is because both philosophy and theology should be directed by one God if God is the one who creates and

150. For further criticism on radical orthodoxy, look at Hankey and Hedley, *Deconstructing Radical Orthodoxy*; Shakespeare, *Radical Orthodoxy*; Robbins, *Radical Theology*.
151. Strauss, "The Inner Reformation of the Science," 193–212.
152. Milbank and Pickstocks, *Truth in Aquinas*.
153. Milbank says, "After the fall, humans lose this original righteousness, and become incapable of obeying the natural law: Aquinas is quite clear, we cannot do any genuinely 'natural' good." Milbank and Pickstock, *Truth in Aquinas*. 39. Cf. Mawson points out that Milbank misuses the theology of Aquinas, because Milbank makes a contradictory argument in using Aquinas' understandings of nature and grace, as I also indicate. Mawson, "Understandings of Nature and Grace."

redeems the whole world.[154] In this respect, radical orthodoxy once again shows a self-contradiction: *everything* is grounded by God, while secular theories are not.

In addition, radical orthodoxy has a problem in that it romanticizes the Church as an absolute institution that overcomes all differences in the world. For example, in another critique made by Stephen Shakespeare, radical orthodoxy romanticizes just one specific Christian assertion rather than seeing an openness of Christian interpretation.[155] On the one hand, as Ward's cultural hermeneutics suggests, radical orthodoxy believes that all revelations are mediated by specific signs, cultures, and practices.[156] In this cultural hermeneutics, all narratives (cultures, and practices) incorporate contingencies in this world. This means that the Christian narrative also has contingencies like secular philosophies. On the other hand, radical orthodoxy believes that "it is the Christian narrative alone can raise this contingency up to its full created potential, revealed in Christ."[157] Based on this belief, radical orthodoxy believes that the union of God and human "is mediated only in and through the Church, especially in the Eucharist."[158] As a result, radical orthodoxy mystifies the language of Christianity and the Church. However, in radical orthodoxy's description of the Church, it is difficult to explain why there exist so many different forms of the Church and why the Church gets revised and self-critical.

Shakespeare points out, "the alternative to exclusivism is not a naïve return to the search for timeless rational or revealed foundations. It is a dialogical form of theology which does not limit the presence and work of god to the confines of a single framework of meaning, because no such narrative framework is a self-contained whole."[159] In this critique of Shakespeare, it is easy to find that radical orthodoxy romanticizes the Church as a divine, complete, and perfect unity, even though the Church has many imperfect contingencies like other human institutions. Here, radical orthodoxy

---

154. Strauss says, "Christians and non-Christians are not doing different things—they do the same things differently. Consequently, within the natural sciences and the humanities, Christian scholarship ought to bear witness to a distinct Christian position even in the apparently most exact sciences such as mathematics." Strauss, "The Inner Reformation of the Sciences," 209.

155. Shakespeare, "The New Romantics," 163–76.

156. Shakespeare, "The New Romantics," 165.

157. Shakespeare, "The New Romantics," 166.

158. Shakespeare, "The New Romantics," 171. Cf. Milbank says, "The Body of Christ is the locus of mutual participation of God in humanity and humanity in God." Milbank, *Radical Orthodoxy*, 381.

159. Shakespeare, "The New Romantics," 175.

overlooks the fact that Christian tradition itself is not a perfect form of God. That is why radical orthodoxy fails to see that the development of Scripture and Church tradition is the result of God's speaking to us.[160] Consequently, even though radical orthodoxy attempts to engage with many secular philosophies, radical orthodoxy is in fact exclusive to worldliness because it fails to see the openness of Christian theology in front of God; the view of radical orthodoxy is problematic.

Looking at many critiques on radical orthodoxy, I believe that radical orthodoxy's response to worldliness is problematically incomplete. Especially, I think that this is because radical orthodoxy often defines secularity in negative terms and shows a fundamentalist viewpoint: holding Christianity's superiority over other cultures and substituting Christian theology as the absolute answer of the political sphere. When this is true, which it often is, radical orthodoxy brings a contestation rather than a peace. For example, Ward explicitly wrestles with a fundamentalist assumption in his book, when he asks, "What other voices have I silenced or with some intellectual integrity struggled with, or what ignorances am I concealing such that I can claim some superiority?"[161] This implies that radical orthodoxy theologians claim Christianity's superiority over modern secularism, which radical orthodoxy criticizes. This attitude, of course, is scandalous in the postmodern society because postmodernity advocates plurality and is hostile to the fundamentalist argument. Furthermore, Ward openly claims that the time demands theologians to be impolite to the voices of secularity, because theologians should present only the Christian perspective to change the world radically. As a result, radical orthodoxy is even called "indecent theology."[162] In this sense, what radical orthodoxy brings is contestation between the world and Christianity. Ward says, "the recovery of contestation is fundamental. Contestation and dispute are synonyms. Here, the contestation is between Christianity and the secular powers we have already named."[163] In this rhetoric of Ward, it is not hard to find that radical orthodoxy in fact has a hostile to worldliness in its deep heart even though it engages with many secular theories in appearance.

The real problem in this radical orthodoxy's contestation is that radical orthodoxy theologians dispute other secular discourses using the same premises of secular modernity which they sweep and criticize. That is, radical orthodoxy theologians believe that their project, which has a worldly

---

160. Shakespeare, "The New Romantics," 173.
161. Ward, *Politics of Discipleship*, 15.
162. Ward, *Politics of Discipleship*, 22. Cf. Althaus-Reid, *Indecent Theology*.
163. Ward, *Politics of Discipleship*, 168.

and political aim, should supersede all other political projects. This idea is, itself, political.[164] Radical orthodoxy theologians are not, as a rule, self-aware of this paradox in their work. According to radical orthodoxy, the world and the Church do not necessarily "have two opposed realms of activity."[165] Because the Church as a political entity has an ongoing struggle to discern what is true like other political entities, the Church has no difference from other cultural products or institutions in terms of the fact that the Church is also struggling in this world;[166] radical orthodoxy's notion of the Church is full of ambiguity. In radical orthodoxy, the Church is a theological notion, but it is described as a historical cultural, and political phenomenon. As a result, radical orthodoxy leads Christians to struggle in the public sphere, while advocating human freedom in this world. This means that radical orthodoxy falls into the realm of modern secularism (which it criticizes) because there is no exit from their political struggles until the time of *eschaton*. Consequently, radical orthodoxy in fact does not offer the opposite of nihilism.

Examining the paradox of radical orthodoxy, Dalferth argues, "It is easy to see how Radical Orthodoxy turns the tables on secularism by using the same pattern of sweeping argument and generalization from a non-secular or religious perspective rather than from a secular perspective."[167]

---

164. It is noteworthy that Stanley Hauerwas also has a similar view on the Church. He says, "The church therefore is a polity like any other, but it is also *unlike* any other insofar as it is formed by a people who have no reason to fear the truth." Cf. Hauerwas, *Peaceable Kingdom*, 102.

165. Ward, *Politics of Discipleship*, 23. Cf. He also says, "The Church is also a human and earthly institution. Insofar as it is ordered towards the worship and love of God, and participates in the triune operation of that God . . . , then it is the heavenly city. But, Augustine is also aware that those who make up the ecclesial community are subject to the same desires and temptations of those espoused to the *civitas terrena*." Ward, *Cities of God*, 229.

166. Ward says, "Christians can accept that God is not silent, that Christ remains head of his church, and that the Holy Spirit guides this church into all truth. But they also have to accept that it handles interpretations and conflicts among them. It has to make judgments, but there is a provisional nature about these judgments, for only when Christ judges all things will the relationship between these judgments and the truth of the church's vision and mission become evident. The precariousness of all earthly judgment is terrifying; it is a scandalous aspect of acting in faith that we must never understate. This necessary trafficking in interpretations and judgments is inseparable from the more universal trafficking in interpretations and judgments that goes on in the world. The church and the world are not, then, discrete entities. This fact gives rise to the church's ongoing struggle of faith seeking understanding. And this ongoing struggle is the substance of the church's political life." Ward, *Politics of Discipleship*, 23. Cf. Dalferth, *Sünde*.

167. Dalferth, "Post-secular Society," 14.

Although radical orthodoxy tries to reject secular modernity, it ironically accepts the style of argument which secular modernity advocates. This is because radical orthodoxy tends to substitute a realist viewpoint on the world with a confused nominalism. For radical orthodoxy, God gives us freedom to think and struggle in this world as Duns Scotus suggests.[168] That is why the Church, like other political entities, struggles with others in this world. In this point of view, radical orthodoxy defends "a view on authority as centered in the people rather than in God."[169] However, radical orthodoxy does not fully overcome modern secularism, because the theology of radical orthodoxy is still grounded by human activities, while holding an eschatological vision which in fact does not exist in this world yet. At this point of struggle, Dalferth further points out that Christians today are not interested in defending a pre-modern religious society. Rather, they are interested in an autonomous secular life in the presence of God.[170] In this respect, the project of radical orthodoxy remains a scandal rather than giving us a fully satisfactory answer to worldliness. Therefore, we need a further discussion in the rest chapters to correct the problems of contemporary trinitarian theologies (in postliberalism and radical orthodoxy).

---

168. According to Dalferth, it is dangerous to trace the origins of modernity and Reformed theology back to Duns Scotus because "we cannot use the verb *to be* (esse) univocally of both God and humans." Dalferth, *Creatures of Possibility*, 53.

169. Dalferth, "Post-secular Society," 14.

170. Dalferth, "Post-secular Society," 23.

4

A Radical Hermeneutic Reaction (European Continent)

Inviting German (trinitarian) hermeneutic theology to a discussion of contemporary trinitarian theological movements, the fourth chapter will explore the theology of Ingolf Dalferth. To rectify the problems of the former two trinitarian theological movements (postliberalism and radical orthodoxy), this chapter will argue that Christian theology should offer a God-focused-theology as Dalferth suggests. According to Dalferth, when Christians orient their lives within the perspective of transcendence (the Triune God), they can embrace many different understandings and worldly cultures in the world, because it is the Triune God who differentiates understandings and cultures in this world. To show this, the first section of this chapter will attempt to understand the background of Dalferth's theology through investigating the reception of Barth's trinitarian theology in German hermeneutic theology (especially in new hermeneutics). In the second section, I will introduce Dalferth's Christian philosophy of orientation to see how he develops German (trinitarian) hermeneutic theology further to the modern world. Finally, the last section of this chapter will look at how Dalferth understands secularity and how he develops his theology toward the age of post-secularity, which supports peaceful coexistence of the spheres of faith and reason.

THE DEVELOPMENT OF GERMAN HERMENEUTIC THEOLOGY

Post-Barthian Theology in the German-Speaking World

Although the reception of Karl Barth's theology has been bigger in the English-speaking world, the German-speaking world as the home place of hermeneutics also innovated Barth's theology into hermeneutics based on Tübingen and Zürich. In the German-speaking world, Barth's theology has been received by Rudolf Bultmann's pupils, such as Gerhard Ebeling and Ernst Fuchs, who raised a theological movement called *new hermeneutics*.[1] In new hermeneutics, Ebeling and Fuchs try to understand biblical texts not only through the existence of language, but also through event called language-event or word-event (*Sprachereignis* or *Wortgeschehen*) which is actualized in one's individual life.[2] In this theological movement, theologians claim that Christians can understand God through word-event because God reveals Godself through word-event in one's life. In word-event, Christians affirm the presence of God in their life, and thus the love of God, which comes to be word-event, opens up the future toward authentic existence (faith, hope, and love).[3] In this German theological movement, word-event is fundamental for ontology because word-event (based on faith) embraces both linguistic tradition as well as encounter with reality.[4] In this approach, theology's task is primarily hermeneutical because theology interprets biblical texts into the contemporary "existence" of individual life through the process of hermeneutics—"word-events."[5]

---

1. Interestingly, new hermeneutics has been received and popularized in the English-speaking world by the Claremont theologians such as James Robinson and John Cobb. Robinson and Cobb, *The New Hermeneutic*.

2. Ebeling says, "Word is therefore rightly understood only when it is viewed as an event which—like love—involves at least two. The basic structure of word is therefore not statement-that is an abstract variety of the word event—but appraisal, certainly not in the colorless sense of information, but in the pregnant sense of participation and communication." Ebeling, "Word of God and Hermeneutic," in Robinson and Cobb, *The New Hermeneutic*, 103.

3. Ebeling says, "*Thus, the text by means of the sermon becomes a hermeneutical aid in the understanding of present experience.* Where that happens radically, there true word is uttered, and that in fact means God's word." Ebeling, "Word of God and Hermeneutic," 109.

4. Ebeling, "Word of God and Hermeneutic," 98.

5. Ebeling says, "Word serves understanding. Where word happens rightly, existence is illumined (and that naturally always means existence in association with others).... *The precise purpose which the word is meant to serve is that man shows himself as man.* For that is his destiny.... His existence is, rightly understood, a word event which has its origin in the word of God, and in response to that word, makes openings by a right and salutary use of words." Ebeling, "Word of God and Hermeneutic," 104.

After new hermeneutics was initially raised by Ebeling and Fuchs, the approach of new hermeneutics has been developed further by another German theologian, Eberhard Jüngel (who studied and taught in Berlin, Zürich and Tübingen). Engaging with Ebeling and Fuchs, Jüngel combines Karl Barth's doctrine of the Trinity with the hermeneutic discussions of the Bultmann School in his second work, *God's Being Is in Becoming* and his main work, *God as the Mystery of the World*. While connecting (new) hermeneutics and the doctrine of the Trinity, Jüngel basically understands God's revelation as a "language-event" within the individual life. In this theology, he highlights that the communication of God relates to the world because God freely comes to us and communicates with the world through the second person of the Trinity—Jesus Christ (the Word of God).

In the methodology of these German theologians, worldliness is not depicted in negative terms, unlike postliberal and radical orthodoxy theologies.[6] Rather, worldliness belongs to God's free relationality. In contrast to many English-speaking world theologians, who emphasize the separation of Barth's theological method from the nineteenth century liberal theology, German hermeneutic theologians attempt to understand Barth's theology with its connection to Rudolf Bultmann and Martin Heidegger's radical hermeneutics, focusing on the radical changes of one's existential life throughout hermeneutic process. In this sense, German hermeneutic theologians tend not to separate analytic (linguistic) theology from the themes of Continental philosophy such as human existence or ontology. If the endeavor of German hermeneutic theology has a different emphasis from that of the English-speaking world, how is it different specifically and how does it respond to worldliness?

To understand the development of German hermeneutic theology and its distinctiveness, the following section will investigate how Infolf Dalferth elucidates the development of German hermeneutic theology. Currently, German hermeneutic theology—which connects analytic (linguistic) philosophy and trinitarian theology—is further developed by Dalferth who draws on the work of Eberhard Jüngel. In his works, Dalferth also connects the doctrine of the Trinity and radical hermeneutics, while additionally raising the Christian philosophy of orientation to explain the relationship between Christianity and the current secular world. In investigating German

---

6. In this German theological movement, we should not forget Dietrich Bonhoeffer's contribution (Ebeling was also a student of Bonhoeffer). Especially, in his writings from prison, Bonhoeffer developed a new theological appreciation of the secular, so called the post-religious world "without God." In this respect, the reason why Jüngel embraces the secular is connected to his attempt to combine Barth's and Bonhoeffer's theology. Cf. Bonhoeffer, *Letters and Papers from Prison*.

hermeneutic theology, Dalferth claims that Christian theology can be "radical," when the life orientation of faith, hope, and love is placed at the center of theological thinking and Christian practices. This is because the life orientation can change the lives of Christians radically when they orient their lives based on their understanding of God toward new possibilities of truth, hope, and love. To examine the background and uniqueness of Dalferth's work, this section will deal with (1) the types of contemporary philosophical hermeneutics, (2) the types of theological hermeneutics, and (3) the important characteristics of new hermeneutics (radical hermeneutic theology).

The Types of Hermeneutics

Ingolf Dalferth believes that hermeneutics is "the practice and theory of an art" to understand the world and to solve problems arising from the process of understanding.[7] This indicates that hermeneutics for Dalferth is also an art of orientation because the process of understanding presupposes an orientation. That is, human beings always orient themselves in the world, which is always changing, so they constantly enact the process of understanding in changing situations. Here, Dalferth points out that "understanding is a fundamental means of carrying out our lives in relation to the situation in which we live."[8] This is because understanding gives us meaning in relation to ourselves and to the other. In the journey of their lives, human beings always interpret things and themselves because they orient themselves to their life situations. This means that human life is always a process of interpretation because interpretation is the active performance of passively experienced events in one's life. That is why Dalferth argues that human beings are always in the process of understanding because they always orient their lives in the world and find meanings from their orientation process.

In the process of understanding, however, because everybody is situated in different contexts, each specific understanding process brings different outcomes. Because of this, every understanding process has different interpretations and problems. According to Dalferth, although each understanding process offers a truth, that truth is not universal because everything has meaning only for a certain interpreter who understands the truth in a certain situation. That is why the process of understanding always involves "a sign-process in which someone (*interpreter*) interprets something or someone (*interpretandum*) as something (*interpretant*) through something (*interpretants*) for someone (*addressee of interpretation*) with respect to something

7. Dalferth, *Radical Theology*, 9. Cf. Dalferth, *Die Kunst des Verstehens*.
8. Dalferth, *Radical Theology*, 11.

(*point of interpretation*) on the basis of something (*basis of interpretation*) in a particular context and situation (*context of interpretation*)."[9] To relate themselves to the world, human beings interpret things in sign-processes rather than referring to things directly. This means that the process of understanding is intrinsically ambiguous and open because the process of interpretation or understanding basically occurs as sign-processes which refer to their subject indirectly. For Dalferth, the process of understanding can produce either understanding or misunderstanding, sense or nonsense, either truth or falsity. Thus, there can always be many different interpretations and different hermeneutic problems because human beings always use different sign-processes, producing many different understandings in the world.

Looking at the existence of many different interpretation processes, Dalferth points out that there are two different usages of the term "hermeneutics." On the one hand, hermeneutics designates "what one does when one seeks to understand something or to make something understandable."[10] On the other hand, hermeneutics may also indicate "the theory of such a practice."[11] Based on the two usages of the term "hermeneutics," Dalferth notices that hermeneutics does not merely analyze the methods or procedures of understanding, but also elucidates "the phenomenon of understanding as whole."[12] According to Dalferth, the process of understanding comes from self-reflection rather than from a direct universal truth or a direct revelation of said truth. And that is why human beings always have many different interpretations even on the same thing. As a result, the study of hermeneutics should not be limited to explaining one's understanding process of something, but should go further to discuss the general process of understanding with an awareness of this fundamental limitation.

To grasp the complicated process of understanding as a whole, Dalferth points out that the development of hermeneutics in the Western tradition showed three stages in general: "the hermeneutical question moves from a focus on the problem of understanding *something* (classical hermeneutics or hermeneutics of works), through a focus on the activity of *understanding* something (subjective hermeneutics of the modern period: nineteenth century), to the *understanding of understanding* (hermeneutics of event or philosophical hermeneutics: twentieth century)."[13] In explaining these three stages of Western hermeneutics, Dalferth says that the basic question

---

9. Dalferth, *Radical Theology*, 26.
10. Dalferth, *Radical Theology*, 30.
11. Dalferth, *Radical Theology*, 30.
12. Dalferth, *Radical Theology*, 30.
13. Dalferth, *Radical Theology*, 31.

of hermeneutics is what the process of a human being understanding "something" (products of an action such as texts, artefacts, monuments, and buildings) is. In this basic development of hermeneutics, people tried to focus on how they could describe "things" more accurately. Then, the development of hermeneutics was integrated into different practical applications, such as legal, theological, or literary hermeneutics; people began to develop diverse hermeneutic traditions. In this level of development, people focused on the "process" of understanding and they wondered how human beings could understand things in their own "thinking-process." After this development, hermeneutics was revisited to discuss the subject/object issue, engaging one's self-understanding process (one's own hermeneutic tradition) to other hermeneutic processes (other hermeneutic traditions).

Looking at these three stages of the development of Western hermeneutics, Dalferth draws attention to the fact that many twentieth century hermeneutic philosophers finally began to focus on "*the understanding of understanding*," which discusses the subject/object issues of hermeneutics. According to Dalferth, to explain the process of hermeneutic as a whole, twentieth century hermeneutic philosophers develop the philosophical theory of understanding into a *hermeneutical philosophy*. The examples of this trend include Martin Heidegger, Hans-Georg Gadamer, Günter Figal, and Paul Ricoeur.[14] Although twentieth century hermeneutic philosophy has divergence in it, many hermeneutic philosophers try to understand the process of understanding as a whole, so that they concentrate on "the understanding of understanding."

To understand hermeneutic philosophy more clearly, Dalferth summarizes the types of hermeneutical philosophy in three ways: "*the subjectivity-oriented approaches*," "*the approaches of linguistic phenomenology*," and "the *approach of existential phenomenology*."[15] First, *the subjective-oriented approaches* borrow neo-Kantian philosophy and neo-Thomism to explain the process of understanding "as a web of fundamental cognitive and evaluative functions of the human subject that are linked to a patten of *a priori* and universally valid, self-referential, interwoven, and unchangeable operations of the human mind in its construing engagement with the world and itself."[16] These approaches are raised by Ernst Cassier, Bernard Lonergan, and Charles Taylor.[17] Secondly, *the approach of linguistic phenomenology*

---

14. Dalferth, *Radical Theology*, 33.
15. Dalferth, *Radical Theology*, 34–38.
16. Dalferth, *Radical Theology*, 34–35.
17. Cf. Cassier, *An Essay on Man*; Lonergan, *Insight*; Taylor, *Hegel and Modern Society*; Taylor, *Sources of the Self*; Taylor, *A Secular Age*.

criticizes the concept of the subject because the process of understanding does not merely happen in an individual center. In this approach, philosophers focus on linguistic-cultural community rather than individual subject. This approach follows the later Wittgenstein to describe the process of understanding as a language game or a form of life, constituted by the grammar of a certain cultural-linguistic community. George Lindbeck and D. Z. Philips are good examples of this approach. Lastly, *the approach of existential phenomenology* understands the process of understanding as "the fundamental ontological mode of human existence in this world."[18] In this approach, philosophers such as Martin Heidegger, Hans-Georg Gadamer, and Günter Figal, believe that the process of understanding precedes all other specific actions of human beings, and thus the act of hermeneutics is the ontological mode of human beings prior to human subject or human linguistic community.

According to Dalferth, *the existential approach of hermeneutic philosophy* has three different versions: Martin Heidegger's existential-ontological hermeneutics of facticity, Hans-Georg Gadamer's hermeneutics of conversion, and Günter Figal's hermeneutical philosophy of objectivity. To be specific, Heidegger claims that human beings are "*Dasein*"—thrown being-in-the-world. In this view, *Dasein* is marked off from other things because it understands other things within the horizon of time.[19] Heidegger believes that the interpreter, as *Dasein*, always has to be cautious of "the arbitrariness of sudden ideas or of unnoticed narrow mindedness through methodological unfolding of our "fore-having" (Vorhabe), "foresight" (Vorsicht), and "fore-conception" (Vorgriff) in the case of the interpretation in question."[20] Heidegger's hermeneutics leads human beings to realize the arbitrariness (limit) of their understanding process because they always understands things in a certain time or context. On the other hand, Gadamer analyzes the process of understanding in the context of transmission or conversation. He says that understanding is "never a subjective relation to a given 'object' but to the history of its effect; in other words, understanding belongs to the being of that which is understood."[21] For Gadamer, the process of understanding is always mediated through conversions in time and history; human beings develop their understanding from history and

18. Dalferth, *Radical Theology*, 36.

19. Heidegger says, "When something within-the-world is encountered as such, the thing in question already has an involvement which is disclosed in our understanding of the world, and this involvement is one which gets laid out by the interpretation." Heidegger, *Being and Time*, 190–91.

20. Dalferth, *Radical Theology*, 37.

21. Gadamer, *Truth and Method*, xxviii.

conversions. In this hermeneutic method, the process of understanding has to be in communication with others to be proceeded further. Lastly, picking up Heidegger and Gadamer's hermeneutics, Figal establishes "objectivity" as his basic hermeneutic concept to integrate the three dimensions of human understanding: freedom, language, and time. He asserts, "That we are drawn to things and are at the same time impacted by them, that we are surrounded by things yet are different from them, is a key to understanding what 'life' means in reference to us and for us."[22] Instead of using the term "language" or "event," Figal describes life as the space of the process of interpretation. For him, human beings can have the process of understanding, when there is objectivity which opens the possibility of understanding up. In this method, hermeneutics is a fundamental philosophical discipline to seek objectivity. As a result, this hermeneutic method focuses on otherness rather than on one's own subjective understanding formation.[23]

Investigating the development of Western hermeneutics, Dalferth realizes that many contemporary hermeneutic philosophers have attempted to understand the process of understanding on a universal level rather than on an individual level. That is why many hermeneutic philosophers did not merely explain one's subjective-internal understanding process, but recognized many different hermeneutic processes happening like a web. In distinguishing many different hermeneutic processes, many contemporary philosophers began to highlight the importance of otherness outside of one's own subjective interpretation process to explain the existence of many different and conflicting hermeneutic processes in our world. As a result, while highlighting the linguistic aspect in hermeneutic process, modern hermeneutic philosophers started to describe the process of understanding as an "event" to explain many different web-like processes of understanding phenomenologically. In this way, academic interest was established "hermeneutic of event."[24]

Looking at the rise of *hermeneutics of event*, Dalferth draws attention to the fact that theological hermeneutics also has complicated issues like hermeneutic philosophy does. For example, when Christians try to understand the biblical text, all understanding processes include two axial processes (as Schleiermacher suggests): psychological interpretation (*interpretandum* within the context of the works and life of the author) and grammatical interpretation (*interpretandum* within the overall linguistic

---

22. Figal, *Gegenständlichkeit*, 361.
23. Dalferth, *Radical Theology*, 38.
24. It is noteworthy that Heidegger's move from Dasein to event in the thirties and forties of the last century had an important impact on this development.

context of the topic discussed).²⁵ According to Schleiermacher, the process of understanding requires both the psychological and grammatical interpretations because the two perspectives of interpretation cannot be detached. Schleiermacher says, "Both are completely equal, and it would be wrong to call grammatical interpretation the lower and psychological interpretation the higher."²⁶ Through pointing out these two different understanding methods, Schleiermacher indicates that the process of Christian understanding is not monolithic; the movement of Christian interpretation is open and complicated. Consequently, to grasp the complicated process of Christian understanding in a holistic way, Dalferth tries to build his theological hermeneutics through picking up twentieth century hermeneutical philosophy, dealing with hermeneutics of event. In doing so, he attempts to show that interpretation is always an open-ended process because the process of interpretation always happens in a new context.

Theological Hermeneutics

According to Dalferth, if the fundamental problem of philosophical hermeneutics is to seek "the understanding of *understanding*," the fundamental issue of theological hermeneutics is "the understanding of the *understanding of God*."²⁷ Like hermeneutic philosophy, German theological hermeneutics is a field that can be further divided into three different positions. These three positions essentially map onto the three positions outlined in the above section. The first is the *subjective-theoretical approach*, where Christians understand God as "the ultimate ground of the reality and possibility not only of the human subject (self) . . . but also of everything that is an can be understood with and through these operation (world)."²⁸ In this approach, the understanding of God is understood according to the grammar of self-understanding; Christians "construe the understanding of God in terms of the epistemological contrast between subject (self) and object (world) based on the subject-predicate grammar of European languages."²⁹ In this method, Christians attempt to orient their lives toward the cosmological difference between God and the world in this scheme of understanding. A good example of this method is the theology of Karl Rahner that tries to understand God within one's intersubjective

25. Schleiermacher, *Hermeneutics and Criticism and Other Writings*, 8–9.
26. Schleiermacher, *Hermeneutics and Criticism and Other Writings*, 10.
27. Dalferth, *Radical Theology*, 65.
28. Dalferth, *Radical Theology*, 61.
29. Dalferth, *Radical Theology*, 62.

communication.[30] On the other hand, when Christians understand God from the *phenomenology of language* approach, they understand God within a given normative grammar of a religious tradition. D. Z. Philipps is a good example of this approach.[31] In this approach, a Christian way of life is accomplished only when Christians live in a particular Christian linguistic community because it is their linguistic-cultural frame that forms human beings' way of life. In this approach, the proper understanding of God can be done only through using the internal grammar of a certain (linguistic-cultural) religious community or religious text. Lastly, when Christians seek *the phenomenology of existence* approach, they understand God "in the light of the fundamental connection between [other's] understanding and self-understanding by means of existential ontological, effective history, or hermeneutics-of-objectivity analyses."[32] A good example of this approach is Rudolf Bultmann, who borrows Heidegger's analysis of being and time.[33] In this approach, Christians describe the process of understanding God as an event which opens a new, faithful, existential authenticity. In this approach, the understanding process of God occurs in linguistic conversation, while the understanding process as an event constantly leads human beings to change their way of thinking, living, and acting in the world.

Examining different approaches of theological hermeneutics in the twentieth century, Dalferth suggests developing the *phenomenology of existence approach* further in order to understand God in a holistic way. For Dalferth, the event of understanding God requires a hermeneutics, taking seriously that something occurs which is not of our making—and this has to be understood; he focuses on "hermeneutics of (language) event." In pursuing the understanding of *understanding*, he seeks to take "the understanding of something as a particular web of meaning within the context of the entire history of the texts in which a theme has been addressed in writing."[34] This means that Dalferth, through developing a hermeneutics of event, recognizes the multilayered construction of meaning in interpreting other things or oneself. If we apply this method to text-hermeneutics, what produces the meaning-event is not the author of the text but the text itself. This is because it is the text which makes "the concrete weaving units

---

30. For example, in Rahner's theology, God's self-revelation is mediated through one's intersubjective communication. See Rahner, *Foundations of Christian Faith*.

31. Phillips, *The Concept of Prayer*; Phillips, *Faith and Philosophical Enquiry*; Phillips, *Religion without Explanation*; Phillips, *Faith after Foundationalism*.

32. Dalferth, *Radical Theology*, 63.

33. Bultmann, *Glauben und Verstehen 1*, 26–37; Bultmann, *Glauben und Verstehen 2*, 211–35.

34. Dalferth, *Radical Theology*, 47.

of meaning into a text and the manifold connections to other signs, texts, images, monuments, or other units of meaning that are thereby made use of but also made newly possible."[35] According to Dalferth's hermeneutics of event, although every text comes out of a certain historical context, the text always produces new possible meanings and different interpretations to the interpreter. This is because all understanding processes are bound to the concrete act of understanding in a certain time of the interpreter who performs the concrete act of understanding. In this hermeneutic scheme, an interpreter can only understand here and now, while the text can have an impact on human beings who interpret the text in their current life. This means that each concrete act of understanding appears to be an arbitrary act because there can be so many different possibilities of interpreting the text. In fact, a person can generate a different interpretation every time they read a text. In this respect, every process of understanding holds new possibilities of meaning, even though there is also a certain stability in interpreting the same text at different occasions.

The Rise of New Hermeneutics: Radical Hermeneutic Theology

In Dalferth's theological hermeneutics of event, the process of understanding is placed in a human subject who interprets everything in language; the relationship of language and Being becomes important. In this scheme of hermeneutics of event, the process of self-interpretation occurs within the use of language because there is nothing we encounter that is not encountered in a context of meaning.[36] Indeed, when people interpret things, they should match their self-interpretation with language because there is no way to explain their self-interpretation without using language. This implies that it is the use of language which leads human beings to communicate and to orient their self-understanding to others. Looking at the importance of the use of language, Dalferth points out that Gerhard Ebeling, Ernst Fuchs, and Eberhard Jüngel pick up Bultmann's *hermeneutical approach of event* and develop it further to *new hermeneutics*, focusing on the linguistic reflection of hermeneutic events. For new hermeneutic theologians, the "ontological and epistemological priority of language means that a pure phenomenology of existence is impossible."[37] Because every process of interpretation is structured by language, new hermeneutic theologians believe that without

---

35. Dalferth, *Radical Theology*, 48.

36. Dalferth says, "everything that possesses the structure of self-interpretation is language." Dalferth, *Radical Theology*, 84.

37. Dalferth, *Radical Theology*, 85.

paying attention to language we cannot understand human existence. As a result, new hermeneutic theologians regard the process of hermeneutics as "a speech-event," "a language-event," or "a word-event."

In the new hermeneutics approach, theologians pay attention to the human use of language itself rather than the people using the language. In other words, in this method, the interpreter no longer focuses on the intention of the text's author like the hermeneutics of post-Enlightenment era. Instead, they focus on the topic addressed in the text. This is because the method of new hermeneutics is concerned with the meaning disclosed by the text itself. Following Bultmann's theology, new hermeneutic theologians claim that the process of understanding does not occur by the author of the text but the one who interprets the text right now. For new hermeneutic theologians, the process of understanding is a word-event which continuously reveals the meaning of texts themselves; they do not concentrate on the spoken word but on the word-event which discloses truth in itself within one's subjective existence. Although a word-event happens in one's subjective process of understanding, new hermeneutic theologians point out that word-event is always in communication because the nature of language is to help human beings to communicate with others. In this approach, the process of understanding as word-event leads the interpreter to keep communicating with others outside of one's own self-understanding.[38]

Based on this understanding of word-event, new hermeneutic theologians apply their hermeneutical principles to the understanding of God; the world is regarded as the totality of that which God speaks to us. For them, because all dimensions of theological reflection have to be explained in terms of language, they argue that there is something primordial like language before our existence; a word-event is an event that tells us what it is.[39] Based on this understanding, new hermeneutic theologians believe that it is God who leads human beings to have word-events because God is the Creator in Christian theology. In this understanding, human beings understand God within the horizon of a self-interpretative event. However, it is in fact God who allows human beings to understand God's Word. In other words, new hermeneutic theologians believe that "it is not that we interpret the world, God, and ourselves in some original or ultimate way, but rather that we are first and foremost ones who are interpreted and directed toward interpretations that are offered to us."[40] In this methodology, theologians

---

38. To understand the idea of word-event better, see Jenson, *The Knowledge of Things Hoped For*.

39. In this method, it is noteworthy that it is not we who arbitrarily give meaning to events, but they have a meaning which we can understand.

40. Dalferth, *Radical Theology*, 90.

draw attention to the fact that languages have been there even before human beings used their language to proceed the processes of understanding. Similarly, in this frame, although the understanding of God is a self-interpretive event, Christians are inspired to humility by recognizing the fact that their self-understanding is, in fact, given by God. That is to say, Christians seek to understand how God understands Godself in communicating God's understanding to them in this methodology. In this sense, new hermeneutic theologians believe that it is God who leads human beings to understand and to communicate in the world, and thus Christians should understand everything in the light of God.

The distinctiveness of new hermeneutics is that it first concentrates on divine understanding, which is distorted and limited.[41] Following the theological themes from Luther and Barth, new hermeneutic theologians such as Ebeling, Fuchs, and Jüngel put God first in the process of hermeneutics. In their theology, word-event or language-event is not just a linguistic category. For them, the category of word-event implies a Christological or a trinitarian understanding of language, because they believe that language is the "primordial language of God."[42] In this respect, new hermeneutic theologians argue that God's creative activity has an impact on the concrete situations of human life because it is the creative activity of God's Word, leading human beings to have the process of understanding.[43]

Here, because word-event before God reveals an understanding of self, world, and God, the category of word-event illuminates "the *fundamental situation* of humankind before God."[44] In other words, word-event—which is God's activity—determines hermeneutical principles in Christian life. That is why, for new hermeneutic theologians, the key hermeneutical distinction is not between the text's meaning and the act of reading the text, but "between the *authentic* and the *inauthentic meaning* of a text."[45] For them, because God is a foundational event that brings a world into being, it is

---

41. It is noteworthy that there are divergences among new hermeneutic theologians. For example, Ebeling pursued a theological anthropology for his theological hermeneutics. That is why he focused on the doctrines of sins and conscience, while giving a place to the dialectic between God and human. On the other hand, Jüngel developed Christological hermeneutics with an emphasis on the doctrine of the Trinity. So, he highlighted the parallel between God and humankind within the law-gospel dialectic. Dalferth, *Radical Theology*, 147.

42. Fuchs, "Das Christusverständnis bei Paulus und im Johannesevangelium," in Grass and Kümmel, *Jesus Christus*, 17. Cf. Fuchs, *Hermeneutik*; Jüngel, *God as the Mystery of the World*.

43. Dalferth, *Radical Theology*, 150.

44. Dalferth, *Radical Theology*, 152.

45. Dalferth, *Radical Theology*, 152.

God's activity which leads human beings to have the authentic meaning of a text or a life. Consequently, the primary concern of new hermeneutic theologians is to understand everything in the category of word-event within the presence of God who reveals the authentic meaning of reality toward humanity.

Dalferth points out that the scheme of new hermeneutics has a theological application, because Christians believe that the Word of God is the continuous self-revelation of Godself to humanity. In Christian practices, the event of understanding has practical implications for Christian life. For example, in Christian theology, one's own engagement with Scripture changes and corrects one's mind about the text and the notion of God. Because the new event of understanding happens continuously whenever the reader performs the concrete act of understanding Scripture, the reader can be changed whenever he or she engages with the text.[46] In this approach, the text is something to be understood in one's own life; the biblical texts are means to understand one's life in the light of the gospel within the presence of God's love. In this frame of understanding, God comes to us through word-event, and thus word-event makes Christians radically new through showing them new possibilities in their lives and texts every time. So, new hermeneutics of event suggests a *radical theology*, changing human lives new.

According to Dalferth, the strength of this *radical theology* is that it changes human life radically, while using "signs in which the signs do not disguise God but rather make God present."[47] Even though human beings want to understand *something* directly, the process of interpretation always produces different and ambivalent consequences; all understanding processes are mediated by signs. Likewise, in the process of understanding God, human beings necessarily use signs. However, in radical theology, "God does not disappear behind the signs, but becomes so present with them that through these signs, for the one understanding, God becomes

---

46. Dalferth adds, "Theologically, the meaning of a text is not to be sought in the presumed intent of the author or in the facts of its composition, but rather in what is revealed through it to the one understanding it as the truth of his or her life." Dalferth, *Radical Theology*, 52.

47. Dalferth, *Radical Theology*, 67. Dalferth's radical theology here should be distinguished from North American theologians' radical theology which is based on "death of God theology." In the death of God theology, theologians believe that the language of God is no longer meaningful to the secular world. The leading figures of movement are James Robinson, Harvey Cox, Thomas Altizer, and John Caputo. However, Dalferth's use of "radical theology" is different from them. These are important works on the death of God theology: Altizer and Hamilton, *Radical Theology and the Death of God*; Robinson, *Honest to God*; Cox, *The Secular City*; Caputo and Vattimo, *After the Death of God*.

understandable as God."[48] In this way of understanding, although word-events themselves are not God, God allows human beings to have a concrete word-event of God's revelation in this immanent world. As a result, Christians can understand God through the event of God's self-revelation. In this scheme of radical theology, the revelation of God is seen "as an interpretation (to experience something as revelation), not as the designation of that which is to be interpreted (to experience revelation as something)."[49] In this scheme, radical theology does not understand revelation as a particular phenomenon or special experience. Rather, revelation is a sign event that carries its own interpretation in disclosing the presence of God as the presence of creative and redeeming love. In this respect, radical theology changes the lives of Christians by leading them to pursue faith directed by God.

THE RADICAL HERMENEUTIC THEOLOGY: A TRINITARIAN WAY OF ORIENTATION

Modernizing Radical Hermeneutic Theology

Following new hermeneutics, Dalferth's *radical hermeneutic theology* makes several important points. First, it understands God through a symbolic event within human life that discloses God as God. Second, God is understood as the fundamental self-interpreting event that brings a world into being. Third, it is God who differentiates the understandings of God and beings. Fourth, the process of understanding God is always in communication. Fifth, the focus shifts from understanding texts to understanding one's life in the light of the presence of God.[50] Throughout these characteristics, radical hermeneutic theology leads Christian theology to be open and practical because it requires Christians to orient their lives in the perspective of God who is the foundation of the world and to change everything new in

---

48. Dalferth, *Radical Theology*, 68.

49. Dalferth, *Radical Theology*, 70.

50. Dalferth, *Radical Theology*, 134–36. It is also noteworthy to highlight the characteristics of radical hermeneutic theology's textual hermeneutics. In terms of textual hermeneutics, it also has few important points: (1) it replaces "*the author's intent with the divine word-event*"; (2) it identifies "*this word-event with the subject matter of the biblical texts*"; (3) it believes "*structural parallels between the perspectives of a hermeneutic of subject matter and that of a hermeneutic of texts*"; and (4) it understands the biblical texts "within the horizon of the key distinction between law and gospel, in consequential exegesis." With these characteristics, hermeneutic theology believes that reading the biblical text for Christians keeps occurring as "an occurring proclamation of God" again and again. For the treatment of biblical hermeneutics and the communication of the gospel, see Dalferth, *Wirkendes Wort*.

the perspective of God. Consequently, radical hermeneutic theology offers a practical art of orientating one's life in the world within the presence of God, while allowing Christians to recognize others (and other interpretations) in the perspective of God. This scheme of radical hermeneutic theology indicates that theology has a capacity to "communicate" with other immanent understanding processes, while it understands everything in the perspective of God first.

Although radical hermeneutic theology is helpful for Christians to understand God as a whole through advocating communications of many different understanding processes, Dalferth points out that hermeneutic theology today does not have a huge impact as it had before. This is because God is no longer a primary concern for many contemporary societies. As a result, to explain its validity, Dalferth believes that hermeneutic theology today has to engage with the current era. That is why one of the main tasks of Dalferth's theology is to modernize hermeneutic theology.[51] To explain his theology toward the modern era, Dalferth draws attention to the importance of distinctions in our life. According to Dalferth, human beings always use distinctions to orient their lives in the world. Here, Dalferth argues that radical hermeneutic theology makes a distinction between God and the immanent world, which is what allows Christians to orient their lives towards transcendence—the Triune God. In doing so, he argues that radical hermeneutic theology can contribute to the modern world. To see how Dalferth modernizes radical hermeneutic theology for the modern world, this section will investigate the unsolved problems of hermeneutic theology and how Dalferth validifies hermeneutic theology in the contemporary world. For this, the coming section will deal with (1) Tillich's theology to solve the problem of hermeneutic theology, (2) Barth's dialectic theology to explain the necessity of trinitarian understanding in hermeneutical theology, and (3) the usefulness of radical hermeneutic theology in human life.

The Problem of the Phenomenology of Existence Approach

According to Dalferth, although the (theological) phenomenology of existence approach has a great strength in that it allows Christians to seek the process of understanding God as a whole, there still remains an unsolved problem that God appears as to be an imminent phenomenon (event) in this methodology. Because word-events are regarded as immanent events or sign-processes, hermeneutic theology has to explain this phenomenon (event) of God to others. The problem here is that God is not a phenomenal

---

51. Dalferth, *Radical Theology*, 158–59.

object in this world. Ironically, although hermeneutic theology tries to deal with non-phenomenal God, it always talks about what it receives as God's revelation within the realm of phenomenal human experience. This implies that the event of God's revelation or the act of God becomes a "phenomenon" among other phenomena, which we can concretely grasp and talk about within this immanent world, even though God is not phenomenal or graspable within the realm of human experience. On this issue, questions are raised as Dalferth writes: "From what theological positions and with what sort of self-understanding does theology seek such a conversation? Does it understand itself as one version of the social-scientific study of religion, competing on the same field as religious studies . . . ? Or does it present itself as *theo*-logy, which finds its central themes in the topic of God, not in the question of religion?"[52]

To answer these questions, theologians have often described theology as a scientific study of religion because they tried to explain the event of God's revelation as the object of their studies; many theologians made theology as a branch of religious studies or cultural studies to deal with God's revelation within the realm of religious phenomenon or human culture. However, some theologians attempted to focus on the act of "God," rather than explaining God's revelation as one of many religious phenomena. A good example of this trend is Paul Tillich. He describes God's revelation as the "breaking-in" of eternity into time (or of the unconditional into the conditioned). In his distinctive method of correlation, Tillich places the human self in tension between two ontological polar elements: individuation and participation, dynamics and forms, freedom and destiny, and non-being and being.[53] Borrowing Schelling's scheme of real and ideal, the polar structure of the ontological elements carries out the whole self-world structure in Tillich's theology. In this correlational description of human being, it is noteworthy that the tension between two polarities can be reconciled through the dynamic manifestation of God's creative spirit. In his theology, the Absolute appears as God's self-revelation in religion and this unconditioned revelation of God transcends the polar dichotomy between individual life (subjectivity, the conditioned, or real) and universal necessity (objectivity, the unconditioned, or ideal).[54]

---

52. Dalferth, *Radical Theology*, 167. Cf. Dalferth, "Possible Absolutum," in Min, *Rethinking the Medieval Legacy for Contemporary Theology*. In this article, Dalferth further discusses about phenomena as sign-events.

53. Tillich says, "Since the human participates not only in being but also in nonbeing, the very structure which makes negative judgment possible proves the ontological character of nonbeing." Tillich, *Systematic Theology*, 1:187.

54. According to Tillich, even though religion is the substance of human culture,

However, Tillich perceives that human beings cannot express the Absolute without symbolic language; symbol is necessary for human beings to point the Absolute.[55] Regarding the necessity of symbol, Tillich emphasizes three positive functions of symbol in religion. First, religious symbols keep pointing beyond themselves to something else outside of the immanent world. Second, religious symbols allow human beings to participate in the ultimate reality with power and dignity because human beings essentially respect symbols. Third, religious symbols open up levels of reality which are closed for us.[56] Tillich here believes that religious symbols point to the Absolute, which symbolically transcends all finite particularities. However, Tillich also points out that there is always a danger of idolatry in using religious symbols. For Tillich, religious symbols "always have the tendency to replace that to which they are supposed to point, and to become ultimate in themselves . . . and they become idols."[57] As a result, although religious symbols allow human beings to open up towards the new reality of the Absolute, every religious symbol may have potential danger to be idolatrous, because nothing is ultimate other than the ultimate itself.

To break out of this finite circulation of religious symbols, Tillich points out that human beings necessarily find a meaning in the human spirit. According to Tillich, the human spirit moves "back and forth between two poles, the eternal truth of its foundation and the temporal situation in which the eternal truth must be received."[58] In the face of these two different poles in the human spirit, he believes that the human spirit must strive to find a meaning: "the opposition of real and ideal is based on the double relationship of the import to the form of meaning."[59] That is why Tillich claims

---

religion should have an openness to other cultures in order to lead human beings to be grasped by the right subject of our ultimate concern. In Tillich's theology, religion should have an openness to secular or other religious cultures to transform human culture even though it is the substance of human culture. And this openness is coming from God's "breaking-in" into the world (culture or finite time). He says, "Religion is directedness toward the Unconditional, and culture is directedness toward the conditioned forms and their unity." Tillich, *What Is Religion?*, 59.

55. He says, "Man's ultimate concern must be expressed symbolically, because symbolic language alone is able to express the ultimate." Tillich, *Dynamics of Faith*, 47.

56. Tillich, *What Is Religion?*, 41–42.

57. Tillich, "Religious Symbols and Our Knowledge of God," 193.

58. Tillich, *Systematic Theology*, 1:3. Cf. According to Tillich, "philosophy deals with the structure of being in itself; theology deals with the meaning of being for us." This implies that the work of theology is the work of human spirit to find the meaning of being. Tillich, *Systematic Theology*, 1:22.

59. Tillich, *What Is Religion?*, 63.

that "every spiritual act is an act of meaning."[60] He realizes that the relationship between subject and object (or between the eternal truth and the temporal situation) must be mediated by the human spirit. In other words, for Tillich, human reality should entail the structure of meaning-reality in the human spirit to dialectically transcend its finite realities toward the Absolute. In this view, Tillich argues that the human spirit connects particular human meanings to the Unconditional (Absolute or God) through the help of religious symbols.

According to Dalferth, Tillich's theology answers to the question of God's revelation phenomenologically. This is possible because the revelation of God in his theology has a realistic sense.[61] According to Tillich, the symbols of a religion are important not in themselves, but only insofar as they point to the breaking-through of the Absolute into the realm of humanity.[62] For him, religion is not the absolute concept. Instead, what is important for him is God's self-revelation—the breaking-in of the Absolute. In this approach, each religion is a specific and particular cultural phenomenon. However, God's revelation can break the particularities of each religious experience because the unconditional (God) is the base of all the conditioned world of phenomena. In this theological method, God is not a secondary theme of religion but the power to overcome the gap between ideal and real. Thus, Tillich's method successfully explains the role of religion, while explaining non-phenomenal God's activity in the finite world of phenomena.

God First Theology: The Necessity of Trinitarian Theology

Although Tillich's theology explains God's revelation in phenomenological terms, Dalferth believes that Tillich's correlational method does not go far enough compared to Karl Barth's trinitarian theology, because Tillich's theology still gets trapped in the use of religious symbol.[63] For Barth, however, Christian faith does not allow itself to be grasped as a phenomenon or a mere religious symbol because it is considered as the direct self-revelation

---

60. Tillich, *What Is Religion?*, 56.
61. Dalferth, "The Idea of Transcendence," 174.
62. He says, "In the depth of every living religion there is a point at which the religion itself loses its importance and that to which *it points breaks through its particularity, elevating it to spiritual freedom* and with it to a vision of the spiritual presence in other expressions of the ultimate meaning of man's existence." Tillich, *Christianity and the Encounter of World Religions*, 97.
63. Dalferth, "The Idea of Transcendence," 175.

of God in Christ.[64] According to Barth, in biblical testimonies, God has come to this world through the event of incarnation which is a historical occurrence of the self-revelation of God. This means that Christians witness to God's self-revelation in Christ. In Christian theology, God's revelation is not a mere religious symbol, because it appears as Jesus Christ Himself. Here, Jesus is a concrete reality for us because Jesus was born and resurrected in human history; Jesus was with other God's creations in this world, while he was identical with Godself. In this logic, Barth believes that the revelation of God should be regarded as God's self-revelation in Jesus Christ.

Based on this understanding of God's revelation, Barth believes that the primary concern of true religion should be God's revelation itself, which is represented by the historical event of incarnation of God: Jesus Christ. Barth's view on the relationship between religion and God's revelation is well explained in his early work, *Church Dogmatics* §17.[65] In this section of *Church Dogmatics*, he claims that although God's revelation is a self-enclosed circle of Godself, this self-enclosed event encounters the human sphere. He says, "the revelation of God by the Holy Spirit is actual and possible as a determination of human existence. . . . We must recognize that it also has at the very least the character and face of a human, historically and psychologically comprehensible phenomenon."[66] Here, Barth points out that the revelation of God can be grasped historically, psychologically, and phenomenologically, because this revelation is in fact an event which encounters the human sphere; God's revelation is hidden in this world.[67] For him, human beings cannot know God's revelation in a perfect sense. However, God's revelation requires some kinds of human institutions (like religions) because it has come into the human sphere. Consequently, according to Barth, God's revelation is the given reality of the world through the event of incarnation, and thus the standpoint of religion should be the revelation of God.

---

64. Dalferth, *Radical Theology*, 203.

65. There is an alternative translation for this part of *Church Dogmatics*: Barth, *On Religion*. According to Garrett Green, the former title, "The Revelation of God as the Abolition of Religion," gives a false impression to Barth's thought on religion because the former translation allows the readers to simply think revelation replaces religion. Instead, he argues that we can fully grasp what Barth describes here when we understand *Aufhebung* (which translated as "abolition" in the former version) as an equivalent term with "sublate" or "sublation" in Hegel's philosophy.

66. Barth, *On Religion*, 40.

67. Barth says, "God in his revelation has in fact entered into a sphere . . . of human actuality and possibility . . . and thus God's hiddenness in the world of human religion. Because God reveals himself, the divine particular is hidden in a human universal." Barth, *On Religion*, 42.

Barth believes that the truth of religion is thoroughly dependent on God's grace. For Barth, when religion has the revelation of God in faith, it can become a true religion in the same way that we can be righteous with God's grace, even though we are still sinners. He says,

> The true religion is a creature of *grace*. That grace, however, is God's revelation, the same one before which no religion can stand as a true religion, the same one before which no man is justified, the same one that subjects us to the judgment of death. . . . The sublimation of religion by revelation does not only have to mean its negation, not only the judgment that religion is faithlessness . . . religion can be justified by revelation and we must immediately add—sanctified. . . . There is a true religion: just as there are justified sinners . . . we must not hesitate to state that the Christian religion is the true religion.[68]

For Barth, the religion of revelation can be sanctified as the true religion only if it listens to the revelation of God in faith. As a result, he explains that Christianity can be the only true religion, because it has a possibility to be a bearer of God's revelation in the reality of incarnation even though religion by itself is faithlessness.[69] For Barth, Christianity is not the true religion, but can only become it. If it so, it pleases God. In this methodology, Barth highlights the "act of God," rather than the use of phenomenal symbols of God's revelation. In Barth's frame, "God "reiterates" for humans in history who, what, and how God is in Godself from all eternity."[70] In this approach, even though God is a Whole Other who cannot be grasped by human beings, God constantly reveals Godself toward us through God's self-transcending. In this sense, the reason why human beings can grasp God's revelation is because God makes Godself comprehensible to human beings through the creative and graceful self-revelation of God, not because

---

68. Barth, *On Religion*, 111–12.

69. Barth explains that Christianity only can be the bearer of God's revelation because of the name of Jesus Christ which it has through God's election. "The relationship between the name Jesus Christ and the Christian religion has to do with an act of divine election. Because the Christian religion neither possessed, nor ever can possess, a reality of its own, and because, considered by itself, it reduces to merely one possibility among many others—for this reason it did not and does not have anything of its own to bring to the name Jesus Christ that would make it worthy of being his creation and as such the true religion. . . . Christian religion, by the power of Jesus Christ, is reality and not nothingness." Barth, *On Religion*, 147.

70. Dalferth, "The Idea of Transcendence," 175. Cf. Jüngel says, "In reiteration, that which is reiterated lets itself be known. In God's being for us, God's being for himself makes itself known to us as a being which grounds and makes possible God's being-for-us." Jüngel, *God's Being Is in Becoming*, 121.

God's revelation is an immanent event in the realm of human experience. Thus, in this method, God keeps communicating with us through God's self-revelation.

According to Dalferth, because the understanding of God is based on God's self-revelation and God's grace, what is important in Barth's approach is "how God understands Godself and us."[71] This is because the revelation of God can be known only in the light of God's self-revelation itself. In this way, God must be known for us within the trinitarian, christological, and pneumatological dimensions. Because God can be known for us through the event of incarnation, human beings can know about God through the event which is done by the Trinity who reveals Godself as Jesus Christ with the power of the Holy Spirit. In this positive affirmation of God's self-revelation, Christ is the phenomenal God who can be discussed in this world, while he is considered as God's action. In this dialectical way of understanding God, the point of Christian communication becomes totally new, because Christians can understand the phenomenal revelation of God in the perspective of God rather than the perspective of human experience.

The New Way of Distinction by God

Borrowing Barth's insight, Dalferth believes that the distinction between Christian and non-Christian becomes not important anymore in the perspective of God, because everybody is God's creature, invited to God's trinitarian fellowship. Instead, he highlights that the perspective of God can show how every individual human life can be true, right, and good in front of many different understanding processes. According to Dalferth, there are as many forms of lives as there are many different human lives. That is why one can get involved with many different forms of religion in one's own historical background.[72] In front of many different forms of lives, what is important is how human beings orient their lives to the current communicational situation.

Here, Dalferth draws attention to the fact that each of us experiences "the differences between actuality and possibility."[73] In human life, human beings try to make their life truer, more upright, and better. In this human striving for a better life, human beings are often familiar with lack and deficiency and always experience the brokenness of the world. However, they are not familiar with perfectness, abundance, and fulfilment because they

---

71. Dalferth, *Radical Theology*, 205.
72. Dalferth, "Mitmenschlichkeit," 151.
73. Dalferth, *Transcendence and the Secular World*, 42.

are always confined within the boundaries of what they can see, do, and achieve. That is why human beings many times want to posit new possibilities and to make those possibilities happen in their life. In postulating new transcendent possibilities in human life, human beings challenge themselves and others to have better, more upright, and truer lives. Consequently, new distinctions lead human beings to orient their lives toward better possibilities, and thus human beings need new ways of distinctions to posit their life toward new possibilities of truth, uprightness, and goodness.

Highlighting the importance of distinctions in human life, Dalferth thinks that the task of metaphysics (philosophy) in human life is to make distinctions.[74] According to Dalferth, science, theology, and philosophy have different roles in human life. For example, sciences describe and explain phenomena by using different methods of description and explanation. In science, human beings explain things located in experience; the task of science is to describe and explain the world. However, philosophical discussions of God do not refer to any distinction in the realm of experience. This is because God is not an object of experience. As Kant indicates, God is rather the precondition for the possibility.[75] As a result, philosophy deals with what causes phenomena rather than merely explaining phenomena in this world. Because philosophy reacts to a different problem from science, philosophy is not a theoretical or explanatory enterprise like science. Instead, (metaphysical) philosophy asks human beings critical questions about everything by exploring the grammar of distinctions that cause confusions in human life and thought. Dalferth says, "Philosophy is not a science. It is an art—the art of exploring and clarifying distinctions that we make in different spheres of life and in different areas of thought."[76] In this respect, the mission of (metaphysical) philosophy for Dalferth is to "draw a distinction" toward the formal ground for logics beyond explaining the realm of experience.[77]

Regarding the role of philosophy, Dalferth clearly argues that philosophy is an art of orientation toward new possibilities by exploring and clarifying the distinctions we use.[78] As Niklas Luhmann points out, human beings cannot not communicate in situations of communication.[79] This is because

74. Dalferth, "On Distinctions," 172.
75. Kant, *Critique of Pure Reason*, 559–85.
76. Dalferth, "On Distinctions," 173.
77. Cf. To have a logic and mathematics, we first need to "draw a distinction," as G. Spencer Brown suggests in *Laws of Form*.
78. Dalferth, "On Distinctions," 175.
79. Luhmann, *A Systems Theory of Religion*. In *A Systems Theory of Religion*, Luhmann attempts to answer the question: "How does one identify certain social

even when one ignores the questions, the one needs to understand the question to ignore it. Here, human beings' life in communication presupposes distinctions because they can only communicate when they know how to make and understand distinctions. In the process of communication, human beings cannot make any possible action without drawing distinctions. Looking at communications by distinctions, Dalferth finds that all human beings have different positions of orientation. In order to make a distinction, human beings first need to know where they are to locate others and themselves in schemes of communication. In human lives, orientation is the way to overcome confusions by drawing distinctions; explanation presupposes orientation.

However, Dalferth points out that people often fail in seeking to orient themselves. Sometimes, human beings do not know where they are in the map although they do have a map. Or, they sometimes do not know how to locate themselves in a map even though they know where they are.[80] The failure of orientation in our lives implies that explanations are intrinsically insufficient. To correct this problem, Dalferth argues that "we need orientation strategies in our precarious worlds of meaning."[81] Because life is complicated, our orientation should be holistic, plural, and pragmatic. Without employing the whole scheme of communications, we cannot use any particular distinction. As a result, in order to orient ourselves in a meaningful way, Dalferth suggests two premises: we "must *order* the world for us in a meaningful way" and we "must make it possible for us to *find our place* in

---

appearances as religion" (1). Regarding this question, Luhmann believes that social systems are systems of communication. If religion is understood at the level of society, the most encompassing social system, it has to be understood in terms of communication. Based on this understanding, Luhmann believes that religion could be explained better if we permeate the distinction between religion's self-reflection and the religious outsider's reflection through communication. Luhmann argues that "meaning" is the medium that leads us to draw a distinction between a religious system and its environment (the self-reflection of religion and its observation of other references). Here, Luhmann thinks that drawing "the distinction between self and other-reference has the significant advantage of being capable of connection on both sides" (16). This is because "'Draw a distinction!' is telling us to cross this boundary" (17). For Luhmann, drawing a distinction allows us to "re-enter" to the distinction between self and other references. As a result, according to Luhmann, this re-entry process produces "the capacity for connection by making distinctions" (21). In other words, drawing a distinction enables us to cross the boundaries between unmarked and marked spaces through the process of re-entry. Based on this description of social systems, Luhmann claims that the concept of religion cannot be deconstructive because it reproduces new meanings in the process of communication constantly. Thus, for Luhmann, religion functions for us to have "the evolution of the communicative system of society" (31).

80. Dalferth, "On Distinctions," 176.
81. Dalferth, "On Distinctions," 178.

this ordered world."[82] Suggesting the two premises, Dalferth realizes that philosophy (metaphysics) can work as a practical enterprise which leads us to open to explore new ways of orientation. Thus, in Dalferth's theology, philosophy as a way of orientation helps us to orient our lives with others.

According to Dalferth, when human beings regard philosophy as an orientation strategy, they can clearly distinguish the roles of science, theology, and philosophy in human life. He proclaims, "*Science* searches for explanations, *theology* unfolds the orientation implicit in the practice of faith, *philosophy* clarifies the schemes of distinctions and procedures of location that we use in different spheres of life and areas of thought, and *philosophy of religion* does so in the sphere of our religious practices and ultimate existential orientations."[83] For him, philosophy and theology have different agendas from science, because their concern is not to explain a mere phenomenon in the realm of human experience. Instead, the task of theology and philosophy is to unfold the schemes of orientation in the practice of faith or the metaphysical schemes of everyday life. In this point of view, metaphysics (philosophy) is a practical enterprise because it offers ultimate explanations in regard to its fundamental structure of human lives. For Dalferth, the purpose of metaphysis is not to explain the world, but to orient ourselves in the world in a specific way. Consequently, he points out that philosophers must critically reflect on the basic distinctions that they use to orient their lives in the world, because their job is to orient their lives in a specific way (suggesting a metaphysics as a new distinction). And that is why philosophers must be sensitive to scientific, social, and cultural changes.[84]

In the same way that philosophy is a practical enterprise as an orientation strategy, Dalferth suggests that Christian theology is also a way of orientation. However, for Christians, the term "God" is not a mere hypothesis, referring to the most perfect and necessary entity.[85] For Christians, "God" is the way of orientation. To be specific, when Christians orient their lives by reference to God, they confess God as the Creator, and thus live as God's creatures. In doing so, Christians locate themselves as a created being among other creatures so that they try to live their lives with the dignity of other creatures. Here, the most important distinction in the way of Christian orientation becomes the distinction between God (transcendence) and God's creature (immanence). As a result, Christians can gain a better and deeper understanding of the phenomena of their life when Christians orient

---

82. Dalferth, "On Distinctions," 178.
83. Dalferth, "On Distinctions," 179.
84. Dalferth, "On Distinctions," 182.
85. Dalferth, "On Distinctions," 180.

their life by the reference to God because their life gets changed by this new transcendental Christian way of distinction. In this sense, Christians use the language of "God" for a practical orientation, not for theoretical explanation. And that is why Christians must be open, like philosophers, because their concern is not to explain the world like scientists, but to orient their lives in the current communications around them with their new way of distinction—God. Therefore, in Dalferth's theology, Christian faith is about understanding how one is understood by God and how one can live according to this new distinctive understanding with others in the web-like world of communication.

In the theology of Dalferth, the point of radical hermeneutic theology is to orient one's life by the new distinction—God (transcendence). By orienting their lives towards God, Christians can rightly understand what a true human life is.[86] When human beings understand their lives by God's perspective, they finally can develop co-creativity with others, because all people in this new distinction are called to be the neighbor of the Triune God who incarnated to us. In this way, Christianity offers the ideal of human life articulated by the transcending love of God. In Christianity, although the ideal (authentic) form of life is in this phenomenal world, it has many different forms because it is transformed every time when human beings orient their life toward God in new situations by their new distinction from God. In this respect, Dalferth claims that God's revelation is never abstract because it refers to the concrete (phenomenal) human life and practice. Rather, it occurs as many differentiated self-activities of the non-phenomenal God, while changing the way of human orientation dynamically.

In short, to apply the phenomenological hermeneutic theology of existence in the modern world, Dalferth develops the Christian philosophy of orientation. To do this, Dalferth introduces the concept of the breaking-in of God in Tillich's theology. In Tillich's methodology, even though Christians understand God phenomenologically through using religious symbols, their religious symbols have a realistic sense. Furthermore, Dalferth shows a more advanced version of theology in Karl Barth, arguing that the reason why Christians can understand the non-phenomenal God is because God reveals Godself through God's self-revelation in this world. From this theology of Barth, Dalferth points out that Christian theology should be based on the perspective of God because the subject-matter of Christian theology is none other than the Triune God and God's self-revelation, not immanent human experience or tradition. Consequently, Dalferth believes that Christians should orient their lives within the presence of the Triune God.

---

86. Dalferth, "On Distinctions," 163. Cf. Dalferth, "Mitmenschlichkeit," 158.

In doing so, he makes theology practical, and thus his theology promotes changing the lives of Christians new within the perspective of the Trinity.

THE ORIENTATION OF CHRISTIAN LIFE IN A POST-SECULAR WORLD

Christian Theology as Way of Orientation

As discussed, the aim of Dalferth's works is to demonstrate how Christians should orient themselves in the world to the presence of God. If Christian theology is a way of orientation in the world by a new distinction from God, how should Christian theology react to other modern cultures? On this question, Dalferth critically engages with the modern secular world like other post-Barthian theologians in the English-speaking world. However, unlike postliberal and radical orthodoxy theologians, he argues that, for Christians, secularity is not necessarily to be understood in negative terms. Rather, he says, "Christian theology ought to be adopting a critical attitude to the current swan song of secularization and the fashionable heralding of a new post-secular religious era."[87] According to Dalferth, Christians have engaged with their current culture to change people's lives within God. He points out, "Paul, Augustine, Luther, Barth, Bohnhoeffer, Gogarten, Ebeling, and Jüngel remind us that in any case Christian faith is not *per se* in opposition to a secular world, but is actually a contributory factor to it in certain respects."[88] For Dalferth, secularity constitutes the present world because we all live in that secular world as a matter of fact. In this respect, he claims that the task of theology is to engage with the current secular age based on the Christian perspective rather than ignoring or denying the current situation.

To be specific, Dalferth does not describe the modern secular world in negative terms because he realizes the rise of post-secularity. In Dalferth's theology, Christianity is not an opposite concept against worldliness. Instead, Dalferth believes that Christianity is a practical enterprise which contributes to the human life in a post-secular society. That is why his engagement to the secular world is different from other post-Barthian movements such as postliberalism and radical orthodoxy. To investigate the unique response of Continental radical hermeneutic theology, this section will look at how Dalferth understands the concept of secularity and how he postulates his theology toward other cultures in a post-secular world.

87. Dalferth, *Transcendence and the Secular World*, x.
88. Dalferth, *Transcendence and the Secular World*, 12.

For this, the following section will include (1) how Dalferth understands the concept of post-secularity, (2) how he orients Christian life toward the age of post-secularity, and (3) the evaluation of Dalferth's unique trinitarian response toward worldliness as the conclusion of this chapter.

The Rise of Post-secularity

Although many postmodern theologians (in the cases of postliberalism and radical orthodoxy) understand secularity as the opposite concept of religion with a negative nuance, Dalferth tries to understand the term "secular" as vertical antithesis of divine and worldly. In other words, he recognizes the term "secular" in a neutral sense. To do this, he suggests the concept of post-secularity "as the recovery of the religious-that is to say, the possibility of the religious-at the end of modernity (weak post-secularity), or as the overcoming of the distinction between the religious and the secular (strong post-secularity)."[89] According to Dalferth, post-secularity is a social state in which many different public spheres coexist; in post-secularity, religious sphere does not need to be described as the opposite realm of secularity. For example, the *Consolidated Version of the Treaty on European Union* announces that the European Union is founded "from the cultural, religious and humanist inheritance of Europe, from which have developed the universal values of the inviolable and inalienable rights of the human person, freedom, democracy, equality and the rule of law."[90] In this article of EU, it is interesting that the current societies (the contemporary union of states) value pluralism, non-discrimination, tolerance, and equality without the help of any specific religious tradition, and religions do not play a political or constitutional role. This means that secularity is no longer defined as the opposition of the religious because the state members do not refuse any specific religious tradition. In fact, it is more right to say that the current post-secular societies are indifferent to religions. Because post-secularity is neutral and indifferent to the religious, post-secularity instead offers "a differentiation of various 'public spheres.'"[91]

To explain the concept of post-secularity clearer, Dalferth draws attention to the fact that the view of modern sociology on secularity is broken by Jose Casanova, Charles Taylor, Peter Berger, Jürgen Habermas, and many

---

89. Dalferth, *Transcendence and the Secular World*, 13.

90. Dalferth, *Transcendence and the Secular World*, 14. Cf. *Consolidated Version of the Treaty on European Union*, C83/15.

91. Dalferth, *Transcendence and the Secular World*, 36. Cf. Dalferth, "Öffentlichkeit, Universität, Theologie," 68.

other postmodern sociologists. According to Dalferth, in explaining the relationship between religion and society, many postmodern sociologists emphasize "social differentiation (religion is one social subsystem among others)" more than "privatization (religion is a private matter, not a public affair)" and "rationalization (religion must earn its legitimacy by justifying itself in the forum of reason)."[92] After the Wars of Religion in Europe, many modern social theorists developed the concept of secularity, referring to "the move from confessional strife to secular peace in the 16th and 17th centuries (political motive); the move from a monopolist state economy to a free market economy in the 18th and 19th centuries and the move from an authoritarian religious past to a liberal modernity in the 19th and 20th centuries (cultural motive)."[93] In this modern theorist concept of secularity, religion is a private matter, while the state promotes policies to make peace among people. As a result, the realm of secularity should be dominant over the realm of religion in modern societies, and many modern religious thinkers refuse this concept of secularity which has a negative nuance on religion.

However, according to many postmodern sociologists, the current post-secular age affirms social differences and promotes a peaceful dialogue between the different spheres of faith and reason. Many postmodern sociologists such as Charles Taylor, Niklas Luhmann and Jürgen Habermas, point out that secularity does not always have a negative meaning against the religious in the age of post-secularity, because post-secularity values social differences. For them, the term "secular" can be used either positively or negatively in the ethos of post-secularity. That is why many postmodern sociologists such as Jose Casanova and Charles Taylor develop counter-narratives against the universal modern sociology.[94] In addition, in the light of the concept of post-secularity, Niklas Luhmann rediscovers the importance of religion since he realizes that religion is the basic prerequisite for all social reality, even though religion may not play a role in every individual human life.[95] Likewise, instead of separating the spheres of faith and reason, Jürgen Habermas popularizes the concept of post-secularity to re-think the role of religion in the public spheres.[96] In this respect, many postmodern so-

92. Dalferth, *Transcendence and the Secular World*, 20. Cf. Casanova, *Public Religions in the Modern World*.

93. Dalferth, *Transcendence and the Secular World*, 27.

94. Cf. Casanova, *Public Religions in the Modern World*; Taylor, *A Secular Age*.

95. Cf. Luhmann, *Die Religion der Gesellschaft*.

96. Habermas says, "For the normative self-understanding of modernity, Christianity has functioned as more than just a precursor or catalyst. Universalistic egalitarianism, from which sprang the ideals of freedom and a collective life in solidarity, the

ciologists today believe that religion does not need to be the enemy of modernity or the anti-thesis of secularity. Rather, promoting social differences, they embrace the perspective of religion as one of many sub-cultural systems. As a result, they proclaim the end of secularism, while promoting a peaceful dialogue between the spheres of religion and secularity through highlighting the differentiation of many social sub-systems.

Looking at the rise of post-secularity from many postmodern sociologists today, Dalferth argues that "post-secular" does not merely mean to change the meaning of "secular," because "post" implies a totally changed meaning of "secular." For him, post-secularity refuses the inherent meaning of secularity; post-secularity is not just "an indicator for the recovery of the religious within the secular world of modernity, but for a dismissal of the antithetical relationship between the secular and the religious."[97] To give a clear description of post-secularity, Dalferth explains four types of state: "*religious, tolerant, secular* and *post-secular.*"[98] First, religious states incentivize specific religious practices to their citizens. A good example of this is the European nations of the sixteenth and seventeenth centuries. Second, tolerant states do not prescribe any specific religion with tolerance for their citizens, but do assume that their citizens will practice a specific religion more intensively. The examples of the second case are Great Britain (the Anglican church) and the Scandinavian countries (the Lutheran churches). In these countries, the state assumes that their citizens are involved with their main religion, even though they do not persecute other religions. The third case is secular states, which prohibit religious interferences from political issues. In this case, religion becomes a private matter and a state defines itself as neutral toward religious issues. That is why these states give a free choice of religion to their citizens. Within a secular state, there can be many religious as well as non-religious people. Because religion is a private matter in secular states, however, secular governments tend not to discuss about religion in their political spheres. Lastly, post-secular states no longer describe themselves as neutral to the religious or non-religious. Instead, they are

---

autonomous conduct of life and emancipation, the individual morality of conscience, human rights and democracy, is the direct legacy of the Judaic ethic of justice and the Christian ethic of love. This legacy, substantially unchanged, has been the object of a continual critical reappropriation and reinterpretation. Up to this very day there is no alternative to it. And in light of the current challenges of a post-national constellation, we must draw sustenance now, as in the past, from this substance. Everything else is idle postmodern talk." Habermas, *Religion and Rationality*. 149. Cf. Habermas and Ratzinger, *The Dialectics of Secularization*; Habermas, "Notes on Post-secular Society"; Calhoun et al., *Habermas and Religion*.

97. Dalferth, *Transcendence and the Secular World*, 31.

98. Dalferth, *Transcendence and the Secular World*, 32.

indifferent to religious questions and give no prominence to the religious systems or other social spheres. In other words, post-secular states accept many different public spheres, while allowing individuals to live either religious or non-religious lives. In a post-secular state, the religious sphere is regarded as one of many contingent spheres in its society.[99] And that is why the religious sphere does not carry greater weight for the political or other subsystems of a post-secular society. Because a post-secular society is not affected by any specific stance or social subsystem, a post-secular state leads different communities to coexist together and to interact with one another in accepting "a differentiation of various 'public spheres.'"[100] Accordingly, a post-secular state does not combine religions with the topics of privatization or rationalization, but with the topic of social differentiation.

The Orientation of Christian Life in Post-secularity

If the post-secular societies respect the difference of each public sphere equally, why does religion still matter? According to Dalferth, because the project of the Enlightenment tries to determine what we can know and what we ought to do through the mere use of reason, the Enlightenment's concept of publicness is distorted. In the project of the Enlightenment, a concept of rationality is emphasized to seek neutrality, universality, and public good. However, as Jürgen Habermas suggests, the concept of the public sphere in the Enlightenment project is usually reduced to a private matter, because there is no transcendental authority which determines what is the public or who is right in the discourse of modern philosophy.[101] And that is why everybody determines what the truth is by themselves in modern societies. As a result, modern liberal theology fells into the same problem of the Enlightenment: "I Determine What God is!"[102] In the modern understanding of the public, what becomes "right" and "public" attracts a majority, even if this majority's opinion might be wrong. That is why many modern theologians attempt to accommodate their faith into the understanding of reason or secular theories in order to appeal their private faith to the majorities. In this project of the Enlightenment, nobody has the public opinion, and

---

99. Dalferth says, "religions exist not in *vacuo*, but in cultures." Dalferth, "Religions in a World of Many Cultures," 153. Cf. Tanner says, "culture is the defining mark of human life." Tanner, *Theories of Culture*, 25.
100. Dalferth, *Transcendence and the Secular World*, 36.
101. Habermas, *The Structural Transformation of the Public Sphere*.
102. Dalferth, "I Determine What God Is!," 10.

everybody has to fight to appeal that their own private perspective is public and valid to the majorities.

To overcome the problem of the Enlightenment project, Dalferth draws attention to the development of analytic philosophy and theology. For example, following Wittgenstein and Clifford Geertz, George Lindbeck argues that religion is "a communal phenomenon, that shapes the subjectivities of individuals rather than being primarily a manifestation of those subjectivities."[103] In this cultural-linguistic frame of religion, the one who determines God is not just an individual person but a community, because religions are comprehensive cultural-linguistic systems. In this perspective, the Yale school theologians (including George Lindbeck) no longer continue the liberal theology's attempt to justify the Christian narrative to the modern world. Instead, they try to go back to the ancient practice to interpret the Christian narrative in "the proper relation of Christians to their cultural environment."[104] Here, Dalferth agrees on that faith is a communal way of life which goes beyond one's own subjective experience. However, he argues that it is not enough to understand religion as a mere communal practice. This is because a communal interpretation does no guarantee that its understanding can be a public opinion to other different communities. In this sense, Lindbeck's communal understanding of religion suggests another problematic claim like other liberal theologians: "We determine what God is."[105]

Although Dalferth agrees with Lindbeck that theology should speak from the perspective of the participants, he claims that theology is not the only absolute perspective, because theology is "one particular approach to reality."[106] Dalferth here distinguishes "between *God's reality* and *faith in God's reality*."[107] For him, theology does not have an full access to the entire reality of God, because there are many different public spheres in our world which we cannot ignore. In Dalferth's theology, every attempt to prove the entire reality from a neutral perspective is impossible, because every perspective has its own way of observation which is different from the reality itself or other public spheres. This means that faith community is always surrounded by cultural environments, and it always communicates and interacts with other public spheres; theology belongs to the place where our society debates about truth publicly. In this inevitable communication process of community, each community has their own perspectives, but they

103. Lindbeck, *The Nature of Doctrine*, 33.
104. Dalferth, "I Determine What God Is!," 12–13.
105. Dalferth, "I Determine What God Is!," 15.
106. Dalferth, "I Determine What God Is!," 16.
107. Dalferth, "I Determine What God Is!," 17.

do not establish the *truth*. Rather, what we can only believe is that the truth "exists only within the communication of faith."[108] As a result, in Dalferth's description of community, it is not difficult to find that there are always conflicts between self-reflections and reflections upon other references, between community's internal perspective and perspectives from external communities, and between faith in God's reality and God's reality itself.[109]

To relieve the inconsistency between self-reflection and other references, Dalferth borrows Luhmann's theory, believing that the concept of transcendence is necessary for human life to imagine a boundary between immanent self-reflection and reflection upon other references.[110] According to Dalferth, the notion of transcendence enables us to have "a re-entry of the distinction into what it is distinguishing."[111] Dalferth believes that the religious system does not merely observe its own particular view from one side, but rather the paradoxical unity of the difference between the observable and the unobservable through the using the notion of transcendence.[112] As a result, although a religious system perceives the world in the realm of the observable or immanence, its point of reference comes from the outside of the immanent world; a religious system can pursue the unity of the difference between immanence and transcendence through positing a distinction from the perspective of transcendence. In this respect, Dalferth believes that we can relate to two different points of view (a particular religious community and external perspectives) that cannot be taken together at the same time, when we establish the distinction between transcendence and immanence with the help of religion. Thus, in the face of different public spheres of post-secularity, he claims that the right principle to understand the world is not "we determine what God is," but rather "God determines

---

108. Dalferth, "I Determine What God Is!," 19. Cf. Fischer, "Pluralismus," 507–8.

109. For a similar view, see Grosshans, "And the Truth Will Set You Free."

110. Dalferth said, "In Luhmann's theory, the paradoxes arise because we cannot observe the point of view from which we observe. So, we always must say two things: (1) what we see and (2) from where we see it. But, (1) and (2) are not two positions on the same line, but divided by a shift of the point of view. It is not a continuous line that is divided up by the distinction so that we have two polar opposites with a lot of gradual steps in between." From personal class notes in "The Theory of Religion," Claremont Graduate University, Spring 2020.

111. Luhmann, *A Systems Theory of Religion*, 58.

112. Borrowing Karl Jaspers' idea of transcendence, Dalferth believes that the notion of transcendence is inevitable in human life. Dalferth, "The Idea of Transcendence," 146. Cf. Jaspers says, "In some way or other man becomes certain of transcendence.... It is impossible for man to lose transcendence, without ceasing to be man." Jaspers, *The Origin and Goal of History*, 219.

what we are."¹¹³ According to Dalferth, in this perspective of *God first theology*, human beings can move beyond the worldly contradiction between self-reflection and other references.

Based on Luhmann's theory, Dalferth claims that Christianity, as an art of orientation, can contribute to Christians' lives because they face many different public spheres (of post-secularity).¹¹⁴ To be specific, Dalferth believes that Christian theology can offer transformative insights into the world (of communication), such as the fundamental distinction between the creator and creation—that is, the distinction between transcendence and immanence. According to Dalferth, Christians believe that God shows God's love to us in Jesus Christ. In this Christian faith, Christians decide to live a life in the fellowship with God and others.¹¹⁵ For Dalferth, being a Christian basically means to have a new orientation of life within God's presence. In such a Christian orientation, God through Jesus Christ makes Godself our neighbor so that all human beings are called to be the heirs of God; "In this new community of God's neighbors there are—as Paul says—no longer Jews or Greeks, slaves or free, men or women (Gal. 3:28)."¹¹⁶ In this Christian orientation of life, the distinction between faith and unbelief is not based on particular characteristics or human experiences, while the true distinction comes instead from the perspective of transcendence—God.

According to Dalferth, the Christian way of orientation "is different from all other public spheres of our life, which are constituted by *communication between human beings*."¹¹⁷ For him, believers are distinguished from others because they orient their lives in God's presence as the ground;¹¹⁸ their distinction comes from the transcendental God rather than the immanent communication among human beings. In this Christian orientation, God is relational to the world, because the God is triune in nature. That is why believers can illuminate others in the perspective of transcendence rather than staying in a worldly horizon or a particular human ideology. From there, Christians can live a totally different life because they become a being for others through opening the new possibilities of transcendence beyond the immanence of a secular world. In this respect, Dalferth's work offers a necessary corrective to the perspective of animosity between the Church

113. Dalferth, "I Determine What God Is!," 18.

114. The following portion of this section published in my book review on Dalferth's book to introduce Dalferth's theology further to the field of academic theology. This portion is revised for a further discussion.

115. Dalferth, *Transcendence and the Secular World*, 3.

116. Dalferth, *Transcendence and the Secular World*, 4.

117. Dalferth, *Transcendence and the Secular World*, 278.

118. Dalferth, *Transcendence and the Secular World*, 279.

and the rest of the world. He summarizes, "the Christian life orientation moves beyond the alternative between religious and non-religious life . . . rather, it is the self-mediating presence of God, and the distinction, established by this presence of God within the possibility space of the world, between a life that orients itself to that presence (faith), and a life which does not (unfaith)."[119] Thus, Dalferth's radical hermeneutic theology promotes a truer life to Christians within God's presence through suggesting a distinction from transcendence—the Triune God.[120]

In conclusion, looking at the rise of post-secularity which highlights the differentiation of social sub-systems, Dalferth argues that Christianity can help us to reconcile with many different social cultures and worldviews.[121] According to Dalferth, when human beings orient their lives from the perspective of transcendence, they can relate to two different points of view (a particular view of a certain community and a different view of external communities) through positing a transcendental distinction beyond two different (immanent) worldviews. In this respect, he believes that Christianity can offer a way of orienting our lives toward the perspective of transcendence because Christian theology leads us to think from the perspective of the Triune God—that is the distinction between the Creator (transcendence) and creature (immanence). In Dalferth's theology, Christianity have an impact on other cultures because Christianity's engagement with a culture brings transformation to the culture through utilizing the notion of transcendence which overcomes immanent differences.[122] As a result, Dalferth's theology of orientation shows us how Christian theology can contribute to the current world of post-secularity.

---

119. Dalferth, *Transcendence and the Secular World*, x.

120. Cf. Ingolf Dalferth, "Mitmenschlichkeit." 161.

121. It is to see how Dalferth characterizes culture. He suggests six important characteristics of culture. First, "culture is a relative to a group or community." Second, culture "varies with social group or community." Third, "cultures are trans-individual, but they are not based on agreement." Fourth, "cultures are not dependent on social consensus." Fifth, "cultures are products of historical process, and they are contingent." Sixth, "cultures are adaptable to changing contexts because they are internally differentiated." In this understanding culture, Dalferth believes that cultures are receptive to changes in their contexts, because each culture always engages with others. Dalferth, "Religions in a World of Many Cultures," 154–55.

122. Even though religions always carry their own culture with them, Dalferth believes that religion has a special function to other cultures. That is, religion offers a transformation when it engages with other cultures; religion offers a new (contemplative) form of life to its believers. He says, "The Christian faith, for example, is not tied to a particular culture but a way of transforming, modifying, improving (in some respects), and of ending (in other respects) certain strands in a culture." Dalferth, *Transcendence and the Secular World*, 157.

Conclusion: Highlighting the Public Reason of Christianity

I believe that Dalferth's radical hermeneutic theology makes huge contributions to the contemporary theological studies in three ways. First, it highlights the openness of Christian theology. Unlike other post-Barthian theological movements such as postliberalism or radical orthodoxy, Dalferth claims not to understand worldliness as an opposite or negative concept against the Church. Instead, he draws attention to the fact that we all are the part of the Trinity's creation in Christian theology. Through stressing the relationality of the Trinity, he explains that the world is always in communication; we are all relational before the Triune God. As a result, Dalferth's theology contends that it is in fact the Triune God who differentiates Godself, the world, and even the understanding process within relational unity. In this view, Christianity does not need to fight against or despises worldliness, because it can communicate with worldliness within the presence of God. This theological view implies that the Church has a public reason in the world, even though it has its own unique trinitarian/Christological grammar in terms of interpreting its theology and the world. Consequently, Dalferth's view allows Christians to affirm many different understandings and to realize the relationality of one another in the world of communication.

Another contribution which I think is very helpful is that he focuses on "transcendent God" rather than explaining religious phenomena within the horizon of the immanent world; his theology promotes human beings to seek a truer life. In Dalferth's hermeneutics, the truer distinction for Christians comes from the transcendent God. This means that Christian theology has a power to orient one's life toward a truer life within the perspective of transcendence. Dalferth claims that, through positing transcendental distinctions within the immanent world, Christian theology opens new possibilities to the human life. As a result, Christian theology leads human beings to co-present with others within the perspective of transcendence. When human beings posit new distinctions from the perspective of transcendence, they can see something which is beyond the immanent horizon of human communication. In the same way that a person who lives in a two-dimensional world could only see and understand a square-like spatial graphic, we can only comprehend the things that are within our (immanent) sphere of understanding. However, if a two-dimensional being were to the world from a three-dimensional perspective, they could realize that there is a cube-like spatial graphic.[123] Transcendence would be, for us, like

---

123. Cf. Abbott, *Flatland*.

this three-dimensional world. This implies that when human beings try to see the world from the perspective of transcendence, they can understand the world in a better way. In this way of orientation, human beings can overcome particularities in the immanent horizon, because they can see a truer distinction from the horizon of transcendence. Through offering this new horizon, Dalferth's Christian philosophy of orientation offers truer truth.

Lastly, Dalferth makes Christian theology practical through understanding Christian theology as an art of orientation. He argues that theology has a different enterprise from science or philosophy. In his theology, the view of Christianity can contribute to human life through suggesting a new way of orientation—God-with-us (*Immanuel*). For him, when Christians understand theology as an art of orientation, they can realize the practicality of theology. This, in turn, allows them to better communicate with others based on their new God-focused horizon, which leads them to posit a better possibility in the world. As a result, Dalferth does not despise or ignore worldliness by which Christians are surrounded. Rather, he promotes Christian theology to communicate with worldliness and to contribute to the post-secular society. In doing so, Dalferth's theology focuses on "changing" people's life by the God-focused distinction. Therefore, his theology promotes Christians to be open and practical toward worldliness, while holding a unique Christian view on the Trinity.

So far, I have researched three influential post-Barthian theological movements (postliberalism, radical orthodoxy, and radical hermeneutic theology) in three different regions: North America, Great Britain, and Continental Europe. Investigating these theological movements, each theological movement has shown a common strength that they made theology practical and trinitarian, although they also had different emphases and strengths according to their different local backgrounds. In the concluding chapter, I will evaluate the result of the comparative study of these three different trinitarian theologies. And I will argue that these three theological movements need to go further to examine the current situation of world (global) Christianity. Although these three theological movements suggest helpful trinitarian principles on the hermeneutic attitude of Christians toward worldliness, the limitation of these approaches is that they build on Western philosophies, which is difficult to use for Christians who live in the global South and East (who are a majority of Christians today). Therefore, in the next concluding chapter, to apply trinitarian theology to the context of world (global) Christianity, I will connect trinitarian theology with Korean Protestant hermeneutic theology, while showing that Korean contextual theology can bring a good insight as a non-Western theological response.

The example of Korea is chosen, not only because it is my home country, but also because its history of rapid Christianization and secularization provides windows to how trinitarian theologies can be understood in a global context. To show this, I will highlight that Korean hermeneutic theology's core concept, *inculturation,* can be a key to connect trinitarian theology to the context of world Christianity.

5

Conclusion: Towards a Trinitarian Theology of Inculturation

TOWARDS A GOD-FOCUSED-THEOLOGY

Looking at these three different theological schools of postliberalism, radical orthodoxy, and radical hermeneutic theology, it becomes clear that Christian theology should be done by a *God-focused-perspective* rather than immanent human perspectives. When Christians orient their lives within a God-focused-perspective, they can overcome the differences in theological understandings because they can understand the world as a relational whole before God. Their theological understanding can be changed and reconciled with different understandings of the world. By understanding the world from a transcendental horizon rather than staying in the immanent horizon of human communication, Christians can be defined by their openness to others. This is because it is the Triune God who differentiates the world and all different understandings in Christian theology. In this respect, a God-focused-perspective leads Christians to communicate with others, to be truly open, and to pursue genuine truth, hope, and love within the horizon of transcendence. Therefore, a comparative study of these three theological movements suggests that Christians can see further when they orient their lives toward the current situation, but within a God-focused-perspective.

In this concluding chapter, I will further argue that Christian theology needs to apply a God-focused-theology to the contextual theologies of world Christianity. This is because the next-generation of Christianity will experience the globalization of Christianity and the dynamic works of the Trinity in the context of world Christianity. On the one hand, this chapter will show that Western theories of secularization do not perfectly fit into the context of world (global) Christianity. To explain this, I will use an example of Korean Christianity. In Korea, although the concept of secularization has been introduced by the rapid globalization of the world, Christianity grew up rapidly in the secularization process. For example, the Korean government from the beginning has guaranteed the freedom of religion, the separation between religion and state, and the (free) competition between social sub-systems and religions; Korean society experienced the process of secularization. Interestingly, during this secularization process, Christianity in Korea grew up rapidly unlike Christianity in European countries. Thus, examining this phenomenon of Korean Christianity, this chapter will emphasize the necessity of contextual theologies in the age of world Christianity to explain many different and vital forms of Christianity today.

On the other hand, this chapter will also criticize the problem of Korean contextual theologies for essentializing specific identities or indigenous concepts in highlighting their difference from Western theologies. In many contextual theologies, theologians romanticized their indigenous identities and tried to de-Westernize Christianity. However, as I will show in this chapter, they overlooked that Christianity from the beginning has been a mixture of dynamic of works of God rather than the work of Western missionaries. To correct both problems in European theories of secularization and in contextual theologies, this chapter will highlight the importance of God-focused-theology in the process of contextualization. In doing so, I will try to construct a trinitarian theology of inculturation, connecting trinitarian theology with contextual theology. Also, I will briefly show how it can be applied in the context of globalization.

To construct my *trinitarian theology of inculturation*, this chapter will first draw attention to the theme of *inculturation*, because the subject of inculturation is none other than the Triune God who leads us to achieve a dialectics of *differentiation* and *interdependence*. In this chapter, I will argue that the theme of inculturation (which is a core concept of Korean Methodist tradition) can penetrate both problems of secularization and globalization because it suggests how Christians should react to worldliness in a world where others coexist within the relational reality of the Triune God. To show the validity of this trinitarian theology of inculturation this final chapter will deal with (1) the summary principles of comparing the three theological movements, (2) the rise of world Christianity, (3) the importance of inculturation in world Christianity, (4) the current discourse of the theology of inculturation among Asian theologians, (5) the problem of the current contextual theology of inculturation, (6) the trinitarian (God-focused) theology of inculturation as an alternative answer to the context of world Christianity, and (7) a brief application of the trinitarian theology of inculturation.

A COMPARATIVE STUDY OF THREE THEOLOGICAL MOVEMENTS

Comparing these three cutting-edge trinitarian theological movements (postliberalism, radical orthodoxy, and radical hermeneutic theology), there are three important points I want to highlight. First, all these theological movements support a trinitarian response toward worldliness in facing the age of secularism. Many modern theologians misunderstood the task of theology as explaining Christian theology within the language of modern secular reason; the trinitarian theologians, instead, argue that Christian theology has to emphasize the centrality of the Trinity as its hermeneutical principle. This is because theologians in these movements realize that Christian theology has its own cultural-linguistic grammar. In these theological movements, it is right to interpret the contents of theology with Christianity's internal logic rather than using other philosophical enterprises because theology's internal system has a different concern with other disciplines. For these movements, as Barth suggests, the starting point of theology should be faith in the Triune God, not modern scientific reason. That is why all these theological movements propose that Christians as the witness of the Trinity should engage with worldliness confidently, while stressing the uniqueness of Christian theology. Moreover, these trinitarian theologians even argue that their trinitarian way of understanding fits into the current postmodern thinking because the Triune God leads Christians to accept diversity within the divine love of God. In doing so, these theological movements show that the doctrine of the Trinity is in fact the reflection of God's love in the concrete life of Christians, rather than a theoretical teaching. Through highlighting both God's transcendence and immanence, these trinitarian theologies confirm that God should be found in the practices of Christian lives as their center. Consequently, while highlighting the practicality of Christian theology, these theological movements affirm that Christians should respond to the world within their trinitarian faith, not by theoretical theologies.

Second, an examination of these three movements reveals the strong power of each movement's local sociopolitical context over their theologians' understanding of worldliness. This indicates that every theology is inevitably contextualized into its unique time and situation, and that every theological movement aims to communicate with its own local audience. For example, American theologians have seen that political changes became the primary concern for the Church. Since Jesus Christ should be the primary concern for the Church, postliberal theologians began to develop their unique theology in a way that could address the failings of secularized churches in America. This is why postliberal theologians suggest a linguistic-cultural frame to explain the unique grammar of Christianity, and why post liberal theologians promote that the Church should be the Church first.[1] On the other hand, British theologians have watched Christianity in the West declined rapidly in the age of secular postmodernity. To fight against the dominant secularized theories which highlight the importance of empirical proof, British theologians launched the radical orthodoxy movement and condemned secular reason to explain the validity of Christian theology in the age of postmodernity. In Germany, however, Christianity has already faced post-secularity; German theologians tried to affirm both their theological value as well as openness toward worldly cultures. In doing so, German theologians allowed each individual public sphere to keep their own tradition and to communicate with other public spheres without hatred. Consequently, these different theological responses toward worldliness indicate that theology cannot be free from its own context because each theological movement tries to cope with their own unique sociopolitical situations to respond to the current situation.

Third, even though each theological movement has unique points because they deal with their own theological contexts, it is possible for them to correct one another's theology. That is why it is possible for radical orthodoxy and radical hermeneutic theology to criticize postliberalism for showing a sectarian response toward worldliness. Although postliberalism has a point that the Church has to focus on its own grammar, many postliberal theologians overlook that their theology has to be in communication with worldliness, which theologians from the other two schools studied so far have correctly pointed out. Likewise, although radical orthodoxy is right to explain Christian theology with its social-political historicity, radical orthodoxy overlooks the fact that theology has to be explained by a God-focused-perspective rather than by immanent human horizons. And that is why radical hermeneutic theology criticizes radical orthodoxy, for it is not theologically correct to understand theology within the realm of human freedom. In this respect, a comparative study of these three theological movements shows that it is important to make theological arguments

---

1. Cf. Willimon and Hauerwas, *Resident Aliens*.

CONCLUSION: TOWARDS A TRINITARIAN THEOLOGY OF INCULTURATION 147

carefully, even though each theologian can make different claims according to their own unique context.

CHRISTIAN THEOLOGY IN THE GLOBALIZED WORLD

Although these three theological movements have had a huge impact for the twenty-first century theological studies in facing the age of secularism, I believe that they need to go further to embrace the rise of world (global) Christianity because they only depict Western contexts and theologies. The link between Christianity and Western culture is getting weaker due to the growth of secularism in Western countries, the expansion of globalization, and the missionizing of non-Western people. Although these three theological movements offer good insights for Christians to respond to worldliness in the dominance of secularity, the aforementioned fact that they are contextualized to Western countries limits their use for the Church of the next few generations. In 1900, 83 percent of Christians were in Europe and North America, while the Christian population in Europe and North America had declined to 34 percent by 2013.[2] Today, more than 60 percent of Christians live in the global South and East. If trends continue, it is predicted that by 2050, 72 percent of them will live outside of Europe and North America.[3] These projections regarding to the seismic shift of "world Christianity" raise questions for further research on Christian theology, such as: what are the characteristics of world Christianity? How does Christianity inculturate into the context of world Christianity? And how should Christians respond to worldliness in the age of world Christianity?

Since the term "world Christianity" appeared as the title of a book by Francis John McConnell, "world Christianity" has meant the movement of Christianity that "takes form and shape in societies that previously were not Christian."[4] After Henry Van Dusen marked "world Christianity" not "by multicultural differences but by worldwide, organic unity," the theological area of world Christianity began to be expanded as the population of Christians in the global world has grown up so fast.[5] To study the world-wide phenomena of growing Christianity in the global world, many theological

2. Sanneh and McClymond, "Introduction," in *The Wiley Blackwell Companion to World Christianity*, 3.

3. Jenkins, *The Next Christendom*, xi.

4. Sanneh and McClymond, "Introduction," 4. Cf. McConnell, *Human Needs and World Christianity*.

5. Sanneh and McClymond, "Introduction," 6. For further discussion, see Van Dusen, *World Christianity*; Latourette, *Toward a World Christian Fellowship*; Scott, *The Emergence of a World Christian Community*.

institutions today teach and research world Christianity as an important subject.[6] Even though world Christianity has many different characteristics which make it hard to define what it is exactly, world Christianity as an academic field of theology generally emphasizes the fact that the center of world Christianity is shifting to the global South and East largely due to the growth of the Evangelical, Pentecostal, and Charismatic churches in Africa, Latin America, and Asia.[7] In many cases, indigenous Christians have particular charismatic religious experiences such as speaking in tongues, healing, exorcising, dramatic conversion stories, and receiving direct revelations from God, while "lacking of a fixed structure in worship, doctrine, and decision-making."[8] Because their strong religious experiences have formed their theology and practice, many Christians around the world today show many different reactions to the diverse works of God. That is why many Christians have formed a personal relationship with Jesus Christ rather than sticking to strict doctrinal beliefs.[9] As a result, world Christianity is understood more in terms of spiritual unity in Christ rather than as organizational or doctrinal unity.

Looking at the rise of world Christianity, I believe that the traditional European theory of secularization cannot explain the vitality and growth of world Christianity, although it gives good insights on the relationship between Christianity and dominant cultures of today. This is because there is also a development of multiple secularities in the world, alongside the rise of world Christianity. The traditional theory of European secularization explains European societies as those of "which [postulate] a structural link between social differentiation and religious decline."[10] However, this European theory of secularization does not explain the vitalities of world Christianity. For example, in the case of Korea, the independence of Korea was suddenly given not by their own hands; Koreans established their constitution in a very short amount of time right after their independence. That is why the

6. Good examples include: Harvard, Yale, Princeton, Duke, Emory, Boston University, Boston College, Oxford, Cambridge, etc.

7. Mark Noll believes that the basic Christian spirituality of the global Christianity is made in the US. This is because most missionized countries in the global world were evangelized by so Pentecostal/Evangelical missionaries from the US. Noll, *The New Shape of World Christianity*, 7.

8. Sanneh and McClymond, "Introduction," 15.

9. Grosshans points out that there is a different account of the new Pentecostal churches on the view on Luther's theology, while non-European Luther theologians also present the theology of the cross and the dialectics of law and gospel as the central elements of Luther's theology. Grosshans and Nüssel, "The Meaning and Legacy of the Reformation in a Global Perspective," 92–95.

10. Casanova, "Religion, the New Millennium, and Globalization," 426.

CONCLUSION: TOWARDS A TRINITARIAN THEOLOGY OF INCULTURATION 149

process of secularization in Korea happened in a very short time because the constitution of the Republic of Korea from the beginning has legalized the freedom of religion and the separation of religion and state.[11] In this setting of secularization, Christianity in Korea had rapidly grown up. In 1945, just after the independence from Japanese colonial rule, Christians were about 2 percent of the entire population in Korea. On the other hand, by 1991, more than 25 percent of the population was Christian (8 million of Protestant and 2.5 million Catholic).[12] During this rapid growth, Christianity in Korea had peacefully coexisted with other religions, while competing with other social sub-systems.[13] In this landscape of Korea, the Korean government has not taken anyone's side in regard to religion, while guaranteeing the freedom of religion; each religion could compete one another along with other social sub-systems to contribute to the overall welfare of their society. In this social background of Korea, Christians in Korea had a huge impact on its society. Christians in Korea established modern educational institutions and hospitals, participated in nationalistic movements, and often struggled for human rights and democracy in Korea. As a result, unlike European countries, the rapid growth of Christianity happened along with the process of secularization in Korea. In this situation, many Korean theologians also developed unique theological traditions such as the theology of inculturation, Minjung theology, or other contextual theologies. This indicates that Christian theology needs a better concept to embrace both the secularization of the current society as well as the rapid growth of world Christianity.

Due to globalization, secularization has been introduced to many non-Western countries, while many Christians also have converted and immigrated all around the world and de-territorialized Christianity. As a result, many Christians have inculturated the gospel of Christianity into many different cultures during the continual secularization processes in many non-Western countries. As a consequence of this process, many different Christian groups are now in a common space called the (secularized) global world. Ironically, even though more societies today are experiencing secularization or post-secularization, Christianity is still growing especially due to the growth of Christianity in the global South and East. That is why Christians today are facing so many vibrant forms of Christianity such as Pentecostalism, fundamentalism, evangelism, online-based churches, and

11. "(1) All citizens shall enjoy freedom of religion. (2) No state religion shall be recognized, and religion and state shall be separated." *Constitution of the Republic of Korea*, Article 20.

12. Korean Overseas Information Service, *A Handbook of Korea*, 132.

13. The current Korean society can be considered as a typical post-secular society in many aspects.

all different kinds of contextual/liberation theologies, in addition to the traditional forms of Christianity such as the Roman Catholic, Eastern Orthodox, Coptic, Ethiopian, and Indian Christianity.

In facing many different forms of Christianity today, the study of world Christianity leads Christians to realize that the globalization of the Church brings two counter forces: one toward universal homogenization (globalization) and another toward the celebration of local customs, languages, identities and histories.[14] Investigating these two forces in world Christianity, the task of the future theology must be then balancing these two factors: homogenization and contextualization. As a result, as Anselm Min suggests, the task of contemporary Christian theology is to develop the dialectics of *interdependence* and *differentiation* in the light of Christian tradition, in order to engage with these two forces in world Christianity.[15] If Christian theology has to pursue both *differentiation* and *interdependence*, how can we accomplish these two in the context of world Christianity?

THE INEVITABLE PROCESS OF INCULTURATION IN WORLD CHRISTIANITY

To reach many dynamic forms of Christianity and their vital growth, Christians today need to apply a *God-focused-theology* to the differentiated forms of Christianity. To argue this, I will first highlight the theme of *inculturation* in world Christianity. Inculturation here means a process of cultural, doctrinal, and practical change that stems from the adapting of different cultures into Christianity. Many scholars often use this term with the words such as indigenization, enculturation, or acculturation, while there is no strict distinction between these terms. Although world Christianity as a theological subject stresses many different theological themes, (such as the role of missionaries, Pentecostalism, Evangelical forms of Christianity, Great Awakening movements, secularization, conversions, de-colonization, and liberation,) inculturation is one of the most important themes in world Christianity. In the theme of inculturation, the doctrines of Christianity get adapted in mostly non-Christian cultures, and in turn, Christians evolve their teachings into their localized cultures. In this process of inculturation, it is noteworthy that Christianity changes a culture, and the culture changes Christianity. From this double side of transformation, we can easily realize that there is no pure Christian culture, but only a process of transforming by God. In the process of inculturation, Christians struggle to make a place

14. Yong, *The Future of Evangelical Theology*, 57.
15. Min, *The Solidarity of Others*, 1.

and context where faith in God's presence and love can be lived individually and commonly; Christians believe that the transformation of their culture is the act of God. As a result, the concept of inculturation highlights the transformation of the lives of Christians within the presence of God, while holding the importance of God's differentiation in the world.

Although the process of inculturation becomes more vivid in the context of world Christianity, inculturation has been an inevitable process of the entire Christian mission history. This is because Christianity, from the beginning, has entailed the process of translation which requires transformations in regard to the meaning of the texts and the understanding of God. A World Christianity scholar, Lamin Sanneh, says "translation involves a degree of cultural decentralization—or, at least, cultural retrenchment on the part of the translator, though the receiving culture may eventually compensate the translator with the consolation of adoption."[16] At its beginning, Christianity's embeddedness in an Aramaic- and Hebrew-speaking context was a limitation that it needed to overcome with translation. Since then, translation always has been a part of Christian life, and thus Christianity dialectically used both its root language as well as the vernacular of its new context such as Hellenistic culture and language.[17] As a result, "it was that the two subjects, the Judaic and the Gentile, became closely intertwined in the Christian dispensation, both crucial to the formative image of the new religion [Christianity]."[18] On the one hand, Christianity kept its Judaic roots through taking the Old Testament as its canon. On the other hand, Christianity always adopted gentile cultures and vernacular languages in the process of its extension. In this respect, the mission of the Church always has been done by two different cultural subjects. In this endless process of translation, Christians always fight against as well as adopt other gentile cultures (and vernacular languages) to understand God in their changing contexts.[19] Therefore, the entire Christian history has been *the history of transformation by God* and *the differentiations of Christian understanding*.

In this process of translation, it is noteworthy that, Christian beliefs or concepts also had to endure the process of *inculturation*, which involves both the processes of purification and transformation. For example, if I translate p into q, then the translation only succeeds if the same is being said on both sides of p=q. However, this never works when it comes to cultures. If I want

16. Sanneh, *Translating the Message*, 36.
17. Sanneh, *Translating the Message*, 1.
18. Sanneh, *Translating the Message*, 1.
19. Sanneh, "Bible Translation, Culture, and Religion," in Sannah and McClymond, *The Wiley Blackwell Companion to World Christianity*, 265–81.

to translate Christian faith into a secular culture, I either ruin Christianity (by adapting it to secularity) or I transform secular culture into something else. That is why Christians many times develop unique concepts according to their different cultures and languages.[20] To give an example, the early Christians borrowed the concept of "*Logos*" from Hellenistic culture. The word *Logos* meant ground, word, way, reason, opinion, and discourse in the ancient Greek world. And it became a technical term in western philosophy through Heraclitus, who used the term for a principle of order and knowledge. Aristotle then applied the term to mean to reasoned discourse, while Stoics recognized the term as the divine principle moving the Universe. In short, the term *Logos* was an important philosophical concept in Hellenistic culture. However, the Gospel of John identified the *Logos* as the divine Word which is incarnated in the person of Jesus Christ. In this case, the term was used differently from the Hellenistic philosophical traditions. Although Christians used the language of the Greek, the meaning of *Logos* has been purified and transformed into a new meaning. In this process, Christians acquired a better critical comparative perspective on their own beliefs because of their processes of purification and transformation on their doctrinal concept. Therefore, in the history of Christian mission, the existence of the process of inculturation has been something to be celebrated, because it has transformed the Christian tradition dynamically.

This inevitableness of the process of inculturation is also valid in the current situation of world Christianity because many Christians keeps transforming and developing their Christian understandings, while being aware of the transforming power of God's love and Spirit in their lives. A good example of this is Korean Christianity. Many Western missionaries in Korea tried to change Korean society through adopting a Korean religious ethos. The process of biblical translation is a good example. Protestant missionaries in Korea published Korean dictionaries and translated the Bible into Korean.[21] It is noteworthy that it was the process of Bible translation which popularized and standardized the use of Korean Character—Hangul.[22]

---

20. It is noteworthy that vernacular translation still moves toward supporting for right reading in its (original) tradition, even though it brings little bit of transformations. Griffiths, *Religious Reading*, 68.

21. Clark, *Living Dangerously in Korea*, 18.

22. Bible translation in Korea had a profound impact on Korean society. When Bible translators began to use Hangul instead of Chinese characters, they rediscovered the effectiveness of Hangul. This in turn, brought the rapid and far-reaching spread of not only the Bible, but also of Hangul itself. In addition, the Hangul Bible translation brought Korean society into a new world. With the spread of Hangul catalyzed by Bible translation, people had access to their mother tongue in a written form, and even women and children were finally able to read. Beginning with the use of Hangul

CONCLUSION: TOWARDS A TRINITARIAN THEOLOGY OF INCULTURATION

Before the process of Bible translation, the Korean script was not widely used, and most literate Koreans used Chinese characters. In this process, the missionaries embodied the Korean religious ethos in their translation. For example, they used a local name, "Hananim," which literally means "master of Heaven" or "only one master," for referring to God, in order to reflect the Korean vernacular culture.[23] Although the name "Hananim" was from the term of Shamanism, the missionaries published some books, including hymnals and tracts, with the term "Hananim" to refer to God. Afterward, Horace Underwood, a leading Presbyterian missionary, discovered that, at a time when only one god was worshiped in the Kingdom of Kokurei (part of early Korea), that god was also called Hananim. And Underwood concluded this term would be useful because Korean readers might easily recall its original sense.[24] Significantly, the Korean Bible translators wanted to be sure that their readers would not only understand the individual words of the Bible, but the concepts within, and so they had to use Korean traditional vocabularies.[25] However, when they used vernacular vocabularies, they used them in a totally new way; they enriched and transformed not only the lives of Koreans, but also the understandings of God.

In this process of inculturation, when Korean Christians understand God as "Hananim" and the *Logos* as the *Dao* (道), their doctrinal concepts have different nuances, although their terms depict the same thing. If someone asks me to achieve "the *Dao*" through believing in "*Hananim*," I would interpret that someone is asking me to achieve the Truth (or the Word of God) through believing in God. However, in this process of thinking, I would first think of the usage of the *Dao* in Laozi and Hananim in shamanism. So, I will understand the Truth (the *Dao*) as something eternally changing, and God (Hananim) as the one ruler of the Heaven. In the Eastern concept of *Dao*, there is no eternal truth, but the eternal truth is that everything is constantly changing.[26] As a result, I will understand the truth in a different nuance be-

---

by Christians, the education system was totally reformed and Koreans began to enjoy a base of increased economic-social development. In sum, Korean Christianity was able to contribute in an unparalleled way to women's and children's rights, a stable public education system, and the social unity between the rich and poor through its use of Hangul in Bible translation. This shows that the process of translation (as well as inculturation) has a huge impact not only on the culture of local Christians, but also on the vernacular culture. This process of translation in Korea reminds us of Martin Luther's Bible translation.

23. Underwood, *Underwood of Korea*, 126.
24. Underwood, *Underwood of Korea*, 344.
25. For further discussion, see Oak, *The Making of Korean Christianity*.
26. One of the oldest usages of the Dao appears in *Laozi*. And it says that the Dao cannot be changed because it is constantly changing. For Eastern philosophy, the truth

cause the term *Dao* suggests additional nuance other than just the Truth or the Word of God, although I still recognize the *Logos* (the *Dao*) as God's Word or the truth. In this example, the process of inculturation involves the processes of purification and transformative elevation of doctrinal concepts in Korean Christianity through the dialectical movements of two different forces (the gospel of Christianity and the new local cultural/linguistic aspect). Consequently, the process of inculturation brings the differentiation of the understanding of God within the presence of God.

A more important point here is that the evidence of inculturation is deeply penetrating not only the doctrinal or institutional aspect but also *the practical aspect* of Christians. For example, in the case of Korean Methodist Church (KMC), the second biggest Protestant denomination in Korea, there are five guidelines for KMC theology: Wesleyan Quadrilateral (Scripture, Tradition, Reason, and Experience) and Localization in the Korean situation (the Tradition of the Theology of Inculturation).[27] This last principle of theology is an addition to the (American) United Methodist Church's four core principles. This means that Korean Methodist Church, as a part of world Christianity, highlights the theme of inculturation more than the Western churches. Within their expressive stress on inculturation, the theme of inculturation becomes clearer in the practices of Korean Christians. From the beginning, many Korean Christians converted to Christianity through a strong Pentecostal repentance revival movement. Western missionaries report that people began to cry and beat their heart, some lay down on the floor and hit the ground, some pulled out their hair, some shouted to the heaven, and some jumped repeatedly, while confessing their sins in the Pyongyang Great Revival Movement (1907).[28] Since Korean Christians converted to Christianity from a distinctive context, they developed distinctive practices by themselves in their churches. They pray loudly on the mountains all night long like Shamans do. Some other examples of distinctive Korean practices are all-night mountain prayer services, evangelism contests, Korean prayer (Tong-Sung prayer), and daily morning prayer service.[29] These examples show that the localization of Christianity involves

---

is that everything is constantly changing. Laozi, *The Daodejing of Laozi*, 106: "The Dao that can be told is not the eternal Dao. The name that can be named is not the eternal name."

27. Korean Methodist Church, *The Book of Discipline*, 2.2.48—2.2.58.

28. It is noteworthy that the Pyongyang Great Revival Movement is the extension of the Wonsan Great Revival Movement (1903), which is started by Korean Methodists. "Letter of W. L. Swallen to A. J. Brown (Jan. 18, 1907)." For further discussion, see Kim, "The Role of Robert Alexander Hardie."

29. For further discussion, see Lee, *Born Again*.

CONCLUSION: TOWARDS A TRINITARIAN THEOLOGY OF INCULTURATION

both the doctrinal and practical aspects. Therefore, we can find that God's work of transformation and inculturation has a huge impact not only on the doctrinal understanding of God, but also on the lives and practices of Christians who live in many different contexts.

THE THEOLOGY OF INCULTURATION

In Protestant theology, the theology of inculturation (or the theology of indigenization) was first suggested by Korean theologians.[30] Although Korean Protestantism has roughly one-hundred thirty years history, its serious academic theological discourse began in the 1960s, after the first-generation theologians (who received PhDs in theology) began to work.[31]

---

30. In the case of the Roman Catholic Church, the term enculturation or inculturation began to appear for the first time in John Paul II's Apostolic Exhortation, *Catechesis in Our Time* in 1977: "The term *acculturation* or *inculturation* may be a neologism, but it expresses very well one factor of the great mystery of the Incarnation. We can say of catechesis, as well as of evangelization in general, that it is called to bring the power of the Gospel into the very heart of culture and cultures. For this purpose, catechesis will seek to know these cultures and their essential components; it will learn their most significant expressions; it will respect their particular values and riches" (no. 53). It is also interesting that many Protestants preferred to use the term contextual theology rather than using the term inculturation (other than Asian scholars). The reason why picked the term *inculturation* in the discussion is the influence of Korean theologians who brought the theology of inculturation for the first time in Protestant theology.

31. Although the theology of indigenization was popularized and theorized by Korean theologians, many first-generation Korean theologians were influenced by Japanese Christian leaders. This is because many indigenous Christian movements appeared first in Japan around the early twentieth century. The best example of this is the non-church movement which was led by Uchimura Kanzo. Japanese indigenous Christian leaders such as Uchimura Kanzo or Kawai Shinsui thought that Japanese received direct revelation of God so that only Japanese churches had more authority than the western church. Uzimura Kanzo says for example: "Christianity is received by Japanese directly from God without any foreign intermediary; no more, no less ... missionaries come to us to patronize us, to exercise lordship over us, in a word, to convert us" (38). For him, this direct encounter with God comes about through reading the scriptures with one's own eyes and heart. That is why he insisted on the need for indigenous Christian response in his non-church movement: In addition, many indigenous Christian leaders claim the distinctiveness of Japanese Christian experience. One Japanese indigenous Christian leader, Kawai Shinsui, reports: "I am sure they (Buddha, Confucius, Wan yang-Ming) would discover something in addition to what Peter, James, John, and Paul had found. This being so, some greater truth beyond the Christianity conveyed from the west may be revealed by embodying the minds of these saints and thus providing the west with the secret of truth found also in Japan" (82). In this respect, Japanese indigenous Christians argue that the experience of God should be in the form of indigenous culture and that it should be distinctive from the western Christianity. Mullins, *Christianity Made in Japan*.

Since the 1960s, Korean theology has developed three distinctive theological traditions: religious conservativism (based on the majority of Presbyterian and other Evangelical denomination seminaries; fundamentalist theology), social progressivism (the progressive Presbyterian seminary; Minjung theology), and cultural liberalism (the Methodist seminaries; indigenous theology).[32] In Korea, the fundamentalist theologian group has defended historic Christian beliefs such as hyper-Calvinism, while conflicting with the World Council of Churches (WCC) for advocating pluralism and ecumenism. Minjung theology, on the other hand, identified the oppressed Korean people (*Minjung*) with the *Ochlos* of Jesus' early movement and developed a contextual liberation theology to fight against military dictatorship and capitalism. However, the indigenous theology group tried to de-Westernize Christian theology and to harmonize Christianity with traditional Korean religions and cultures. In doing so, many Korean Methodist theologians tried to understand "conversion" not as conversion to Western Christianity but as being opened to the presence of God's love in people's current lives and contexts. So, the words "inculturation" or "indigenization" first appeared in the discourse of first-generation Methodist theologians in 1962.[33]

After the concept of inculturation was first introduced, many Korean theologians began to work on inculturating the gospel of Christianity into their traditional (religious) culture. The founding figures of Korean indigenous theology include Sun-bum Yun, Tong-Sik Ryu, and Seon-hwan Pyeon. Although these theologians studied in Western countries, they borrowed eastern religious concepts to inculturate Christian theology into their own context. For example, Yun mainly focused on Barth and Jasper's works when he studied at Basel for his doctoral work.[34] However, after coming back to his country, he believed that establishing the subject of Korean theology was the most urgent work in the context of Korea's post-colonial effort. That was why he developed and published *the theology of Sincerity* (誠), and "Jesus was none other than a filial Son (孝子) of the Father." Throughout his

32. See Ryu, *Veins of Ore in Korean Theology*.

33. Ryu, "The Inculturation of the Gospel and Its Missiological Task." After this article (which is considered as the first article on the concept of inculturation) published, many Korean theologians began to debate on the concept of "inculturation" through many theological journals in Korea. These are examples of articles published in 1963 via journal called *Christian Thought*. These are English titles: "The Understanding of Inculturation in Christianity (Tong-Sik Ryu)"; "The Task of the Gospel's Inculturation"; "Dankun Myth Is Vestigum Trinitas (Sung-bum Yun)"; "The Inculturation of Christianity Is the Task of Our Age (Jang-sik Lee)"; "The Function and Malfunction of Inculturation (Hyun-seol Hong)"; "The Philosophical Foundation of Inculturation (Kyu-ho Lee)."

34. Yun, "My Two Teachers."

writings, he was groundbreaking in his borrowing of Confucian concepts to demonstrate the Triune God. Likewise, after studying Bultmann, Ryu argued "the scripture itself is the product of the western culture; that is why I began to use the word, inculturation, in the Korean theology. . . . I firmly believe that the gospel of Christianity needs to be de-kerygmatized in the ethos of Korean."[35] With his belief, he wrote many books such as *Korean Religions and Christianity*, *Korean arts and Christianity*, *Logos and Dao*, while focusing on the relationship between Christianity and shamanism. In the case of Pyeon, although he often mentioned that he "studied between three 'B's: Barth, Bultmann, and Buri,"[36] he was open to religious pluralism and developed a *religion liberation theology* as his theological method. To develop his theology, Pyeon borrowed Buddhist concepts like Zen, emptiness, and even Buddha to describe Christian theology and develop his religion liberation theology. These theologians not only discussed the theology of inculturation in Korea, but also invited to many ecumenical activities internationally; they were well-received by fellow theologians all around the world.[37]

In the context of post-colonialism, one of the most urgent tasks for Korean theologians was to re-construct their Korean identity through borrowing Korean traditional religious and philosophical concepts in their theologies. And this trend overlaps with diasporic Asian theologies in America. For example, a leading first-generation Korean American theologian, Jung-Young Lee, developed "the theology of Change" through applying Christian theology to an Eastern religious book—the *Book of Change*.[38] In his work, he tried to borrow Eastern religious/philosophical concepts to develop Asian theology. And, this school of thought has been continued to the works of third-generation Asian theologians today.[39] In this school,

35. Yoo, "The Controversy and Assessment," 80.

36. Pyeon, "My Theology Class," in Dean, *Pyeon Sunwhan's Retirement Memorial Articles*, 21.

37. KNCC Theological Committee, *Minjung and Korean Theology*.

38. See Lee, *The Theology of Change*.

39. Current feminist Korean theologians who work in the US engages with Korean traditional philosophical concepts such as Jung, Han, and Wisdom. However, I find huge problems in their works. This is primarily because they do not understand Eastern philosophical concepts well enough, while misusing and romanticizing the concepts in the context of America. For example, they do not use any primary resource when they deal with the Korean concepts of Han and Jung. Han (限) and Jung (情) have deep and broad philosophical meanings in Korean philosophy. Those are huge concepts like the concepts of *Logos* in Western philosophies. Even though there are tremendous meanings and knowledge in Han and Jung (the Shamanism discourse of Han-puri, the controversy of Mencius' Dispute of Four Beginnings and Seven Feelings, and so on., they do not show any deep understanding on the concepts' philosophical and historical backgrounds. Even if I take their shallow usages of Jung or Han, they do not notice

many Asian theologians believe that the western Christianity has to be deconstructed and reconstructed with the help of Eastern philosophies. They argue that western philosophies are not helpful for Asian theologians to reconstruct their localized theology and identities. Rather, they think that Western philosophies cause dualism, orientalism and colonialism.[40] So, they try to use Asian identities and concepts to inculturate theology into their new cultures, while attempting to overcome the problems of Western philosophies with the help of Eastern thoughts and identities. That is why these theologians try to recover the traditional Asian values such as filial piety, faithfulness, or Jung (情) in their Christian theologies, even though these values are lost in the lives of most Korean people today.[41]

This trend of Asian theology today is often connected to postmodern philosophies, which highlight the importance of differentiation. Many postmodern thinkers today point out that stereotyping or having a certain local identity is unavoidable because the standards of truth, beauty, and ritual are inherited from other context. For example, Michael Foucault argues that the individual subject is always enmeshed in political power relations.[42] According to Foucault, the subject always struggles against authorities. However, he points out that "to live in society is, in any event, to live in such a way that some can act on the actions of others. A society without power relations can only be an abstraction."[43] According to Foucault, the individuals are confined by their society's stereotypes because power relations operate everywhere. In other words, the individuals' local identities are given by power relations. Because one's identity is given by others as Foucault suggests, many Asian theologians have attempted to read one's local identity with post-colonial sensibility to establish one's differentiated identity from others. Consequently, to break the prevalent stereotypes to one's indigenous

---

the danger of Jung/ Han community. For example, often my Korean church community people blame the concepts of Jung and Han because there are many dark sides of these concepts, which the outside observers of the Korean community cannot notice. See Joh, *Heart of The Cross*; Kim, *The Grace of Sophia*; Kim, *Colonialism, Han, and the Transformative Spirit*.

40. One of the most important works in this trend is Said, *Orientalism*.

41. Interestingly, even though traditional cultural values were lost in Korea, the religious affiliation for two main religions (Buddhism and Christianity) was increasing in Korea until 1990s.

42. Foucault, "The Subject and Power," in *Power*.

43. Foucault, "The Subject and Power," 343. Cf. Min, *The Solidarity of Others*. In this book, Anselm Min argues that Derrida and Levinas' postmodern philosophies also support indigenous contextual theologies through stressing the importance of different identities.

identity, the discipline of Asian theology has developed their own theologies with the awareness of post-colonial sensibility.

THE PROBLEM OF CONTEXTUAL THEOLOGY

Although Korean/Asian theologies are helpful for local Christians to recover their unique local identity, these theologies have a critical problem in essentialism which romanticizes and absolutizes local identities and indigenous cultural values. In the development of Korean/Asian theology, many theologians eventually began to formulate theological reflection through utilizing their own unique experiences and traditional philosophical concepts. That was why many Asian theologians affirmed their ethnic/racial identity positively in order to prove their equal status with the Western, while trying to break the hegemony of orientalist prejudice. In these attempts of affirming their unique identity, Asian theologians increased their self-esteem through romanticizing their identity. In this respect, they argued, "Asian/Korean (ness) is beautiful and chosen by God," even though we are all mixed of many different identities before God. Thus, many Asian theologians absolutized their unique identities or cultural values in their theologies.

To highlight the different identity of Korean people, the concepts that theologians from the school of Korean inculturation theology have used concepts from Asian philosophies, which were already not in circulation by the time of their work. In their quest for inculturation, self-identity, and the celebration of differences, these theologians inculturated Christianity into a culture that, in many ways, no longer existed. For example, many Korean indigenous theologians brought the concepts of Dao, Buddha, and Sincerity in their theologies to relate their unique traditional philosophies into Christian theology. In doing so, they often praised the superiority of eastern philosophical concepts. However, in this process, they often romanticized and absolutized their traditions, while overlooking that their traditional philosophical concepts are not the primary concern of Christians today. As a result, only a few elite Korean Christians, who understood traditional philosophical concepts, could engage with Korean indigenous theology. Unfortunately, only a few Koreans today can understand and get interested in Eastern philosophies.

Likewise, Asian American theologians expressed similar ideas to Korean indigenous theologians. For example, Jung-Young Lee emphasizes the importance of the marginalized or "in-between" experience of Asian Americans, while writing about his own marginalized experience. In his autographical theology, the experience of in-betweenness becomes holistic because there are many similarities between the concept of incarnation and the experience of being in-between.[44] Lee concludes his autography like this: "I hope that someday this beautiful mosaic (his marginalized experience from both Korean and American societies) will be realized in America."[45] For, Lee, his experience of in-betweenness is essential to fulfill and imitate the love of God; his "in-between" experience is something beautiful. And this idea of the experience of "in-betweenness" as an immigrant is a common subject in many other diasporic Asian theologians' works.[46] In many Asian American theologies, the experience of "in-betweenness" becomes an essential concept to understand God's love and Christology. For them, in order to understand God's genuine love, Christians have to have the experience of in-betweenness like Jesus Christ; they believe that the experience of in-betweenness is something special which helps people to understand God's love clearer. However, in absolutizing the concept of in-betweenness, they overlook that not all Asians have the experience of in-betweenness or immigration at all.

In the works of Korean/Asian theologians, theologians often criticize Western colonial hegemony by undermining the orientalist dogma, and by romanticizing their unique (or oppressed) experiences as something beautiful that can help overcome Western philosophies or sociopolitical oppressions. In this process, many Asian theologians claim their ethnic/indigenous group's superiority to deny the universal validity of Western culture or oppression.[47] That is why, for many Asian theologians, the oppressed experience or their unique traditional heritage is a gift of God to break the dominant power of western colonialism and to fulfill the Kingdom of God in this world. This belief hinges on the understanding that Asian cultures and heritages are essentially different from the Western culture.

However, this Asian theologians' claim relies upon a strong binarism of "we-the oppressed" and "they-the-oppressor." In order to support this binary difference between Western colonialism and the power of the specific

---

44. To look at other Asian American theologians' work on eastern concepts, see Lee, *From a Liminal Place*; Joh, *Heart of the Cross*. These theologians also utilized many Korean religious concepts. Also, look at Lee's books: *The Trinity in Asian Perspective*; *Embracing Change*; *The Theology of Change*.

45. Lee, "A Life In-Between: A Korean-American Journey," in Phan and Young, *Journeys at the Margin*, 37.

46. There are so many Asian American theologians who highlights the experience of immigration or in-betweenness. See Phan and Young, *Journeys at the Margin*; Chow, *The Protestant Ethnic and the Spirit of Capitalism*; Yong, *The Future of Evangelical Theology*; Joh, *Heart of The Cross*; Tan, *Introducing Asian American Theologies*; Lee, *From a Liminal Place*.

47. Kang, "Who/What Is Asian," in Keller, *Postcolonial Theologies*, 103.

CONCLUSION: TOWARDS A TRINITARIAN THEOLOGY OF INCULTURATION   161

ethnic/racial group, many Asian theologians tend to essentialize the experience of specific people. In this theological trajectory, Asians described themselves as the poor, the oppressed, or the chosen. However, in these descriptions, the diversity and complexity of peoples have been overlooked. As a result, Asian theologians paradoxically created occidentalism in the same manner with orientalism, through internalizing the same orientalist model of a monolithic view on a differentiated (racialized) religious community that they criticize.[48]

For Asian theologians, it is strategically better to essentialize their ethnic identity to heal and restore peoples' suffering more powerfully, rather than totally destroying their unique identity. Because the racial/ethnic identity of minority communities has been damaged by brutal colonial powers, many Asian theologians argued that their own unique identity is essentially different from others, and furthermore that their identity is better than the other identities. Naturally, Asian theologians even claim that their unique experience and heritage are a beautiful gift of God to heal the broken world. Gayatri Spivak calls this phenomenon "strategic choices of essentialism."[49] In this strategy, Asian theologians often choose to have a fixed (essentialized or nationalistic) identity which is represented by poverty, oppression, or uniqueness.

Looking at the danger of essentialism in Asian inculturation theologies, third-generation Korean indigenous theologians argue that the strong nationalistic concept of ethnicity has to be de-constructed with postmodern philosophical concepts such as "hybridity" and "the multitude."[50] These are all concepts borrowed from postcolonial thinkers such as Homi Bhabha, Antonio Negri, and Michael Hardt. Although first and second-generation indigenous theologians regarded their ethnicity (Koreanness) as the main subject of their theology, third-generation theologians realize that the concept of ethnicity cannot be valid any more in the age of postmodernity. Postmodernity requires them to realize that the concept of ethnicity or nation is the byproduct of nationalism and imperialism, as Negri and Hardt suggest in their book *Empire*.[51] Rather than using the concept of ethnicity, third-generation theologians claim that the "in-betweenness" of the multitude should be the place of Korean theology. They point out that Korean society already has many immigrant laborers and families who cannot be

---

48. Kang, "Who/What Is Asian," 104; Cf. Coronil, "Beyond Occidentalism," 56.

49. Spivak, "Criticism, Feminism, and the Institution," in *The Post-colonial Critic*, 11–13.

50. See Pyeon Seon-hwan Archive, *The Third Generation Indigenous Theology*.

51. See Hardt and Negri, *Empire*.

explained by the traditional concept of ethnicity.[52] Because of this dynamic change, they believe that the concept of ethnicity no longer describes Korean identity.[53] Because Korean society is already constituted by many different peoples, they believe that Korean theology needs to use the concept of the multitude rather than the concept of nationalistic Koreanness. For them, the concept of the multitude leads Korean Christians to understand the hybridity of their identity and overcome the exclusiveness in the (blood-based/nationalistic) concept of ethnicity.

Based on this new understanding of ethnicity, current Korean indigenous theologians suggest focusing on *cultural nationalism* rather than ethnic nationalism.[54] After the criticisms of many third-generation indigenous theologians, Korean indigenous theology today draws attention to the popularity of K-culture. Recently, Korean cultural products have become very popular to the global world. Korean theologians think that Korean cultural products are popular because they are full of hydridic aspects.[55] As a result, many Korean theologians support cultural nationalism, stressing the concept of hybridity in K-culture which makes people get excited, unified, and dynamic. Through overcoming ethnic nationalism with cultural hybridity, Korean indigenous theologians claim that Korean theology should also embrace hybridity and reproduce new hydridic culture to the global world like K-culture does.

Likewise, many leading Asian American theologians such as Nam Soon Kang and Timothy Tseng focus on the concept of hybridity in order to solve the problem of fixed racial/ethnic identity in the discourse of Asian American theology.[56] For example, Kang brings Homi Bhabha's concept of *Third Space of enunciation* in her theology.[57] For her, the Third Space is "not a fixed space, but an indeterminate one, which occurs with cultural

---

52. Jang-seng Kim, "The Understanding of Nationalism and Indigenous Theology," in Pyeon Seon-hwan Archive, *The Third Generation Indigenous Theology*.

53. It is noteworthy that Korea used to be a homogeneous nation. Ethnically, more than 99 percent of Korean is Korean, and this has been unique case in the world. However, this trend has been changed because of international marriages and immigrations.

54. Lee, "From Ethnic Nationalism toward Cultural Nationalism" in Pyeon Seonhwan Archive, *The Third Generation Indigenous Theology*.

55. The Society For Korean Cultural Theology, *Doing Theology through Korean Culture*. In this eight-hundred-page book, many Korean theologians focus on the popularity of K-culture and believe that Korean Christianity can be popular when they embrace hybridity as K-culture does.

56. Tseng, "Beyond Orientalism and Assimilation," in Matsuoka and Fernandez, *Realizing the America of our Hearts*.

57. Cf. Bhabha, *The Location of Culture*, 37.

hybridity."⁵⁸ Realizing the necessity of highlighting the Third Place, she calls attention to the fact that "all cultures are involved in one another; none is single and pure, all are hybrid, heterogeneous, extraordinarily differentiated, and unmonolithic."⁵⁹ Looking at the Third Place, she believes that the concept of hybridity leads Christian theology to invite otherness without essentializing one's identity. Based on this concept of hybridity, she also develops the cosmopolitan theology which highlights the importance of cosmopolitan solidarity in the global world to overcome binarism.⁶⁰ In sum, many leading Korean/Asian theologians today borrow many postmodern concepts such as hybridity, solidarity of others, or cosmopolitanism, to correct the problem of essentialism in Asian contextual theology, while still holding a sensibility on the differentiation of Christianity.

CONCLUSION: THE TRINITARIAN THEOLOGY OF INCULTURATION

Although many (Korean/Asian) theologies of inculturation are correct to celebrate differentiation in the age of world Christianity, I believe that these theologies are missing one important point—the Triune God. Many theologians in this school believed that God has worked in the lives of their ancestors even before Western missionaries brought Christianity into their land. After the age of colonialism, they had to recover their self-esteem as indigenous people; they tried to find a strong history and a rich culture in their traditional heritages before God. In this process, they developed different hermeneutical approaches from Western theologians. Instead of focusing directly on how God talks to their current situation, Asian theologians tried to find the vestiges of the Trinity in their local cultures and identities. As a result, they began to utilize their traditional religious concepts and their own unique experiences in their theology. However, while developing their own unique Christian theology, they emphasized too little that the subject of inculturation has to be the Triune God, not their traditional cultures or unique experiences.

58. Kang, "Who/What Is Asian?" 115.

59. Said, *Culture and Imperialism*, xxv.

60. Kang, *Cosmopolitan Theology*. In this book, Kang argues that Christian theology needs to be done in the context of cosmopolitanism since we live on the age of globalization. Here, borrowing postmodern philosophies from Jacques Derrida and Gayatri Spivak, she highlights the importance of hospitality, love, and solidarity in the age of cosmopolitanism. Cf. Min, *The Solidarity of Others*. In a similar sense as Kang, Anselm Min also brings postmodern philosophies from Levinas and Derrida to suggest "solidarity of others" as the leading concept of postmodern theology.

There are two major problems in these Asian contextual theologies. One is that they failed to convey the uniqueness of Christian theology. The second problem is that they also failed to bring practicality in Christian theology. In the many works of inculturation theologies, the primary concern is their own uniqueness rather that what Christians practice in their actual religious lives. Because they concentrated on their differences, they essentialized, romanticized, and absolutized their uniqueness in the name of God. In this process, they failed to see God's work in the process of inculturation as a whole. Even though many third-generation Asian theologians today attempt to overcome the danger of essentialism in Asian theology, they still do not go far enough to offer a genuine dialectics of interdependence and differentiation within the perspective of the Triune God. This is because they are still offering human-aspect-theologies with a strong attachment to postmodern philosophies. Although the aforementioned Asian theologians were right to highlight the inevitability of the process of inculturation, most of them merely focused on the localization (contextualization) of Christian theology in a theoretical level. As a result, they failed to realize that the process of inculturation is God's action. When theologians merely deal with worldly phenomena such as the contextualization of Christianity, they miss the prior actuality of God in the process of contextualization.

In addition, because much of Asian inculturation theology overlooks the importance of the internal grammar of Christianity and God's action in history, it often becomes a more of a political ideology than a theology, describing God's transcendental economy in this world. The process of inculturation requires both the internal logic of Christianity and its communication (or its translation) to new cultures. However, as I observed above, many Asian theologians did not adapt trinitarian theology seriously in their works. Consequently, even though Asian theologians were good at contextualizing Christian theology, they could not make a Christian-like theology because they were busy accommodating theology into their traditional cultures rather than focusing on the internal logic of Christianity.

However, when Christians understand the process of inculturation in the perspective of the Triune God, they can see that the creation and shaping our identities are never fixed; our identities are not a given that can be preserved, but only something that is in the making. In Christian theology, God is always a God who transforms the imperfect into the more perfect, who creates good out of evil, and life out of death. That is why we have to pay attention to that which will be, and not primarily to that which has been or from where we come. In this God-focused-theology, the distinction between God and creature is primary because it is God who transforms and sanctifies our world in a better way. In Christian theology, Christians confess that they cannot achieve anything by themselves because the final consummation can only be done by God. As a result, Christian theology affirms that the Spirit of God moves everywhere with all different kinds of people and cultures. In addition, the age of world Christianity leads us to reaffirm that no one can have a pure, single, and simple identity before God. That is why many Christians today witness that the migrating work of the Spirit unites, blends, and interbreeds different people and cultures *in Christ*. In this differentiation of Christianity, the reason why Christians can live as a being for others is because the differentiation of many forms of Christianity is the Triune God's work. When Christians admit that it is in fact the work of the Trinity, Christians can communicate with different understandings of God and different cultures within the spiritual unity of God. In doing so, they can look forward to having better possibilities and transformations in their lives, while holding a spiritual unity from the perspective of transcendent God.

Therefore, I, as a fourth-generation Asian theologian, claim the necessity of *the trinitarian theology of inculturation* which highlights the Triune God's action in the process of inculturation. When human beings seek the solidarity of others or the identity of hybridity within human perspectives, they again fail to explain the existence of specific particularities and differentiations in our world because they are merely offering human ideologies which remains in the realm of finite human horizon. However, when they explain every particularity in the perspective of the Triune God, they can see further to explain transcendences within their different particularities. In this trinitarian theology of inculturation, Christians can posit a better possibility by the transcendent God who differentiates all different cultures within trinitarian unity. Through highlighting the Triune God's work in the process of inculturation, Christian theology can debate not only in its private place but also in public places because all places in this world can be reconciled one another in the relational God who transcend everything. As a result, in the perspective of the Triune God, Christians can reconcile with others and different understandings, and they can realize that everything is connected and interdependent one another within God's presence. Therefore, the trinitarian (God-focused) theology of inculturation can achieve a genuine dialectics of interdependence and differentiation within the *horizon of God*.

My trinitarian theology of inculturation is an attempt to connect trinitarian theologies and contextual theologies, in order to affirm both aspects of differentiation and interdependence in our world. In trinitarian theologies, theologians did not emphasize the processes of inculturation and globalization enough in facing the rise of world Christianity. That was why trinitarian theologies in postliberalism and radical orthodoxy showed ignorance or hostile toward worldly cultures. On the other hand, in Asian contextual theologies, there were not many theologians who focused on trinitarian theology or Christianity's internal logic; they lost practicality in their theologies. However, in my theology, I am trying to link these two different theological traditions through highlighting God's perspective and God's transformation in the process of inculturation.

To outline my trinitarian theology of inculturation, I want to stress two important points, as it is indicated in its name: trinitarian (God-focused) perspective and God's work in the process of inculturation. First, the trinitarian theology of inculturation primarily focuses on the work of the Trinity. In other words, its primary distinction comes from the Triune God, not human spheres. One of the essences of trinitarian theology is to precisely focus on the distinction between what we can do and what God is doing; it allows the space we need for our own actions, but it insists on the prior actuality of God in all we do. When Christians orient their lives in the perspective of transcendent God, they can expect better understandings in the world and act according to these better understandings. Within the perspective of God, Christians can finally embrace all different understandings because they believe that it is God who differentiates the world; the binary human/cultural distinctions between gender, ethnic group, or denomination are not important anymore in God's horizon, because we all are God's heir and we all can reconcile in Jesus Christ (Gal 3:28).

Second, it emphasizes the Triune God's transformation in the process of inculturation. In the globalized world, Christians today face many different forms of Christianity and culture. While holding its internal logic (the perspective of God), the trinitarian theology of inculturation humbly admits that different cultures also bring transformations into Christianity; it is more open and practical. In this theology, on the one hand, Christians are aware of that the process of inculturation can happen everywhere, including liturgies, doctrines, translations, and even the individual/communal lives of Christians who live in the globalized world. On the other hand, they are also aware of that it is the Triune God who brings these *transformations in their lives*; it tries not to lose the internal logic of Christian theology, while expecting the Triune God's divine transformation through different vernacular cultures. In doing so, this theology realizes that everything is codependent in the perspective of the Triune God. Through believing that we are all connected within the Triune God, the trinitarian theology of inculturation can hope for what God will do for us with the divine love, because this theology leads Christians to invite all other differentiations to the fellowship of the Trinity within Divine love.

Here, to highlight the role of the Trinity in the process of inculturation, it is noteworthy to draw attention to the relational persons of the Trinity,

CONCLUSION: TOWARDS A TRINITARIAN THEOLOGY OF INCULTURATION

leading us to achieve a genuine dialectics of differentiation and interdependence. In Christian theology, although human beings are not able to understand the transcending (non-phenomenal) God, God reveals Godself in this immanent world through the dynamic works of the Trinity's relational persons. That is why Christians have developed the concept of persons to describe the relational economies of the Trinity in this phenomenal world. In the biblical narrative, God speaks to humanity with a certain personality, because God enters the human world with personalities. That is why Christians have confessed that God is *"one being (substance) in three persons."*[61] In this understanding of the Trinity, God is described as a personal one who intimately communicates with us. To be specific, in the Old Testament, God appears us to be *the Father of all* who created all of us (Exod 22:20; 23:9; Deut 14:29). In the Old Testament, the Israelites hold a siblinghood with others through a concept of a common Father. This is because they believe in one God who is the Father not only of Israel, but also of all; theologically, the Israelites do not have a national god, but a supranational one. That is why they must welcome strangers (Exo 23:9; Lev 19:33–34; 24:22; Deut 10:19; Jer 7:5–7; 22:3) to invite and unite others to the fellowship of the one common Father. Following this lineage of the Old Testament, Christian theology also describes God as the Father of all who does not leave us orphaned and comes to us constantly (John 14:18).

In addition, Christian theology understands God to be a relational being who communicates with us through the concept of God's incarnation (John 1:1–18); the relativity of God can be seen in the *Logos* (the Word of God) who is sent from and sent for (John 1:3; 20:21). In the biblical narrative, Jesus (who is incarnated as the second person of the Trinity) has a direct relationship with the Father (John 5:19; 10:30; 15:5; 17:11). This indicates that God is a relational and communicative being.[62] Based on this understanding of God, Christians have understood the world as a result of God's relational communication because God created this world and human beings through verbal events: "Then God said, 'Let there be light'; and there was light. . . . Then God said, "Let us make humankind in our image, according to our likeness" (Gen 1:3, 26). In a similar sense, Christians also

---

61. In the Eastern tradition of Christianity, the Cappadocian Fathers (St. Basil the Great; Gregory of Nyssa; Gregory of Nazianzus) established the terms such as *ousia* and *hypostaseis*, to describe the Trinity, while highlighting the perichoretic nature of God. In the Western (Latin) tradition, one the other hand, the languages of the Trinity first developed in the works of Tertullian. While using the terms such as substance, economy, trinity, and persons, Tertullian described God as the one "who has three persons in one substance." Tertullian, *Adv. Praxeam*, xxv.

62. Ratzinger, "Concerning the Notion of Person in Theology."

believe that Jesus's teaching is not a product of human learning, but it originates from a face-to-face dialogue with the Father (John 20:21). This means that Christian faith comes from an active communication of the Trinity. In this understanding of Christian faith, having a Christian faith means to have a personal relationship (communication) with the Triune God and to understand the world in this relational reality (communication) of the Trinity. As a result, the trinitarian understanding of Christian faith shows that being a Christian is to change one's life new through participating to the intimate communication of the Trinity.

Furthermore, in the biblical narrative, the Holy Spirit, as the third person of the Trinity, invites all different beings (others) to a personal relationship with the intimate God.[63] In the New Testament, one of the most important roles of the Spirit is to testify the Father and Son to connect others to the fellowship of God: "When the Advocate comes, whom I will send to you from the Father, the Spirit of truth who comes from the Father, he will testify on my behalf" (John 16:26). In this description of the Spirit, the Triune God does not merely speaks to Godself, but also invites others to the fellowship of the Father and Son.[64] This means that the Holy Spirit as the third person of the Trinity connects others to the communication of God.[65] That is why the outpouring of the Spirit empowers Christians to bear a witness to the love of the Father and Son in their concrete lives; the work of the Spirit leads Christians to bear diverse gifts to testify the love of the Trinity.[66] Here, it is noteworthy that the diverse gifts of the Spirit are not for

---

63. In the Scripture, it might be controversial whether the Spirit is also the object of worship. On this question, Gregory of Nazianzus focuses on the nature of the Holy Spirit in his homily, *On the Holy Spirit*. Gregory of Nazianzus, *Catechetical Oration No. 5*, §6. Here, Gregory points out that it is difficult to support the doctrine of the Holy Spirit because the Spirit is barely mentioned in Scripture, while the doctrine of the Son is clear in the Bible. However, he says that the Holy Spirit was a *procession* from God, although the Holy Spirit and the Father were divided in names. He thinks that the Holy Spirit has a certain superiority and it must be active before the creation because God cannot create the world without the Holy Spirit. He explains this with the concept of the procession. For him, the Holy Spirit proceeds from the Father so that it is not generated by God, but proceeding from God. In this respect, he argues that we should worship the Father, the Son, and the Holy Spirit as the single Godhead and power.

64. See Moltmann, *God in Creation*.

65. Zizioulas says, "Here, the Holy Spirit is not one who aids us in bridging the distance between Christ and ourselves, but he is the person of the Trinity who actually realizes in history that which we call Christ, this absolutely relational reality, our Savior. . . . The Holy Spirit, in making real the Christ-event in history, makes real *at the same time* Christ's personal existence as a body or community." Zizioulas, *Being as Communion*, 110–11.

66. In Scripture, the Spirit has many roles (and gives us many gifts). Min points out, "the Spirit is the subject of verbs such as searching (1 Cor 2:10), knowing (1 Cor 2:11),

CONCLUSION: TOWARDS A TRINITARIAN THEOLOGY OF INCULTURATION 169

celebrating diversity or human works, but to connect all of us to the body of Christ in love (1 Cor 12). Consequently, the person of the Spirit allows Christians to invite and connect others to the mysterious fellowship of the Trinity in divine love.

Looking at the dynamic roles of the Trinity's persons, we can notice that it is in fact the Triune God who initiates our understanding of God because human beings can know about God when God appears to be a personal being to communicate with them. Here, the person of the Father reminds us of that we are all created by the relational God. Also, the second person of God through the event of God's incarnation teaches us that God is a relational being who wants to communicate with others to have a personal relationship. Lastly, the witness of the Holy Spirit connects all our differences to the body of Christ without harming one's different identities or cultures in love through giving us many gifts and different ways of understanding God. In this trinitarian understanding, it is the Triune God who enables Christians to continuously communicate with God and to invite others to the communication of God in love. In this respect, because the persons of God keep inviting others to the intimate relationship of the Trinity, the trinitarian understanding of God leads Christians to realize that we are all relational one another in the perspective of transcendent God.

Concerning the economy of the Trinity's persons in the process of inculturation, we can further realize three important points. First, *God, as a one who has persons, communicates to us so that God becomes the Father, Jesus (the Word of God), and the Spirit, in order that we would understand God.* This implies that the process of understanding God is primarily initiated by the Triune God who incarnates into the world and communicates with us (as radical hermeneutic theology suggests). In this trinitarian understanding of God, Christians can understand who God is because God communicates and speaks to us in Jesus Christ with the power of the Spirit. In this trinitarian hermeneutics, even though God is a non-phenomenal being, God speaks to us in the life and preaching of Jesus Christ (and in the Word of God). In this way of understanding, God invites Christians to understand the world as a relational reality because God creates the reality through the relational communication of the Trinity.[67] Here, because Chris-

---

teaching (1 Cor 2:13), giving life (2 Cor 3:6), dwelling (Rom 8:11), crying out (Gal 4:6), having desires (Gal 5:17), leading (Gal 5:18), bearing witness (Rom 8:16), interceding (Rom 8:26–27), strengthening (Eph 3:16), inspiring, apportioning and willing (1 Cor 12:11), speaking and sending (Acts 13:2, 4), and being grieved (Eph 4:30)." Min, *Solidarity of Others in a Divided World*, 117.

67. Grosshans says, "In the case of the triune God something real, a reality, refers via language to the presence and asserts itself: that is, God's story and history with

tians confess that God is the creator of everything, their worldview is first and foremost in its primordial sense—a relational attribute of God. Thus, in this trinitarian way of understanding, it is the Triune God who enables us to communicate with God and to understand God and this world through the process of God's self-revelation.

Second, *because God appears to be a relational and communicative being, God continuously inculturates into a certain cultural/linguistic context; God invites all of us to the fellowship of the Trinity in a relational way—that is the process of incarnation, translation, and inculturation.* In Christian theology, the Triune God has to be incarnated into the world to be understood. Likewise, the incarnated Word of the Trinity has to be translated and inculturated into a certain context to be understood. Within the reality of the Trinity, God communicates with us through the event of inculturation; Christians can understand the non-phenomenal God because of Jesus Christ who lives a life within a concrete body and context. In this life of Jesus Christ, we can also notice that Jesus, as a one who is confined in a specific cultural context, has to understand his mother language and culture to preach the Word of God. In this mystery of God's incarnation, although human beings cannot understand the non-phenomenal God, God kindly reveals Godself in a specific culture to be understood in a creative and relational way. In other words, our understanding of the Trinity can be accomplished in and through certain a priori mediums such as body, language, and culture. This implies that Jesus (the Word of God) does not only enflesh but also inculturates to a concrete human situation to be understood, because the Triune God with freedom chooses to ceaselessly communicate with us in this world. As a result, the followers of Jesus Christ have to use their own vernacular language and culture to understand the Word of God in their distinctive context. In the freedom of God, the communication of God does not end as a one-time event at the incarnation of God but continues as an ongoing process through the process of inculturation. And that is why the entire history of Christian mission has been the process of inculturation, which can be considered as the extension version of God's incarnation, revealing God in a finite cultural background.

---

himself, the world and the human being. . . . In this respect, the trinitarian understanding of God is central in Christian faith. Starting with the trinitarian name of God it has to be developed, what in Christian faith is understood as real in respect of God and his relation to the world and the human being. This concerns the reality of the creative power of the free God; this concerns the reality of the creative power of the free God; this concerns the reality of the reconciling love, in which God binds himself to the human being and his world; and this concerns the reality of the moving power of God's spirit, who saves the human being and his world." Grosshans, "Internal Realism and the Reality of God," 77.

Third, *the Spirit has given Christians a mandate and a tool to share the gospel (the Word of God) with all different people and cultures; the Spirit intends for the gospel to made available to all cultures, with the same completeness that Jesus made the gospel available to the Israelites.* In the Bible, the Spirit constantly leads Christians to bear diverse gifts and fruits to enrich their understanding of God in love. That is why the story of the Holy Spirit in the Bible shows that Christians can obtain a power and a commitment when they are filled by the Holy Spirit. For example, when the Holy Spirit poured a fire on the apostles, the Holy Spirit enabled them to speak in other tongues on the day of Pentecost (Acts 2:1–4). After the disciples of Jesus Christ were filled by the Holy Spirit, they could not stop going out to preach the gospel to the ends of the earth where people have different languages and cultures (Acts 1:8); many (new) people from all around the world accepted the gospel, received the gift of the Holy Spirit, and shared their gifts and possessions in the fellowship of the Trinity (Acts 4:37–47). In this work of the Holy Spirit, the Triune God invited many different people and cultures through allowing us to have the processes of interpretation, translation, and inculturation, while holding a spiritual unity in love.[68] In this way, the communication of the Trinity became more dynamic and fruitful to us even in different languages and cultures. And thus, Christians within the spiritual unity of the Trinity can pursue many different means of grace, ways to worship the Triune God, and plentiful mediums to interpret the Word of God (God's self-revelation) such as literature, music, visual art, political situation, activism, internet, and academic study. In this respect, the process of inculturation for Christians can be understood as a gift and a commandment of the Trinity because the process of inculturation changes the actual lives of people and enriches people' understanding of God with the power of the Spirit.

Accordingly, when Christians understand the ongoing process of inculturation as the work of the Trinity, they can realize that being a Christian

---

68. Grosshans says, "The claim of the Bible is, that it is the actual word of the living Triune God, the Father, Son and Holy Spirit. It is not only a message from the past. To be actual, the word of God has to be understood by all people in their languages they speak and live with. This is the ambition especially of Protestant Christianity. . . . The idea of Christianity is not to create copies of its cultural and communal forms at its beginnings in the first century AD. It is about God speaking to people in their diverse contexts, addressing them, comforting and challenging them and empowering them to create their own individual and communal responses within their historical, cultural, societal and political contexts. These responses may be very different—and they are different. Therefore, Christianity exists in a diversity of denominations, which reflect different cultural, historical, intellectual, political contexts and traditions." Grosshans, "The Interpretation of Holy Scripture," 10–13.

does not mean to observe some dogmatic statements but to live in the presence of the relational God who constantly communicates with others in love. In this trinitarian understanding of inculturation, the persons of the Trinity endlessly invite all of us to participate to the fellowship of the Triune God, in order to change one's personality, virtue, and culture to the profound relational reality of transcendence. In this fellowship of the Trinity, Christian theology can be open and practical in the concrete lives of Christians through inviting all different people and cultures to the better possibility of transcendence, promoting both differentiation and interdependency within relational love. Therefore, facing the ages of post-secularism, globalism, and world Christianity, the trinitarian theology of inculturation offers a genuine dialectics of differentiation and interdependence from the perspective of relational transcendence in love.

THE APPLICATION OF THE TRINITARIAN THEOLOGY OF INCULTURATION

If the trinitarian theology of inculturation is necessary for the age of world Christianity, how can we apply this theology to specific problems in the global context? I believe that my trinitarian theology of inculturation can contribute to pursuing genuine reconciliation in a globalized world, because it stresses both the differentiation and interdependence of different cultures within the spiritual unity of the Trinity. Because the process of globalization leads us to live all together in a (connected) web-like world, people today face so many different cultures in a common place. As a result, we see that many different human ideologies and differentiated theologies conflict with one another. As Anselm Min writes, one of the examples of these conflicts is "the conflict between imperialist forces trying to impose their economic and political interests on the rest of the world . . . and the indigenous forces trying to secure even a minimum of autonomy and dignity against the pressures of global imperialism."[69] However, we also realize that the reconciliation between these two different forces or groups is almost impossible in the realm of human spheres or human traditions.

In America, for example, we often see that both extreme parties of people quote biblical passages to prove that they are right over another party of people; it is not difficult to see two different parties of Christians quote Jesus Christ to highlight the wickedness of their opponents, while arguing that Jesus is on their side. Looking at this complicated irony, it somehow makes sense for Stanley Hauerwas to argue that the primary job of the

---

69. Min, *The Solidarity of Others*, 93.

CONCLUSION: TOWARDS A TRINITARIAN THEOLOGY OF INCULTURATION 173

Church is to be the Church first, even while it might be valid for Graham Ward to recover the classical Christian tradition to fight against different worldviews, and while it is probably right to point out that God works for the oppressed like many contextual theologians claim. Looking at these different views above, it is easy to find out that theologians often use binarism to deal with differences in the realm of human thought. That is why when Christians try to understand the world with binarism or with their own theological tradition, they fell into the realm of finite human ideology, instead of thinking from the perspective of the Triune God who transcends our differences in a relational way.

As I indicated above, highlighting the differentiation (contextualization) of theology becomes more important in the age of world Christianity. However, there exists the danger of essentialism, which is already prevalent in many contemporary theologies. Unfortunately, in many contextual theologies, theologians often remain in the realm of human ideologies to advocate a specific group of people (or a specific cultural movement).[70] One of the best examples is the corpus of work of James Cone, who is known as the father figure of Black liberation theology. In his works, Cone attempts to center the experiences of African Americans as the key to his theological project.[71] According to Cone, the aim of Black theology is "the complete emancipation of black people from white oppression."[72] Here, in order to achieve this project of liberation, Cone claims that the oppressed Black people need to regain their identity through Black liberation theology. Cone says, "they (Black people) must affirm the very characteristic which the oppressor ridicules—Blackness."[73] For Cone, white America remains unable to accept the beauty of Blackness. Hence, there cannot be peace and integration. Rather, he thinks that Black people can initiate an emancipation from America's distorted reality, because they have the experience of oppression. Because the oppressed experience of Blackness has a consequent power to overcome racism, Cone finds the beauty of Blackness precisely in its oppressed experience. So, he believes that Black is beautiful and Black power

70. One of the most famous Old Testament theologians in the twentieth century, von Rad points out that "the most important item in the whole ceremonial [Deuteronomy 26:1–11] is the declaration to be made by the offeror" who recites the chain of the actions of salvation." Rad, *Deuteronomy*, 158.

71. It is noteworthy that James Cone's doctoral dissertation topic was Karl Barth. However, his interest is criticizing Barth's anthropology. For example, he says, "What could Karl Barth possibly mean for black students who had come from the cotton fields of Arkansas, Louisiana and Mississippi, seeking to change the structure of their lives in a society that had defined black as non-being?" Cone, *God of the Oppressed*, 5.

72. Cone, *Black Theology and Black Power*, 6.

73. Cone, *Black Theology and Black Power*, 18.

can bring peace.⁷⁴ These quotes highlight the way that, for Cone, there are two diametrically opposed categories of Black and white, within which he makes sense of embodied theology.

Another example can be found in feminist and womanist theologies. For example, Shawn Copeland, a renowned Catholic Black feminist theologian, argues that Black women's presence is absence in our culture, because white supremacy is so deep into our culture.⁷⁵ She points out that major Enlightenment thinkers such as Kant, Hegel, and Hume understood the Black bodies in the light of their own prejudices. Kant, for example, says, "Fundamental differences between blacks and whites were in their mental capacities."⁷⁶ Within these biased notions in western philosophies, she thinks that a field of vision threats us to exclude further information or data. However, she believes that there is a solidarity in the subject of Black female body because "the memory of back bodies invokes dangerous memories which protest our forgetfulness of human others, forgetfulness of what it means to enflesh freedom in our time and place."⁷⁷ In her theology, the theologies of white (male) people are something to be abandoned, while the body of Black women should be embraced. As much as Cone, then, she uses the binary categories of Black and white as the foundation of the constructive aspect of her work.

This trend of binarism continues even to the Third-world liberation theologies. To give an example, Suh Nam-Dong, who is known as one of the father figures of Korean Minjung theology, claims that the manifestation of the Jesus-event can be found in the oppressed experience of Korean Minjung (literally "oppressed people"). He believes that Jesus' ministry is about liberating the oppressed people in the sociopolitical setting. He says, "Jesus was truly a part of the minjung, not just for the minjung therefore, Jesus was the personification of the minjung and their symbol."⁷⁸ In his description of Korean history, the Korean Minjung were the objects of the ruling power, but the Minjung prepared the way to bring about a historical transformation.

---

74. Cone says, "The black theologian must reject any conception of God which stifles black self-determination by picturing God as a God of all peoples. Either God is identified with the oppressed to the point that their experience becomes God's experience, or God is a God of racism. . . . The blackness of God means that God has made the oppressed condition God's own condition. This is the essence of the biblical revelation." Cone, *A Black Theology of Liberation*, 67.

75. Copeland, *Enfleshing Freedom*.

76. Copeland, *Enfleshing Freedom*, 10.

77. Copeland, *Enfleshing Freedom*, 53.

78. Suh, "Historical References for a Theology of Minjung," in Suh, *Minjung Theology*, 159.

CONCLUSION: TOWARDS A TRINITARIAN THEOLOGY OF INCULTURATION 175

According to Suh, the experience of the Korean Minjung is Christ Himself because it is the Korean Minjung who cuts off the power of regime and oppressive systems just like Jesus did. He declares, "the subject matter of Minjung theology is not Jesus but the Minjung."[79] Because he understands the Jesus-event as the definitive political liberating event of history, Suh argues that the oppressed Korean Minjung should be the subject of Korean theology. For Suh, the Korean Minjung should be Jesus Christ Himself who cuts off the oppression of colonial dictators through sociopolitical revolutions. Thus, in Minjung theology, Jesus must be Minjung first who overturns the oppression of the colonial powers on the side of the oppressed Minjung. This example shows how Suh's theological work fails to center God.

Looking at these examples of contextual theologies, it is easy to find that many contextual theologies became human ideologies which advocate a specific group's opinion with a strong binarism; they remain in the realm of human horizons. I believe that contextual theologians are right to name the violent sins of the oppressors and the criminals because a genuine reconciliation can only be done when the sinners repent first. Also, it is recommended to utilize human experiences, embodiedness, or racial identities as lenses for Christian theology, because everything here is God's creation. I also recognize that dividing groups and making distinctions between people are sometimes necessary because many bad people are still hurting and oppressing others; we need to ask a repentance from bad people through naming their faults. I additionally believe that we need to celebrate different identities in the age of globalization because it is in fact God who differentiates us and our different understandings in Christian theology. However, while highlighting their different identities (or understandings), many contextual theologians missed one important point—the Triune God.

Many contemporary theologies today have a strong binarism as we have seen above: religion and secularity, Black and white, female and male, the oppressed and the oppressor. Even though it is important to highlight the different understandings to make a better world, contemporary theologians should go further to think from *the perspective of the Trinity*. So, I ask: what if contextual theologians understand the divisions of the world from the perspective of the Trinity who shows us Divine love? If so, I believe that a lot of our theologies will be changed radically, because we can go further to pursue a genuine (divine) reconciliation from the perspective of relational transcendence.

One of the essential teachings in the Bible is that Christians should live and think according to the perspective of God. For example, in the Book of

---

79. Suh, "Historical References for a Theology of Minjung," 160.

Jonah, God commands Jonah to preach against the city of Nineveh. However, Jonah refuses to go there and heads to Joppa instead. In the human perspective, Jonah should not go to Nineveh because the Ninevite people are the enemies of the Israelites. That is why God forces him to go there through a big fish and leads him to preach in the city of Nineveh; Ninevite people repent and get saved by God. After that, Jonah gets angry and protests against God (Jonah 4:2–3).[80] In this story, although it is right to complain in the perspective of the prophet, God has a different view—Divine forgiveness (reconciliation). In my human perspective, I cannot forgive Japanese people. Even though they killed and raped more people in China and Korea than at the Holocaust, they still do not offer any authentic apology, while even economically retaliating against the Korean government for asking a war compensation.[81] In the perspective of God, however, my attitude has to be changed because God's love invites even my enemies to the fellowship of God. When I remain in the realm of a human ideology, I cannot offer a genuine gesture of reconciliation. When I see the world in the perspective of the Triune God, however, I can participate into the mysterious fellowship of the Trinity who offers a genuine reconciliation even with my enemies' culture.

In addition, our interpretation of many parables of Jesus can be changed, when we focus on God's perspective. According to Jesus, the kingdom of God is something like the parables of the lost sheep, the lost coin, and the lost prodigal son (Luke 15). When the Pharisees criticize Jesus for socializing and eating with sinners, Jesus tells those three parables. Through the stories of compassion, Jesus reveals his mission for sinners. Interestingly, in those stories, a shepherd, a woman, and a father already have ninety-nine sheep, nine coins, and a good son each. However, they keep finding the lost one sheep, coin, and prodigal son. For them, it does not matter whether the lost ones are troublemakers or not. Rather, when they find the lost ones again, they call their friends and neighbors at their table to celebrate rejoining of the lost ones. In the stories of Jesus, Jesus calls Christians to invite unexpected persons into the divine fellowship of God. In the parable of the prodigal son, the elder son complains and refuses to join his father's celebration. However, his father says, "Son, you are always with me, and all that is mine is yours. But we had to celebrate and rejoice, because this brother of yours was dead and has come to life; he was lost and

---

80. "O Lord! Is not this what I said while I was still in my own country? That is why I fled to Tarshish at the beginning; for I knew that you are a gracious God and merciful, slow to anger, and abounding in steadfast love, and ready to relent from punishing. And now, O Lord, please take my life from me, for it is better for me to die than to live."

81. For further information, see Wikipedia, s.v. "Japan-South Korea Trade Dispute," https://en.wikipedia.org/wiki/Japan%E2%80%93South_Korea_trade_dispute.

has been found" (Luke 15:31–32). When we read these biblical passages from the perspective of God, we can realize that a genuine reconciliation can be done in the perspective of transcendence—the Triune God. If God is the Father of all who wants to communicate with all of us, the Father should also invite our enemies or lost ones. Although we cannot forgive our enemies, the Triune God will.

Based on these biblical understandings, Christians can practice embracing other cultures and different identities in their practices, while hoping God's transformation (inculturation) in the broken world. In particular, the Eucharist imprints a new image upon Christians, an image which they, in turn, impress upon the world. The strength of the Eucharist is that it allows Christians to participate in the Christian form of life through embracing all different broken bodies of the world. The Eucharist has a performative effect upon participants: "Come and eat! This is my body, broken for you!" This implies that the Eucharist performs or enacts community even as it invites Christians to the realization of human finitude existence and brokenness. In the Eucharist, Christians declare that the body of Christ is broken for us; what we partake of in the Eucharist is a *broken body of God*. This suggests that the Christian community calls people to participate in a kind of radical hospitality, to embrace broken bodies, relationships, and realities within God.

In the table of Christ, Jesus overcomes the brokenness of the world through embracing all different broken bodies. When Jesus had meals, he ate with people who were marginalized, such as prostitutes, the sick, and tax collectors. Even when Jesus invited his disciples to the table, he knew that some of them would betray him soon; nobody was perfect at his table. Even more, Jesus already knew that he was going to be crucified and dead (cf. Matt 16:21).[82] In the table of Jesus, however, Jesus is independent of death, because "death has no claim on him."[83] Thus, if the Holy Communion is to be observed faithfully, we must reimagine the transformative possibilities of brokenness in the perspective of God. This is because the brokenness of the world makes the liturgy holy and the subject of the liturgy is none other than the Triune God who sanctifies the imperfect to the more perfect and who creates life out of death. As a result, in his table, Jesus transforms and overcomes death. Look at what Paul Griffiths says:

> The church's liturgy, what the LORD's people do when they are gathered together to praise and worship him, is the clearest and fullest ordinary foreshadowing of heavenly existence given

82. Guardini, *The Lord*, 137.
83. Guardini, *The Lord*, 134.

> to us. . . . At any particular assembly, there are those present whose lives and thoughts are ordered in such a way as to place a great distance between themselves and the LORD; and this is recognized in the very order of the liturgy, which stutters and stammers, constantly underscoring in its very form its own impossibility, repeatedly approaching the LORD with eagerness, and then withdrawing by confessing its unworthiness.[84]

Here, what makes Jesus' table holy is the brokenness of the world. Clearly, in the Eucharist, God reveals Godself, because the human realization of finitude transforms to the desire for God's presence. In addition, we can also notice that it is God who works at the table because it is God who invites and transforms our broken bodies to the fellowship of the Trinity in love. As a result, in the Eucharist, God changes the perspective of Christian; Christians can share and practice God's divine nature through inviting many different broken bodies to God's table. In this respect, the Eucharist is not only a sacrament of our union with Christ, but also a sacrament of our communion as the body of Christ in the reality of Christ. Therefore, in the Eucharist (which is the act of God), Christians share God's divine nature through inviting broken bodies, relationships, and realities to the fellowship of the Trinity in love.

In arguing the necessity of the trinitarian theology of inculturation, I point out that many contemporary theologians missed one of the most important perspectives in Christian theology—the Triune God first. In being sensitive for social transformations, Christians should confess that the transformation of the world can be done primarily by the Trinity, not by human traditions or ideologies. That is why I claim the necessity of the trinitarian theology of inculturation which highlights God's transformation through diverse cultures, recalling the wisdom in Scripture on ministering to gentiles. When we orient our lives by the perspective of the Trinity, we can finally cooperate and reconcile with different cultures and even our enemies within God's presence. In the perspective of the Trinity, the purpose of repentance can be reconciliation, not total destroying or revenge. Forgiving one's enemy is impossible in the realm of human ideologies. In the perspective of the Trinity, however, everyone can be the Trinity's neighbor because the Triune God invites all of us to the divine fellowship of the Trinity through the ongoing process of inculturation; in the Trinity, we can understand different cultures and find the interdependence of one another. As a result, in the perspective of the Trinity, our life and culture can be totally changed by the Trinity's relational love. When we live within the

---

84. Griffiths, *Decreation*, 101.

CONCLUSION: TOWARDS A TRINITARIAN THEOLOGY OF INCULTURATION

perspective of the Trinity, we can realize that God is love (1 John 4:7–21).[85] Also, when we think and live by the perspective of Trinity, we can finally achieve a *Catholic Spirit* which my denominational father, John Wesley, suggests: "Though we cannot think alike, may we not love alike? May we not be of one heart, though we are not of one opinion? Without all doubt, we may."[86] Thus, when we understand the process of inculturation as the work of the Trinity, we can achieve a better reconciliation so that we can celebrate the coming of the kingdom of God all together in the spiritual unity of the Trinity, while also celebrating each one's different spiritualities in the perspective of relational transcendence.

---

85. John Wesley also points out that love is the most important characteristic of God: "Beloved, let us love one another, because love is from God; everyone who loves is born of God and knows God. Whoever does not love does not know God, for God is love. God's love was revealed among us in this way: God sent his only Son into the world so that we might live through him. In this is love, not that we loved God but that he loved us and sent his Son to be the atoning sacrifice for our sins. Beloved, since God loved us so much, we also ought to love one another. No one has ever seen God; if we love one another, God lives in us, and his love is perfected in us." Wesley, "On Zeal," in *John Wesley's Sermons*, 468.

86. Wesley, "Catholic Spirit," in *John Wesley's Sermons*, 305.

Bibliography

Abbott, Edwin Abbott. *Flatland: A Romance of Many Dimensions*. New York: Dover, 1952.
Althaus-Reid, Marcella. *Indecent Theology: Theological Perversions in Sex, Gender, and Politics*. London: Routledge, 2000.
Altizer, Thomas J. J., and William Hamilton. *Radical Theology and the Death of God*. Indianapolis: Bobbs-Merrill, 1966.
Anderson, Svend, ed. *Traditional Theism and Its Modern Alternatives*. Aarhus : Aarhus University Press, 1994.
Ashford, Bruce R. "Wittgenstein's Theologians? A Study of Ludwig Wittgenstein's Impact on Theology." *Journal of the Evangelical Theological Society* 50 (2007) 357–75.
Auerbach, Erich. *Mimesis: The Representation of Reality in Western Literature*. Translated by Willard R. Trask. Princeton: Princeton University Press, 2013.
Augustine. *The City of God*. Translated by Henry Bettenson. Harmondsworth: Penguin, 1984.
———. *Four Anti-Pelagian Writings: On Nature and Grace; On the Proceedings of Pelagius; On the Predestination of the Saints; On the Gift of Perseverance*. Edited by William J. Collinge. Translated by John A. Mourant. Washington, DC: Catholic University of America Press, 1992.
———. *On Baptism: Against the Donatists*. In vol. 4 of *Nicene and Post-Nicene Fathers, First Series*, edited by Philip Schaff, translated by J. R. King. Buffalo, NY: Christian Literature, 1887.
———. *The Trinity*. Translated by John E. Rotelle. 2nd ed. The Works of Saint Augustine 1.5. Hyde Park, NY: New City, 2012.
Barker, Hannah. *Paul F. Knitter's Soteriocentric Theology of Religions*. Bristol: University of Bristol, 2006.
Barth, Karl. *Church Dogmatics*. Translated by G. T. Thomson et al. Edinburgh: T. & T. Clark, 1936–77.
———. *Dogmatics in Outline*. London: SCM Press, 1966.
———. *The Epistle to the Romans*. Translated by H. Milford. London: Oxford University Press, 1933.
———. *Evangelical Theology: An Introduction*. Translated by Grover Foley. Grand Rapids: Eerdmans, 1963.
———. *Humanity of God*. Translated by Thomas Wieser. Atlanta: John Knox, 1982.
———. *On Religion: The Revelation of God as the Sublimation of Religion*. Translated by Garrett Green. London: T. & T. Clark, 2006.
———. *Protestant Theology in the Nineteenth Century*. London: SCM, 2001.

Bellah, Robert N., and Hans Joas. *The Axial Age and Its Consequences.* Cambridge: Belknap, 2012.

Bhabha, Homi K. *The Location of Culture.* London: Routledge, 1994.

Bonhoeffer, Dietrich. *Letters and Papers from Prison.* Edited by Christian Gremmels et al. Translated by Isabel Best et al. Minneapolis: Fortress, 2010.

Brown, G. Spencer. *Laws of Form.* London: Allen & Unwin, 1969.

Bultmann, Rudolf. *Glauben und Verstehen 1.* Tübingen: Mohr, 1965.

———. *Glauben und Verstehen 2.* Tübingen: Mohr, 1965.

Calhoun, Craig, et al., eds. *Habermas and Religion.* Malden, MA: Polity, 2013.

Calvin, John. *Institutes of the Christian Religion.* Translated by Henry Beveridge. Grand Rapids: Eerdmans, 1962.

Caputo, John D., and Gianni Vattimo. *After the Death of God.* Edited by Jeffrey W. Robbins. New York: Columbia University Press, 2007.

Carter, Craig. *The Politics of the Cross: The Theology and Social Ethics of John Howard Yoder.* Grand Rapids: Brazos, 2001.

Casanova, José. *Public Religions in the Modern World.* Chicago: University of Chicago Press, 1994.

———. "Religion, the New Millennium, and Globalization." *Sociology of Religion* 62 (2001) 415–41.

Cassirer, Ernst. *An Essay on Man: An Introduction to a Philosophy of Human Culture.* Translated by Louis Stern Memorial Fund. Oxford: Oxford University Press, 1944.

Certeau, Michel de. *The Writing of History.* New York: Columbia University Press, 1988.

Clark, Donald N. *Living Dangerously in Korea: The Western Experience, 1900–1950.* Norwalk, CT: EastBridge, 2003.

Cochrane, Arthur. *The Church's Confession under Hitler.* Philadelphia: Westminster, 1962.

Comte, Auguste. *The Crisis of Industrial Civilization: The Early Essays of Auguste Comte.* Translated by Ronald Fletcher. London: Heinemann Educational, 1877.

Cone, James H. *Black Theology and Black Power.* New York: Orbis 1997.

———. *A Black Theology of Liberation.* New York: Orbis, 2010.

———. *God of the Oppressed.* Maryknoll, NY: Orbis, 1997.

Confucius. *The Analects: Chapter 7.* https://china.usc.edu/confucius-analects-7#:~:text=The%20subjects%20on%20which%20the,bad%20qualities%20and%20avoid%20them.%22.

Consolidated Version of the Treaty on European Union. https://eur-lex.europa.eu/resource.html?uri=cellar:2bf140bf-a3f8-4ab2-b506-fd71826e6da6.0023.02/DOC_1&format=PDF.

Constitution of the Republic of Korea. https://www.refworld.org/docid/3ae6b4dd14.html.

Copeland, M. Shawn. *Enfleshing Freedom: Body, Race, and Being.* Minneapolis: Fortress, 2010.

Coronil, Fernando. "Beyond Occidentalism: Toward Nonimperial Geohistorical Categories." *Cultural Anthropology* 11 (1996) 51–87.

Cox, Harvey. *The Secular City: Secularization and Urbanization in Theological Perspective.* Princeton: Princeton University Press, 2016.

Crockett, Clayton. *A Theology of the Sublime.* London: Routledge, 2001.

Cross, Richard. *Duns Scotus.* New York: Oxford University Press, 1999.

———. *The Physics of Duns Scotus: The Scientific Context of a Theological Vision.* Oxford: Oxford University Press, 1998.

Cross, Terry. *Dialectic in Karl Barth's Doctrine of God*. Issues in Systematic Theology 7. New York: Lang, 2001.

Dalferth, Ingolf U. *Creatures of Possibility: The Theological Basis of Human Freedom*. Translated by Jo Bennett. Grand Rapids: Baker Academic, 2016.

———. *Crucified and Resurrected: Restructuring the Grammar of Christology*. Translated by Jo Bennett. Grand Rapids: Baker Academic, 2015.

———. *Die Kunst des Verstehens: Grundzüge einer Hermeneutik der Kommunikation durch Texte*. Tübingen: Mohr Siebeck, 2018.

———. "'I Determine What God Is! Theology in the Age of 'Cafeteria Religion.'" *Theology Today* 57 (2000) 5–23.

———. "The Idea of Transcendence." In *The Axial Age and Its Consequences*, edited by Robert N. Bellah and Hans Joas, 146–88. Cambridge: Harvard University Press, 2012.

———. "Mitmenschlichkeit: Das Christliche Ideal Der Humanität." *Neue Zeitschrift Für Systematische Theologie Und Religionsphilosophie* 62 (2020) 149–66.

———. "Öffentlichkeit, Universität, Theologie." In *Wie viel Theologie verträgt die Öffentlichkeit?*, edited by Edmund Arens and Helmut Hoping, 38–81. Freiburg: Herder, 2000.

———. "On Distinctions." *International Journal for Philosophy of Religion* 79 (2016) 171–83.

———. "Post-secular Society: Christianity and the Dialectics of the Secular." *Journal of the American Academy of Religion* 78 (2010) 317–45.

———. *Radical Theology: An Essay on Faith and Theology in the Twenty-First Century*. Minneapolis: Fortress, 2016.

———. *Sünde—die Entdeckung der Menschlichkeit*. Leipzig: Evangelische Verlagsanstalt, 2020.

———. *Transcendence and the Secular World: Life in Orientation to Ultimate Presence*. Translated by Jo Bennett. Tübingen: Mohr Siebeck, 2018.

———. *Wirkendes Wort: Bibel, Schrift und Evangelium im Leben der Kirche und im Denken der Theologie*, Leipzig: EVA, 2018.

Davidson, Donald. *Inquiries into Truth and Interpretation*. Oxford: Oxford University Press, 1984.

Davis, Creston, et al. *Theology and the Political: The New Debate*. Durham: Duke University Press, 2005.

Deleuze, Gilles. *Différence et répétition*. Paris: Presses Universitaires de France, 1968.

Dorrien, Gary. "Truth Claims: The Future of Postliberal Theology." *The Christian Century*, July 18, 2001. https://www.christiancentury.org/article/2001-07/truth-claims.

Duns Scotus, John. *Ordinatio: (Prologus et Libri I—III)*. Turnhout: Brepols, 2010.

Durkheim, Émile. *The Elementary Forms of Religious Life*. Translated by Karen E. Fields. New York: Free, 1995.

Eckerstorfer, Bernhard. "The One Church in the Postmodern World: Reflections on the Life and Thought of George Lindbeck." *Pro Ecclesia* 13 (2004) 399–423.

Figal, Gunter. *Gegenständlichkeit: Das Hermeneutische und die Philosophie*. Tübingen: Mohr Siebeck, 2007.

Fischer, Johannes. "Pluralismus, Wahrheit und die Krise der Dogmatik." *Zeitschrift für Theologie und Kirche* 91 (1994) 487–539.

Ford, David F. "Radical Orthodoxy and the Future of British Theology." *Scottish Journal of Theology* 54 (2001) 385–404.

Foucault, Michel. *Power*. Edited by James D. Faubion. Translated by Robert Hurley. New York: New, 2000.

Frank, Manfred. *Das individuelle Allgemeine: Textstrukturierung und Textinterpretation nach Schleiermacher*. Frankfurt am Main: Suhrkamp, 1977.

Frei, Hans W. "The Doctrine of Revelation in the Thought of Karl Barth, 1909 to 1922: The Nature of Barth's Break with Liberalism." PhD diss., Yale University, 1956.

———. *The Eclipse of Biblical Narrative: A Study in Eighteenth and Nineteenth Century Hermeneutics*. New Haven: Yale University Press, 1974.

———. *The Identity of Jesus Christ: The Hermeneutical Bases of Dogmatic Theology*. Eugene, OR: Wipf & Stock, 1997.

———. "Response to 'Narrative Theology: An Evangelical Appraisal.'" *Trinity Journal* 8 (1987) 21–24.

———. *Types of Christian Theology*. New Haven: Yale University Press, 1992.

———. "Unpublished Pieces." https://divinity-adhoc.library.yale.edu/HansFreiTranscripts/Freitranscripts/Freicomplete.pdf.

Fuchs, Ernst. *Hermeneutik*. Tübingen: Mohr Siebeck, 1970.

Geertz, Clifford. *The Interpretation of Cultures: Selected Essays*. New York: Basic, 1973.

Grass, Hans, and Werner Georg Kümmel, eds. *Jesus Christus: das Christusverständnis im Wandel der Zeiten, eine Ringvorlesung*. Marburg: Elwert, 1963.

Gregory of Nazianzus. *Catechetical Oration No. 5*. In vol. 5 of *Nicene and Post-Nicene Fathers, Second Series*, translated by William Moore and Henry Austin Wilson. Buffalo, NY: Christian Literature, 1893.

Griffiths, Paul J. *Decreation*. Waco, TX: Baylor University Press, 2014.

———. *Problems of Religious Diversity*. Malden, MA: Blackwell, 2001.

———. *Religious Reading: The Place of Reading in the Practice of Religion*. New York: Oxford University Press, 1999.

Grosse, Sven. *Theologie und Wissensahftstheorie*. Paderborn: Schöningh, 2019.

Grosshans, Hans-Peter. "And the Truth Will Set You Free: On the Relationship between Religion, Truth, and Power." *Studies in Interreligious Dialogue* 17 (2007) 183–204.

———. "Internal Realism and the Reality of God." *European Journal for Philosophy of Religion* 6 (2014) 61–77.

———. "The Interpretation of Holy Scripture—God's Word in Diverse Contexts and Historical-Critical Exegesis." Paper presented at Exploring Christianity in Asia, Münster, December 2020.

Grosshans, Hans-Peter, and Friederike Nüssel. "The Meaning and Legacy of the Reformation in a Global Perspective." *Dialog* 58 (2019) 92–95.

Guardini, Romano. *The Lord*. Chicago: Regenery, 1954.

Habermas, Jürgen. *Auch eine Geschichte der Philosophie*. Berlin: Suhrkamp, 2019.

———. "Notes on Post-secular Society." *New Perspectives Quarterly* 25 (2008) 17–29.

———. *Religion and Rationality: Essays on Reason, God, and Modernity*. Translated by Eduardo Mendieta. Cambridge: MIT Press, 2002.

———. *The Structural Transformation of the Public Sphere: An Inquiry into a Category of Bourgeois Society*. Cambridge: MIT Press, 1991.

Halsey, A. H., et al., eds. *Education, Economy, and Society: A Reader in the Sociology of Education*. New York: Free Press of Glencoe, 1961.

Hankey, W. J., and Douglas Hedley. *Deconstructing Radical Orthodoxy: Postmodern Theology, Rhetoric, and Truth*. Burlington, VT: Ashgate, 2005.

Hans-Georg, Gadamer. *Truth and Method*. Translated by Joel Weinsheimer and Donald G. Marshall. New York: Crossroad, 1982.
Hardt, Michael, and Antonio Negri. *Empire*. Cambridge: Harvard University Press, 2000.
Hauerwas, Stanley. *The Hauerwas Reader*. Edited by John Berkman and Michael G. Cartwright. Durham: Duke University Press, 2001.
———. *The Peaceable Kingdom: A Primer in Christian Ethics*. Notre Dame: University of Notre Dame Press, 1983.
———. *The State of the University: Academic Knowledges and the Knowledge of God*. Malden, MA: Blackwell, 2007.
———. *With the Grain of the Universe: The Church's Witness and Natural Theology*. Grand Rapids: Baker Academic, 2013.
———. *The Work of Theology*. Grand Rapids: Eerdmans, 2015.
Heidegger, Martin. *Being and Time*. Translated by John Macquarrie. London: SCM, 1962.
———. *What Is Called Thinking?* Translated by Fred Wieck. New York: Harper & Row, 1968.
Heim, Mark. *The Depth of the Riches: A Trinitarian Theology of Religion*. Grand Rapids: Eerdmans, 2001.
Henry, Carl. "Narrative Theology: An Evangelical Appraisal." *Trinity Journal* 8 (1987) 3–19.
Hick, John. *God and the Universe of Faiths: Essays in the Philosophy of Religion*. New York: St. Martin's Press, 1973.
———. *God Has Many Names*. Philadelphia: Westminster, 1982.
———. *The Metaphor of God Incarnate*. London: SCM, 1993.
———. "On Grading Religions." *Religious Studies* 17 (1981) 451–67.
———. "The Philosophy of World Religions." *Scottish Journal of Theology* 37 (1984) 229–36.
———. "Pluralism and the Reality of the Transcendent." *The Christian Century*, January 1981.
Hick, John, and Paul F. Knitter, eds. *The Myth of Christian Uniqueness: Toward a Pluralistic Theology of Religions*. Faith Meets Faith Series. Maryknoll, NY: Orbis, 1987.
Hobbes, Thomas. *Leviathan*. Translated by Richard Tuck. Cambridge: Cambridge University Press, 1996.
Hume, David. *A Treatise of Human Nature*. Edited by L. A. Selby-Bigge. Oxford: Clarendon, 1739.
Hunsicker, David B., Jr. *The Making of Stanley Hauerwas: Bridging Barth and Postliberalism*. Downers Grove, IL: IVP Academic, 2019.
Hunsinger, George. *Karl Barth and Radical Politics*. Eugene, OR: Cascade, 2017.
———. "Postliberal Theology." In *The Cambridge Companion to Postmodern Theology*, edited by Kevin J. Vanhoozer, 42–58. Cambridge: Cambridge University Press, 2003.
Hyman, Gavin. *The Predicament of Postmodern Theology: Radical Orthodoxy or Nihilist Textualism?* Louisville: Westminster John Knox, 2001.
James, William. *The Varieties of Religious Experience*. New York: Open Road, 2015.
Jaspers, Karl. *The Origin and Goal of History*. London: Routledge, 2010.

Jenkins, Philip. *The Next Christendom: The Coming of Global Christianity*. Oxford: Oxford University Press, 2007.

Jenson, Robert W. *The Knowledge of Things Hoped For: The Sense of Theological Discourse*. Oxford: Oxford University Press, 1999.

———. *Systematic Theology*. Vol. 1, *The Triune God*. New York: Oxford University Press, 1999.

———. *Systematic Theology*. Vol. 2, *The Works of God*. New York: Oxford University Press, 1999.

Joh, Wonhee Anne. *Heart of the Cross: A Postcolonial Christology*. Louisville: Westminster John Knox, 2006.

John Paul II, Pope. *On Catechesis in Our Time: Apostolic Exhortation Catechesi Tradendae of His Holiness John Paul II to the Episcopate, the Clergy, and the Faithful of the Entire Catholic Church on Catechesis in Our Time*. Washington, DC: United States Catholic Conference, 1997.

Jonas, Hans. *Die Maxcht des Heiligen: Eine alternative Geschichte von der Entzauberung*. Berlin: Suhrkamp, 2019.

Jones, Robert P., and Melissa C. Stewart. "The Unintended Consequences of Dixieland Postliberalism: Theology, Democracy, and the Project of Liberalism." *Cross Currents* 55 (2006) 506–21.

Jüngel, Eberhard. *God as the Mystery of the World: On the Foundation of the Theology of the Crucified One in the Dispute between Theism and Atheism*. Grand Rapids: Eerdmans, 1983.

———. *God's Being Is in Becoming: The Trinitarian Being of God in the Theology of Karl Barth: A Paraphrase*. Grand Rapids: Eerdmans, 2001.

Kang, Nam-soon. *Cosmopolitan Theology: Reconstituting Planetary Hospitality, Neighbor-Love, and Solidarity in an Uneven World*. St. Louis: Chalice, 2013.

Kant, Immanuel. *Critique of Pure Reason*. Edited by Allen W. Wood. Cambridge: Cambridge University Press, 1998.

———. *Religion and Rational Theology*. Edited by Allen W. Wood. Cambridge: Cambridge University Press, 2001.

Kaufmann, Gordon. *God, Revelation and Authority*. Waco, TX: Word, 1976.

Keller, Catherine, et al. *Postcolonial Theologies: Divinity and Empire*. St. Louis: Chalice, 2004.

Kim, Chil-sung. "The Role of Robert Alexander Hardie in the Korean Great Revival and the Subsequent Development of Korean Protestant Christianity." PhD diss., Asbury Theological Seminary, 2012.

Kim, Grace Ji-Sun. *Colonialism, Han, and the Transformative Spirit*. New York: Palgrave Macmillan, 2013.

———. *The Grace of Sophia: A Korean North American Women's Christology*. Cleveland: Pilgrim, 2002.

KNCC Theological Committee. *Minjung and Korean Theology*. Seoul: Institute for Korean Theology, 1982.

Knight, John Allan. "The Barthian Heritage of Hans W. Frei." *Scottish Journal of Theology* 61 (2008) 307–26.

———. *Liberalism versus Postliberalism: The Great Divide in Twentieth-Century Theology*. New York: Oxford University Press, 2013.

Knitter, Paul F. "Interreligious Dialogue: What? Why? How?" In *Death or Dialogue? From the Age of Monologue to the Age of Dialogue*, edited by Leonard Swidler et al., 19–44. London: SCM, 1990.

———. *No Other Name? A Critical Survey of Christian Attitudes toward the World Religions*. Maryknoll, NY: Orbis, 1985.

The Korean Methodist Church. *The Book of Discipline of Korean Methodist Church 2019*. Seoul: The Korean Methodist Church, 2019.

Korean Overseas Information Service. *A Handbook of Korea*. Seoul: Korean Overseas Information Service, Ministry of Culture and Information, 1978–.

Laozi. *The Daodejing of Laozi*. Translated by Philip J. Ivanhoe. Indianapolis: Hackett, 2003.

Latourette, Kenneth Scott. *The Emergence of a World Christian Community*. New Haven: Yale University Press, 1949.

Lee, Jung Young. *Embracing Change: Postmodern Interpretations of the I Ching from a Christian Perspective*. Scranton: University of Scranton Press, 1994.

———. *The Theology of Change: A Christian Concept of God in an Eastern Perspective*. Maryknoll, NY: Orbis, 1979.

———. *The Trinity in Asian Perspective*. Nashville: Abingdon, 1996.

Lee, Sang Hyun. *From a Liminal Place: An Asian American Theology*. Minneapolis: Fortress, 2010.

Lee, Timothy S. *Born Again: Evangelicalism in Korea*. Honolulu: University of Hawaii Press, 2009.

Lindbeck, George A. *The Nature of Doctrine: Religion and Theology in a Postliberal Age*. Philadelphia: Westminster, 1984.

Lonergan, Bernard. *Insight: A Study of Human Understanding*. New York: Philosophical Library, 1957.

Lubac, Henri de. *The Mystery of the Supernatural*. London: Chapman, 1967.

Luhmann, Niklas. *A Systems Theory of Religion*. Edited by André Kieserling. Stanford: Stanford University Press, 2013.

Marshall, Bruce. *Trinity and Truth*. Cambridge: Cambridge University Press, 2000.

Matsuoka, Fumitaka, and Eleazar S. Fernandez. *Realizing the America of Our Hearts: Theological Voices of Asian Americans*. St. Louis: Chalice, 2003.

Mawson, Michael. "Understandings of Nature and Grace in John Milbank and Thomas Aquinas." *Scottish Journal of Theology* 62 (2009) 347–61.

McConnell, Francis John. *Human Needs and World Christianity*. New York: Friendship, 1929.

Michener, Ronald T. *Postliberal Theology: A Guide for the Perplexed*. London: Bloomsbury, 2013.

Milbank, John. *Being Reconciled: Ontology and Pardon*. London: Routledge, 2003.

———. *Beyond Secular Order: The Representation of Being and the Representation of the People*. Chichester: Wiley-Blackwell, 2013.

———. *The Politics of Virtue: Post-liberalism and the Human Future*. Lanham, MD: Rowman & Littlefield International, 2016.

———. *Theology and Social Theory: Beyond Secular Reason*. Cambridge, MA: Blackwell, 1990.

———. *The Word Made Strange: Theology, Language, Culture*. Oxford: Blackwell, 1997.

Milbank, John, and Catherine Pickstock. *Truth in Aquinas*, London: Routledge, 2001.

Milbank, John, et al. *Radical Orthodoxy: A New Theology*. London: Routledge, 1999.

Milbank, John, et al. *Paul's New Moment: Continental Philosophy and the Future of Christian Theology*. Grand Rapids: Brazos, 2010.

———. *Theology and the Political: The New Debate*. Durham: Duke University Press, 2005.

Min, Anselm Kyongsuk, ed. *Rethinking the Medieval Legacy for Contemporary Theology*. Notre Dame: University of Notre Dame Press, 2014.

———. *The Solidarity of Others in a Divided World: A Postmodern Theology after Postmodernism*. London: T. & T. Clark International, 2004.

Moltmann, Jürgen. *The Crucified God*. Translated by R. A. Wilson. Minneapolis: Fortress, 2015.

———. *God in Creation: A New Theology of Creation and the Spirit of God*. Translated by Margaret Kohl. London: SCM, 1985.

———. *In der Geschichte des dreieinigen Gottes: Beiträge zur trinitarischen Theologie*. München: Kaiser, 1991.

———. *The Trinity and the Kingdom: The Doctrine of God*. Translated by Margaret Kohl. Minneapolis: Fortress, 1993.

Moyaert, Marianne. "Postliberalism, Religious Diversity, and Interreligious Dialogue: A Critical Analysis of George Lindbeck's Fiduciary Interests." *Journal of Ecumenical Studies* 47 (2012) 64–86.

Müller-Lauter, Wolfgang. *Heidegger und Nietzsche. Nietzsche-Interpretationen III*. Berlin: de Gruyter, 2000.

Mullins, Mark. *Christianity Made in Japan: A Study of Indigenous Movements*. Honolulu: University of Hawaii Press, 1998.

Nation, Mark Thiessen. "The Ecumenical Patience and Vocation of John Howard Yoder: A Study of Theological Ethics." PhD diss., Fuller Seminary, 2000.

Niebuhr, H. Richard. *Christ and Culture*. San Francisco: HarperSanFrancisco, 2001.

Nietzsche, Friedrich Wilhelm. *The Birth of Tragedy*. Edited by Douglas Smith. Oxford: Oxford University Press, 2000.

———. *On the Genealogy of Morals*. Translated by Horace B. Samuel. Oxford: Oxford University Press, 2006.

———. *The Portable Nietzsche*. Translated by Walter Kaufmann. London: Penguin, 1977.

———. *The Will to Power*. Edited by Walter Kaufmann. London: Weidenfeld & Nicolson, 1968.

Noll, Mark A. *The New Shape of World Christianity: How American Experience Reflects Global Faith*. Downers Grove: IVP Academic, 2009.

Oak, Sung-Deuk. *The Making of Korean Christianity: Protestant Encounters with Korean Religions, 1876–1915*. Waco, TX: Baylor University Press, 2013.

Panikkar, Raimondo. *Invisible Harmony: Essays on Contemplation and Responsibility*. Minneapolis: Fortress, 1995.

———. *The Unknown Christ of Hinduism*. London: Longman & Todd, 1964.

Pannenberg, Wolfhart. *Systematic Theology: Volume 1*. Translated by Geoffrey William Bromiley. Grand Rapids: Eerdmans, 1991.

———. *Systematic Theology: Volume 2*. Translated by Geoffrey William Bromiley. Grand Rapids: Eerdmans, 1991.

———. *Theology and the Philosophy of Science*. Translated by Francis McDonagh. Philadelphia: Westminster, 1976.

Phan, Peter C, and Lee Jung Young. *Journeys at the Margin: Toward an Autobiographical Theology in American-Asian Perspective*. Collegeville, MN: Liturgical, 1999.

Philipps-Universität Marburg. Theologische Fakultät. *Jesus Christus: das Christusverständnis im Wandel der Zeiten, eine Ringvorlesung*. Edited by Hans Grass and Werner Georg Kümmel. Marburg: Elwert, 1963.

Phillips, D. Z. *The Concept of Prayer*. London: Routledge, 1965.

———. *Faith and Philosophical Enquiry*. New York: Schocken, 1970.

———. *Faith after Foundationalism*. London: Routledge, 1988.

———. "Lindbeck's Audience." *Modern Theology* 4 (1988) 133–54.

———. *Religion without Explanation*. Oxford: Blackwell, 1976.

Pickstock, Catherine. "Duns Scotus: His Historical and Contemporary Significance." *Modern Theology* 21 (2005) 543–74.

Placher, William C. "Paul Ricoeur and Postliberal Theology: A Conflict of Interpretations?" *Modern Theology* 4 (1987) 35–52.

———. "Revisionist and Postliberal Theologies and the Public Character of Theology." *The Thomist* 49 (1985) 392–416.

———. "Scripture as Realistic Narrative: Some Preliminary Questions." *Perspectives in Religious Studies* 5 (1978) 30–39.

Pseudo-Dionysius the Areopagite. *Dionysius, the Areopagite, on the Divine Names and Mystical Theology*. Translated by C. E. Rolt. London: SPCK, 1940.

Pyeon Seon-hwan Archive. *The Third Generation Indigenous Theology*. Seoul: Moshineu Saramdle, 2010.

Pyeon, Sunhwan. "My Theology Class." In *Retirement Memorial Articles: Religious Pluralism and Korean Theology*, by Korea Theological Study Institute, 15–30. Seoul: Hankukshinhak, 1992.

Rad, Gerhard von. *Deuteronomy*. The Old Testament Library. Philadelphia: Westminster, 1966.

Rahner, Karl. *Foundations of Christian Faith: An Introduction to the Idea of Christianity*. New York: Crossroad, 1982.

Rashkover, Randi. *Revelation and Theopolitics: Barth, Rosenzweig, and the Politics of Praise*. London: T. & T. Clark International, 2005.

Ratzinger, Joseph. "Concerning the Notion of Person in Theology." *Communio* 17 (1990) 440–54.

Ratzinger, Joseph, and Jürgen Habermas. *Dialectics of Secularization: On Reason and Religion*. Edited by Florian Schuller. San Francisco: Ignatius, 2006.

Reno, R. R. "Stanley Hauerwas." In *The Wiley Blackwell Companion to Political Theology*, edited by William T. Cavanaugh and Peter Manley Scott, 302–16. 2nd ed. Hoboken, NJ: Wiley-Blackwell, 2019.

Ricœur, Paul. *From Text to Action*. Translated by Kathleen Blamey and John B. Thompson. Evanston: Northwestern University Press, 1991.

Robbins, Jeffrey W. *Radical Theology: A Vision for Change*. Bloomington: Indiana University Press, 2016.

Robinson, James M. *Honest to God*. Philadelphia: Westminster, 1963.

Robinson, James M., and John B. Cobb, eds. *The New Hermeneutic*. New York: Harper & Row, 1964.

Ryle, Gilbert. *The Concept of Mind*. London: Hutchinson, 1969.

Ryu, Dong Sik. "The Inculturation of the Gospel and Its Missiological Task." *Methodist Theological Journal* (November 1962) 46.

———. *Veins of Ore in Korean Theology*. Seoul: Chongmangsa, 1982.

Said, Edward W. *Culture and Imperialism*. New York: Knopf, 1993.

———. *Orientalism*. London: Penguin, 1979.
Sanders, Andy F. *D. Z. Phillips' Contemplative Philosophy of Religion: Questions and Responses*. Aldershot: Ashgate, 2007.
Sanneh, Lamin. *Translating the Message: The Missionary Impact on Culture*. Maryknoll, NY: Orbis, 1989.
Sanneh, Lamin, and Michael J. McClymond, eds. *The Wiley Blackwell Companion to World Christianity*. Hoboken, NJ: Wiley & Sons, 2016.
Schleiermacher, Friedrich. *The Christian Faith*. Edited by H. R. Mackintosh and J. S. Stewart. Edinburgh: T. & T. Clark, 1999.
———. *Hermeneutics and Criticism and Other Writings*. Edited by Andrew Bowie. Cambridge: Cambridge University Press, 1998.
———. *On the Glaubenslehre: Two Letters to Dr. Lücke*. Translated by James Duke and Francis Fiorenza. Chico, CA: Scholars, 1981.
———. *On Religion*. Translated by John Oman. Louisville: John Knox, 1985.
Scott, Kenneth. *The Emergence of a World Christian Community*. New Haven: Yale University Press, 1949.
Shakespeare, Steven. "The New Romantics: A Critique of Radical Orthodoxy." *Theology* 103 (2000) 163–77.
———. *Radical Orthodoxy: A Critical Introduction*. London: SPCK, 2007.
Slater, Angus M. *Radical Orthodoxy in a Pluralistic World: Desire, Beauty, and the Divine*. New York: Routledge, 2018.
Smith, Adam. *The Theory of Moral Sentiments*. Edited by Dugald Stewart. London: Bell and Sons, 1892.
Smith, James K. A. *Introducing Radical Orthodoxy: Mapping a Post-secular Theology*. New York: Baker Academic, 2004.
The Society For Korean Cultural Theology. *Doing Theology through Korean Culture: K-Culture and K-Christianity*. Seoul: Dongyeung, 2013.
Spivak, Gayatri Chakravorty. *The Post-colonial Critic: Interviews, Strategies, Dialogues*. Translated by Sarah Harasym. New York: Routledge, 1990.
Strauss, D. F. M. "The Inner Reformation of the Sciences: An Ambiguity in the Radically Orthodox Thought of John Milbank?" *Acta Theologica* 36 (2016) 193–212.
Suh, Nam-dong. *Minjung Theology: People as the Subjects of History*. Maryknoll, NY: Orbis, 1981.
Tan, Jonathan Y. *Introducing Asian American Theologies*. Maryknoll, NY: Orbis, 2008.
Tanner, Kathryn. *Theories of Culture: A New Agenda for Theology*. Minneapolis: Augsburg Fortress, 1997.
Taylor, Charles. *Hegel and Modern Society*. Cambridge: Cambridge University Press, 1979.
———. *Modern Social Imaginaries*. Durham: Duke University Press, 2004.
———. *A Secular Age*. Cambridge: Belknap, 2007.
———. *Sources of the Self: The Making of the Modern Identity*. Cambridge: Harvard University Press, 1989.
Tertullian. *Adv. Praxeam*. In vol. 3 of *Ante-Nicene Fathers*, translated by Peter Holmes. Buffalo, NY: Christian Literature, 1885.
"Theologe gegen Berliner 'Fakultät der Theologien.'" https://www.katholisch.de/artikel/13208-theologe-gegen-berliner-fakultaet-der-theologien.
Tillich, Paul. *Christianity and the Encounter of World Religions*. Minneapolis: Fortress, 1963.

———. *Dynamics of Faith*. New York: Harper & Row, 1957.

———. "Religious Symbols and Our Knowledge of God." *The Christian Scholar* 38 (1955) 189–97.

———. *Systematic Theology*. 3 vols. Chicago: University of Chicago Press, 1951–63.

———. *What Is Religion?* New York: Harper & Row, 1969.

Tracy, David. *Blessed Rage for Order: The New Pluralism in Theology*. New York: Seabury, 1975.

Troeltsch, Ernst. *The Social Teaching of the Christian Churches*. Translated by Olive Wyon. New York: Macmillan, 1931.

Underwood, Lillias H. *Underwood of Korea: Being an Intimate Record of the Life and Work of the Rev. H. G. Underwood, D.D., LL.D., for Thirty-One Years a Missionary of the Presbyterian Board in Korea*. Seoul: Yonsei University Press, 1918.

Van Dusen, Henry P. *World Christianity: Yesterday, Today, Tomorrow*. New York: Abingdon-Cokesbury, 1947.

Vanhoozer, Kevin J., ed. *The Cambridge Companion to Postmodern Theology*. Cambridge: Cambridge University Press, 2003.

Wainwright, Geoffrey. *Doxology: The Praise of God in Worship, Doctrine, and Life: A Systematic Theology*. New York: Oxford University Press, 1980.

Ward, Graham. *Cities of God*. London: Routledge, 2000.

———. *Cultural Transformation and Religious Practice*. Cambridge: Cambridge University Press, 2005.

———. *The Politics of Discipleship: Becoming Postmaterial Citizens*. Grand Rapids: Baker Academic, 2009.

———. "Theology and Postmodernism: Is It All Over?" *Journal of the American Academy of Religion* 80 (2012) 466–84.

Weber, Max. *The Protestant Ethic and the Spirit of Capitalism with Other Writings on the Rise of the West*. Translated by Stephen Kalberg. New York: Oxford University Press, 2009.

———. "The Sociology of Religion." In *Economy and Society: An Outline of Interpretative Sociology*, edited by Guenther Roth and Claus Wittich, 399–634. Berkeley: University of California Press, 1978.

Wesley, John. *John Wesley's Sermons: An Anthology*. Edited by Albert C. Outler and Richard P. Heitzenrater. Nashville: Abingdon, 1991.

Willimon, William H. "Answering Pilate: Truth and the Postliberal Church." *The Christian Century*, January 28, 1987. https://www.religion-online.org/article/answering-pilate-truth-and-the-postliberal-church/.

Willimon, William H., and Stanley Hauerwas. *Resident Aliens: Life in the Christian Colony*. Nashville: Abingdon, 1989.

Wittgenstein, Ludwig. *Culture and Value*. Chicago: University of Chicago Press, 1980.

———. *On Certainty*. Edited by G. E. M. Anscombe and G. H. von Wright. Translated by Denis Paul and G. E. M. Anscombe. Oxford: Blackwell, 1969.

———. *Philosophical Investigations*. Malden, MA: Wiley-Blackwell, 2009.

Wolterstorff, Nicholas. "Evidence, Entitled Belief, and the Gospels." *Faith and Philosophy* 6 (1989) 429–59.

Yoder, John Howard. "How H. Richard Niebuhr Reasoned." In *Authentic Transformation: A New Vision of Christ and Culture*, by Glen H. Stassen et al., 31–90. Nashville: Abingdon, 1996.

———. *The Original Revolution: Essays on Christian Pacifism*. Scottdale, PA: Herald, 1971.

———. *The Priestly Kingdom: Social Ethics as Gospel*. Notre Dame: University of Notre Dame Press, 1984.

———. *The Royal Priesthood: Essays Ecclesiological and Ecumenical*. Grand Rapids: Eerdmans, 1994.

Yong, Amos. *The Future of Evangelical Theology: Soundings from the Asian American Diaspora*. Downers Grove, IL: InterVarsity, 2014.

Yoo, Dongsik. "The Controversy and Assessment for the Korean Indigenous Theology." *Christian Thought*, June 1991.

Yun, Sung Bum. "The Dangun Mythology Is Verstigium Trinitatis." *Christian Thought*, October 1963.

———. "Getting Interested in the Dangun Mythology and the Thought of Yulgock." *Christian Thought*, August 1976.

———. *Korean Religion and Korean Christianity*. Seoul: Methodist Theological University Press, 1998.

———. "My Two Teachers." *Christian Thought*, July 31, 1976.

———. *The Theology of Sung*. Seoul: Munhwa, 1973.

Zizioulas, John. *Being as Communion: Studies in Personhood and the Church*. Crestwood, NY: St. Vladimir's Seminary Press, 1985.

Index

Aquinas, Thomas, 46, 50, 66, 69, 99, 100
Auerbach, Erich, 33
Augustine, 64, 66, 79–87

Barth, Karl, 5–7, 18, 33–34, 39–41,
    45–46, 49–50, 53, 55, 65–66, 74,
    91–95, 105–8, 117, 120, 123–26,
    130–31, 145, 156–57, 173
Bhabha, Homi K., 161–62
Bonhoeffer, Dietrich, 107
Bultmann, Rudolf, 106–7, 114–16, 157

Calvin, John, 5–6, 35–36, 55, 73, 156
Casanova, José, 132–33, 148
Catholic spirit, 179
Christian practice, 5, 16, 41, 48, 57, 80,
    84, 91, 108, 118
Cobb, John B, 24, 106
Comte, Auguste, 71
Cone, James H., 173–74
Contextual theology, 16, 23, 141, 143–
    46, 149–50, 155–59, 163–64,
    173–75
Copeland, M. Shawn, 174
Cultural hermeneutics, 90, 94–8, 100–1

Dalferth, Ingolf U., 2, 7, 11–3, 15–16,
    30, 62–63, 103, 105–42
Deleuze, Gilles, 67, 75–78, 88
Dialectics, 16, 75, 134, 144, 148, 150,
    164–65, 167, 172
Differentiation, 8, 15–16, 71, 84, 133–
    35, 139, 144, 148, 150, 151,
    154, 158, 163–67, 172–73

Duns Scotus, 66–69, 78, 104
Durkheim, Émile, 66, 71–72

Enculturation, 150, 155
Eucharist, 101, 177–78

Figal, Günter, 110–12
Foucault, Michel, 75–76, 78, 99, 158
Frei, Hans W., 2, 11, 14, 18, 32–45,
    46–50, 58, 65, 80
Fuchs, Ernst, 15, 106–7, 115, 117

Geertz, Clifford, 30, 42, 95, 136
Genealogy, 67, 69, 73, 75–76, 78
God first theology, 117, 120, 123–31,
    138, 178
Gregory of Nazianzus, 167–68
Griffiths, Paul J, 58–61, 152, 177–8
Grosshans, Hans-Peter, 60, 137, 148,
    169–71

Habermas, Jürgen, 69, 132–35
Hans-Georg, Gadamer, 94, 110–12
Hardt, Michael, 88, 161
Hauerwas, Stanley, 2, 11, 14, 18, 32,
    46–63, 103, 146, 172
Heidegger, Martin, 75–78, 99, 107,
    110–12, 114
Heim, Mark, 30
Hick, John, 19–24, 25, 29
Hobbes, Thomas, 66, 69–71, 74, 79
Hume, David, 70, 174
Hunsinger, George, 32, 59, 94

INDEX

Ideology, 7, 73, 97, 138, 164, 173, 176
In-between, 159–61
Inculturation, 3, 10, 13, 15–17, 142, 143–45, 150–79
Interdependence, 144, 150, 164–65, 172, 178

James, William, 49, 61
Jaspers, Karl, 137
Jenson, Robert, 7–10, 116
Jonah, 176
John Paul II, 155
Jung, 157–58, 174
Jüngel, Eberhard, 7–8, 15, 107, 125, 131

Kang, Nam-soon, 160–63
Kant, Immanuel, 2, 4, 68, 76, 127, 174
Knitter, Paul F., 19, 23–24, 29
Korean Methodist (indigenous) theology, 10, 16, 149, 152–57, 159–63

Language-game, 18, 20, 27–31, 49, 58, 111
Lee, Jung Young, 157, 159–60
Lindbeck, George, 11, 14, 18, 20, 27–32, 47, 49, 59, 65, 80, 95, 111, 136
Lubac, Henri de, 95
Luhmann, Niklas, 127–28, 133, 137–38

Marshall, Bruce, 32, 50–51
Milbank, John, 11, 14, 61–62, 64–90, 99–101
Min, Anselm Kyongsuk, 150, 158, 163, 172
Minjung, 149, 156–57, 174–75
Moltmann, Jürgen, 7–8, 168

Negri, Antonio, 88, 161
Niebuhr, H. Richard, 39, 49, 65
Nietzsche, Friedrich, 67, 75–79,

Orientation philosophy (theology of orientation), 12–13, 15, 105, 107–8, 127–31, 135–39, 141

Panikkar, Raimondo, 19, 25–27, 29
Pannenberg, Wolfhart, 7–9
Phillips, D. Z., 30, 39, 41, 80, 114
Pickstock, Catherine, 12, 65, 67–69, 100
Placher, William C., 32, 57–58
Post-Barthian theology, 3, 64, 106, 131, 140–41
Postliberalism (postliberal theology), 11–14, 18–104, 105, 107, 131–32, 140–41, 143, 145–46, 165
Postmodernity, 12, 64, 75, 80, 87–91, 97, 99, 102, 146, 161
Post-secularity (post-secular society), 12–13, 15–16, 103–5, 131–39, 141, 146, 149, 172
Predestination, 5
Public reason, 140
Pyeon, Seon-hwan, 156, 157, 161–62

Radical Hermeneutics, 107
Radical Orthodox, 11–14, 61, 63, 64–104, 105, 107, 131–32, 140–41, 143, 145–46, 165
Rahner, Karl, 26, 75, 113–14
Ratzinger, Joseph, 134, 167,
Relational love, 15, 90, 172, 178
Religious pluralism, 19–20, 22, 30, 157
Ryle, Gilbert, 33–34, 44, 95
Ryu (Yoo), Dong-sik, 156–7

Sanneh, Lamin, 147–48, 151, 157
Schleiermacher, Friedrich, 4, 37–41, 45, 82, 92, 95, 112–13
Secularization, 131, 134, 142, 144, 148–50
Smith, Adam, 66, 70–71, 74, 98
Spivak, Gayatri Chakravorty, 96, 161, 163
Suh, Nam-dong, 174–75
Strauss, D. F. M., 100–101

Taylor, Charles, 52, 97, 110, 132–33
Tertullian, 167
The doctrine of the Trinity, 6–13, 84–85, 107, 117, 145
The marginalized, 96, 159–60, 177

Theological hermeneutics, 66, 108, 112–15
Tillich, Paul, 17, 120–23, 130
Tracy, David, 39–40
Transcendence, 7, 12–13, 16, 27, 67, 73–75, 78, 88–89, 98–99, 105, 120, 129–30, 137–41, 143, 145, 165, 172, 175, 177, 179
Troeltsch, Ernst, 72–73

Van Dusen, Henry P., 147
Virtue ethics (theories), 14, 46–49, 66

Wainwright, Geoffrey, 11

Ward, Graham, 14–15, 64–65, 87, 90–103
Weber, Max, 66, 72–74
Wesley, John, 154, 179
Willimon, William H., 30, 32, 52–53, 146
Wittgenstein, Ludwig, 14, 18, 20, 27–33, 46–49, 58, 60, 111, 136
Word-event, 8, 106, 116–20
World Christianity, 3, 12–4, 16, 142–5, 147–52, 154, 163, 165, 172–73

Yoder, John Howard, 46, 53–57
Yun, Sung-bum, 7, 10, 156

www.ingramcontent.com/pod-product-compliance
Lightning Source LLC
Chambersburg PA
CBHW070329230426
43663CB00011B/2262